OUTSOURCING THE SALES FUNCTION

THE REAL COST OF FIELD SALES

Erin Anderson
Bob Trinkle

Australia · Canada · Mexico · Singapore · Spain · United Kingdom · United States

THOMSON

™

Outsourcing the Sales Function: The Real Cost of Field Sales
Erin Anderson, Bob Trinkle

Library of Congress Cataloging in Publication Number is available. See page 202 for details.

For more information about our projects, contact us at:

Thomson Learning
Academic Resource
Center 1-800-423-0563

Thomson Higher Education
5191 Natorp Boulevard
Mason, Ohio, 45040
USA

Asia (including India)
Thomson Learning
5 Shenton Way
#01-01 UIC Building
Singapore 068808

Australia/New Zealand
Thomson Learning
Australia
102 Dodds Street
Southbank, Victoria 3006
Australia

Canada
Thomson Nelson
1120 Birchmount Road
Toronto, Ontario
M1K 5G4
Canada

Latin America
Thomson Learning
Seneca, 53
Colonia Polanco
11560 Mexico
D.F.Mexico

UK/Europe/Middle East/Africa
Thomson Learning
High Holborn House
50/51 Bedford Row
London WC1R 4LR
United Kingdom

Spain (including Portugal)
Thomson Paraninfo
Calle Magallanes, 25
28015 Madrid, Spain

TABLE OF CONTENTS

FOREWORD

The choice to establish a Rep network or a direct sales organization is certainly more complex than "paper or plastic" at the grocery store—yet it's been my observation that many invest about as much time and thought in the decision. Executives often ignore many critical factors they should consider, yielding increased challenges and barriers down the road. For example, I was listening to a very well known semiconductor CEO address an audience five years ago at an industry conference where he prognosticated, "all manufacturers' reps would go away" within three to four years. Of course, that prediction and the guidance he gave the market about his stock were both way off base, since the stock went from around $200 a share to the single digits during the same time period—and the quality Reps in the electronics business not only weathered the storm but were stronger for it going into the recovery of 2003/2004.

I'm fortunate in that I had exposure early in my career to the value of the outsourced sales function and what it can do for a firm's agility and business results. I'd just been hired in my second job in the industry; the new organization had high hopes that this "new kid" they had just brought on board could help them penetrate some key applications in the PC/workstation market in North America. We had a Texas manufacturers' representative that had excellent entrenchment into the PC marketplace with other lines, but really was at wits' end with our company. For years they successfully wrote business into this explosive PC account with other lines, and yet the company I'd just joined never "tuned in" to the required business model necessary to penetrate this critical account. Contrary to "common wisdom," this Rep team had relationships throughout the account (executive and working level), tremendous knowledge, and superior access compared to any of our direct guys at the time. I ended up partnering with the Reps, taking their advice, and actually doing an under-the-radar risk development, which ultimately spawned a new product family and multimillion dollar engagement with the customer. I'm convinced today that without the domain expertise and account control of this individual Rep and his company, all of that business wouldn't have materialized.

Bottom line: companies have to focus on what they are really good at—and in many cases, it is the product development or engineering side of the value chain rather than the sales channel.

And if the core competency isn't sales, often a superior channel strategy is to align with manufacturers' representatives that clearly make this their stock in trade.

The other major observation I've made over the last 20 years in this truly volatile business environment is the utter disregard for making Rep selection based on critical and important criteria that are actually available. What's worse, when things don't work out, the model is blamed rather than the flawed decision process. This is analogous to not properly recruiting or training a sports team, losing, and then concluding the sport is flawed!

To quote the authors of this book: "The trend is clear: yesterday's radical idea is today's must-do." What could be truer in these times? It's hard to believe that in 1980 there were no PCs; even in 1995 most people had not browsed the web or even established an e-mail address. EBay, unheard of in 1998, was a household word by the year 2000. The Internet wasn't a trend that came and went—it is a phenomenon that has become the fabric of our environment, often the single resource used for weather, stock analysis, communications, and commerce. To my kids "IM-ing" is as common with their friends as making phone calls was when I was their age. It may be time for some companies to think more radically.

In the electronics world, outsourcing seemed radical when Cisco pioneered outsourcing on a large scale globally with partner companies to build a new model in a new economy. It may not seem radical now, but it certainly was scrutinized then. Outsourcing the sales function may also seem radical, but I would contend that it's become imperative for many companies facing a headwind of global competitors, manufacturing challenges, and dynamics in the business and manufacturing environment to force them to focus on what really is important to them.

This book may be the first ever written that steps the reader through these critical-to-success parameters for model and Rep selection. More important, successful implementation and execution is reviewed in detail so the organizational buy-in and linkage to stakeholders is understood and analyzed by two people who clearly have demonstrated success in this outsourced structure. Bob and Erin not only provide the tools and information to successfully integrate a Rep organization into a high-tech firm, they have backgrounds that inject academic rigor with proven "street experience" from an entrepreneurial standpoint. Had I applied this cost modeling and analysis to my decisions over the years in my organization changes and restructuring, I certainly could have avoided learning these lessons the hard way—which is all too common for executives in this industry.

Who should read this book? There are several obvious answers. My take is anyone in an organization that has manufacturers' representatives or is considering the use of Reps in the channel. There are so many misconceptions, and this book allows the reader to "tune in" to what really motivates and drives their sales organization, not to myths that have sometimes been erroneously passed down over the years. Second, it's a must-read for those considering changes to their sales channel or wishing simply to educate themselves on the use of an outsourced sales resource in the modern 24/7 dynamic times we're living in today. The fact is the CEO I referred to earlier didn't "get it," and chances are his organization that was partnered with manufacturers' rep companies most likely was suboptimized, given the leadership's lack of understanding of the model and its value to the firm.

It's obvious to me that Bob and Erin "get it." Using these breakthrough tools to understand and optimize a sales channel is simply smart business—and in these times of accelerated change and heightened global competition, we simply require additional flexibility and thought leadership in the sales organization. One thing hasn't changed: nothing really matters until someone sells something. This insightful book is thought provoking and allows us to learn to leverage the sales function for higher performance in the modern economy.

Tom Dalton
Vice President Worldwide Sales
Honeywell Sensing and Control

PREFACE

Tiger Woods has earned and retained the "number one ranking" in the golf world for years. When Tiger begins his golf swing, his body coils as though it was spring loaded. Woods then unloads that pent-up energy and launches a golf ball with awesome power and accuracy. Golf buffs, young and old, keep their eyes glued to this man's demonstration of athleticism and intensity. He has established a performance standard that other golfers dream of emulating.

Randy Johnson, a pitcher for the Arizona Diamondbacks, is the recipient of five Cy Young Awards and ten selections as an "All Star"—unbelievable and enviable achievements in baseball. When he uncorks his 99 miles-per-hour fastball, it rockets through the strike zone . . . and as they say in the trade, "When he brings the heat, you may not see it, but you sure can hear it." The "Big Unit," as he is called, is a very special athlete. Both Woods and Johnson make the juices flow and the goose bumps rise in every competitive athlete and sports enthusiast.

In addition to raw talent, these and other remarkable performers have the ability to concentrate on their core competencies. This is what they do best and what they do for a living. As long as they do it well, contribute to the pleasure of their fans, and enhance the success of their sponsors or their team, they will continue to be admired and earn substantial rewards for their performance. Woods' job is to shoot low scores in golf and Johnson's job is to send opposing hitters back to the bench in frustration in America's favorite pastime, baseball. These athletes seek perfection and work very hard at every aspect of their craft to achieve it. They focus on their tasks with laser-like intensity—and it shows.

There is one major difference between the activities of Tiger Woods and Randy Johnson. For the most part, golf is an individual sport and baseball is a team sport. Woods can excel in his individual performance because he plays independently from the other players. Tiger can enjoy an impressive win even if every other player has a bad day. On the other hand, Randy Johnson needs to win as part of a team. He and his teammates are very *interdependent*. Johnson's individual performance could be spectacular. He could strike out thirteen hitters, give up one base hit, and issue zero walks, which, by any standard, would be a great game. But, if his teammates don't score any runs or if they perform poorly on defense, he would still lose, as would the team.

Senior managers in all companies have to juggle many responsibilities in order to fine-tune their winning team. Most important, however, they are responsible for creating the "bottom line" performance of the organization as a whole . . . that's their team score and how they win. Their task is to fill all organizational positions with results-oriented people who can obtain levels of performance just as Woods and Johnson do in their respective sports. As they evaluate the talents within their organization, senior managers determine those things that the company can do best and those things that will create greater differentiation between them and their competitors.

Doing things right *and* doing the right things has always been the quest of professionals in all fields of endeavor. Employees and managers who are able to concentrate and excel in a specific skill are the foundation of the modern-day managerial vision. Individuals as well as organizations can do their very best when they can zero in on their core competencies. This reasoning has spurred today's widely implemented outsourcing phenomenon. It is a strategy used by top management in order to focus the energies and resources of the organization in areas where they can excel and reap greater results for their stockholders and owners.

Too many senior managers consider that having their own in-house field sales organization is a form of status and an indicator of strong, steady sales growth. It's no wonder . . . that's what their college textbooks instructed. Today's thinking is that it is no longer critical for a firm to perform every task, including field sales, within the organization itself. This change in concept was a paradigm shift and a major modification in strategic thinking for senior managers in the past. Now, the objective is to be successful, to win. It's not important who plays a given position; what *is* important is how well the position is played.

Good decisions are made with quality, up-to-date information. Unfortunately, much information regarding manufacturers' representatives (Reps) is obsolete, biased, or just plain inaccurate. For decades, people have been taught that small companies should utilize manufacturers' representatives to sell their products until they grow to a certain size in sales volume, and at that point, a company should change over to a captive (direct) sales force. This didactic position is predicated on the outdated textbook version of the "break-even curve," which illustrates two straight (linear), intersecting lines on a graph that allegedly represent the actual cost of each sales force option. Unfortunately, this fallacious method of illustrating the total costs of either sales force option is still being published and taught to both students and managers alike. To suggest that all costs are linear regardless of sales volume is absurd.

Similarly, it has been preached that Reps cannot sell technical products, nor can they effectively penetrate large, complex, global customers. Some academics teach students and potential managers that manufacturers' Reps are hard to control and that these firms will not invest the necessary resources to develop "long-term sales" opportunities. They suggest that Reps are short-term thinkers. People have been conditioned to accept these statements as gospel. We will explode these and other myths.

Until 1530, scientists, including all astronomers, believed that the Earth was the center of our universe and that all other celestial bodies, including the Sun, rotated around it. This explanation was easily accepted and never challenged. In that year, however, Nicolaus Copernicus (the architect of modern astronomy) theorized that instead, the Earth rotated on its axis once daily and that it traveled around the Sun once yearly. This concept was received with substantial skepticism at that time but was proven to be scientifically correct. In fact, until Copernicus' manuscripts were published, nearly 300 years later, most people still believed in a fallacious concept.

Like those early astronomers, many of today's top managers hold beliefs about manufacturers' representatives that are out of date or that were never true in the first place. Many have been happy to accept those things that they have been taught or told about Reps without question or reservation. We hope to encourage senior managers to re-think these and other issues by reading through the material contained in this book.

This book offers a whole new way of thinking about determining the viability of *outsourcing the field sales function* to professionally managed manufacturers' representatives and the role that Reps can play in maximizing the sales of your company's products or services. Rep firms vary in size. While there are single-person firms, the majority are multiperson firms that employ from five to over one hundred people. A Rep organization can be a significant member of *your team.* The authors hope to dispel some myths about Rep firms and to elaborate on the many values that they can add to principals and customers. We will present some cost analysis data and methodology that have never before been presented. We will illustrate how Rep firms actually finance the cost of sales (interest free) for their principals, a fact that is seldom considered. We give a candid and specific look at the Rep function as it is *today*. Our goal is to prompt you to evaluate this very important aspect of your business. Examining the viability of outsourcing the field sales function has caused companies such as Intel, Honeywell, and others referenced throughout this book to add the expertise of professionally managed Rep firms to their sales strategy. Presenting these possibilities is what this book is all about. We provide a balanced, up-to-date picture of the pros and cons of each of the options available for field sales coverage. Rep, in-house, or a hybrid configuration—whatever option best suits your situation—this book will assist you in making your decision and maximizing your company's sales performance.

Just as Randy Johnson's success and the performance of his teammates are interdependent, a Rep firm's success and that of its principals are equally interdependent. Rep firms may be privately owned and self-financed, but they and their principals are resolutely *interdependent*. They can only be successful if and when they perform for the companies that they represent, and their principals, in turn, perform for them.

In today's competitive world that demands performance from results-oriented companies, a Rep/principal relationship may be one of the best, most predictable, and most loyal examples of the true meaning of "partnering." Unlike distributors, dealers, contract manufacturers, Internet companies, and so on, a Rep firm cannot sell competing products when under contract to its principals. They are a faithful partner that exclusively represents each principal's best interest throughout the entire selling process and whose success is tied inexorably to a winning team result. A Rep firm can be a potent and valuable partner as well as a team player for large or small companies, generating powerful performance and with predictable costs in both good and bad economic times. Costs are one consideration; but excellence and consistency in performance are just as important. Losing any of these criteria can be a short-term solution with unintended, long-term consequences.

The saying, "Nothing happens till somebody sells something," is truer today than ever before, and Reps are doing it better and more professionally now than ever before. Regardless of whether you are currently utilizing a network of Reps or have never even given the idea a second thought, this innovative and revealing book is a compelling read. An academic and a practitioner combine their thoughts and experiences in a one-of-a-kind, up-to-date, thought-provoking book about *Outsourcing the Sales Function: The Real Cost of Field Sales*.

ACKNOWLEDGMENTS

This book has been many years in the making. From Erin's side, it all started in 1980 with Barton Weitz, then a professor at the University of California, Los Angeles. Bart had been a sales manager before becoming an academic. Bart explained the concept of a Rep to Erin and suggested she do a dissertation on when firms use Reps and when they go direct. Dubious, Erin visited Jack Berman, who not only convinced her that the idea was feasible but connected her to his extensive Rep network—starting with Bob Trinkle! Empowered and motivated, Erin committed to studying Reps. Bart chaired her dissertation, which culminated in a very large database that spawned multiple research articles.

Later, Erin and Bart teamed up with Leonard Lodish, a professor at Wharton, and worked together on several research projects involving Reps. Erin, Bart, and Len relied heavily on Ray Hall, of the Electronic Representatives Association, and on a handful of Reps who had plenty of things to do—yet who gave exceptionally generously of their energies to help three professors get out of their ivory tower and into the world of field selling. These Reps include Bruce Anderson, the late Tim Coakley, Russ Diethert, Tim Eyerman, Gene Foster, Jim Jordan, Jess Spoonts, and the late Charles Tindal.

The result of all of this was . . . more academic articles—lots of them. Along the way, Erin's family got to know a lot about Reps (can you imagine the dinner table conversation at that house?). One day, Erin's teenage daughter, Aline Gatignon, suggested that Mom should write a book about Reps. Mom protested that she didn't really know enough to do it alone. Aline replied, "You should do it with that guy you like so much, you know, the one you always phone, that guy in New Jersey. Isn't his name Bob Something?" Mom realized that this was a great idea. As luck would have it, Bob Trinkle had recently sold his representative firm, had begun a new career, and had had similar thoughts about writing a book and was willing to team up with Erin yet again. And now, several years later, Aline is an adult—and this book is a reality.

From Trink's side, a long career as an outsourced sales professional was enabled by a few men who gave a 20-year-old (who was scared stiff) a chance to continue his father's company after his father's sudden death. Three different principals headed by Matt Little, Harry Kalker, and Rudy Hummes promised me that they would "hang in there" while everyone else had bailed out. Their support and mentoring were absolutely essential in many ways, and I will be eternally grateful to each of them.

My dad was an ardent believer in professional selling, the value of the entrepreneurial spirit, and the efficacy of small business. Pop had an insatiable love of people. He loved what he did for a living and believed in giving back to the profession that provided him and his family with a quality of life that we all enjoyed. I am most proud to have had the opportunity of following in his footsteps.

My involvement in industry associations and related activities has served as my classroom and my laboratory. I've learned everything I know from others and there are too many to name. My association with a small group of Reps for over 40 years was a career highlight. We shared experiences, ideas, confidential data, inspiration, and long-term friendship. This same group has contributed greatly to this book. They wish to remain anonymous.

My wife, Betty, has always supported me and encouraged me in everything I have ever done. She has been my personal cheerleader and confidante. She has been prodding me to write a book for years. Her prodding became more intense after I sold my company. Since beginning this effort, she has read every word and critiqued every phrase. Thanks, Babe, for your love, support, and encouragement.

To get there, we required one more element, one more talent. We owe a tremendous debt of gratitude to our editor Lynn Selhat, who worked intensively with both of us to turn our drafts into this book. Lynn's dedication, extraordinary skill, vision, patience, and sheer hard work made an enormous difference. We also thank Paola Soneghet, who unleashed her expertise in preparing and testing our CD for the Cost Calculator.

INTRODUCTION

Put the word "outsourcing"[1] in the title of a book today, and it's bound to sell. Outsourcing is the "reengineering" of the 1990s and the "just-in-time" of the 1980s. Just ten years ago outsourcing would have been unheard of; now, it's as common as such pivotal functions as research and development, manufacturing, and human resources. But beyond this book, you will be hard pressed to find the terms "outsourcing" and "field sales" in the same sentence. Outsourcing has reached far and wide, but it has managed to bypass one major cost center: field sales, whose associated costs account for as much as 40 percent of revenue.

We believe this has to do with a number of factors, many of which are based on misconceptions, while others are based on a simple lack of information.

In this book we argue that too many companies automatically and unquestioningly staff their own dedicated field sales forces without giving serious consideration to outsourcing the field sales function to an institution known as a *manufacturer's representative firm*.[2] These observations stem from our unique perspectives: an academic who has studied field sales forces and channels of distribution for more than 20 years and a practitioner who has owned a Rep firm and has been involved with associated national trade organizations for more than 40 years.

In our experience, one of the major issues that complicate the make (in-house)/buy (Rep) decision is a general lack of understanding of the true costs of running a sales force. Most firms lack a good, sensitive cost accounting system that properly tracks and separates field sales costs from other sales costs. Field sales costs are typically mixed in with other general and administrative costs. Pulling out these costs is a bit like trying to unscramble an egg. So, we turned to Rep organizations themselves, who are "pure selling machines." In other words, all of their costs are devoted solely to sales in the territories that they cover. By studying the costs from multiple

---

1. It is important not to confuse "outsourcing" with "downsizing" (eliminating jobs once and for all) or "offshoring" (transferring jobs to other countries). "Outsourcing" means getting the work done on a contract with another company. The idea is to do the work better—and this actually saves jobs. Outsourcing is a way to keep people in work and to keep that work in the home country.
2. Throughout this book we will refer to manufacturer's representatives as either Reps or OSPs (outsourced sales professionals). Both terms are used in the industry so we will use them interchangeably in the book. In contrast, we will refer to in-house sales forces as either "in-house," "captive," or "direct."

leading Rep firms, we have been able to determine with great accuracy the real costs of field sales (whether in-house or Rep).

We have transformed these heretofore undocumented costs into a forecasting model—the Cost Calculator©—which is included in CD-ROM format with this book. You can use the Cost Calculator to develop estimates, specific to your situation, of what a well-managed field sales force (Rep or in-house) should cost. With the Cost Calculator, you will see the implications of all your decisions (how many salespeople, how much salary, and so forth). The program prompts you for these decisions, then shows you all the hidden costs (payroll, travel, office expense, and so forth) that will be necessary to support your sales force. Further, the Cost Calculator compares an outsourced and an in-house sales organization and shows you where and how they differ. For your situation, you will see whether outsourcing or an in-house sales force would be more cost effective, with a detailed analysis of all the reasons. In other words, you will be able to compare the costs of in-house and Rep on an "apples to apples" basis, something that is nearly impossible to do without this program.

Yet, costs are only one consideration—excellence and consistency in performance are equally as important. Sacrificing either of these criteria can be a short-term solution that has unintended long-term consequences. Thus, in addition to the Cost Calculator (see Chapter 8), we offer many other visions of what a Rep can bring to the field sales process. Specifically, in Chapter 2, we offer an in-depth explanation of what Reps are and aren't, and how they differ—from both a manufacturer's and customer's perspective—from an in-house sales force. This is not to say we are single-mindedly advocating outsourcing the field sales role. In fact, there are instances when a Rep is clearly not the way to go. We review these cases in Chapter 3. In Chapter 4, we look at a third option—a hybrid of Reps and in-house salespeople—that many manufacturers have been using recently. We'll explain when and how they work. Throughout these chapters, we cover how to reengineer sales roles to get the most out of them, whether you use an OSP or an employee sales force.

If you choose to outsource all or part of your sales roles, we offer three chapters that explain how to maximize your results, that is, how to enhance your relationship with an OSP. Chapter 5 focuses on two key variables that every manufacturer working with a Rep firm must work out: time and commission rates. The right answers to the questions, "How much time should I expect from my

Rep, and how much commission should I pay," are not always, "as much time as possible and at the least possible commission rate." Indeed, these answers are often moving targets, and a delicate balance can mean the difference between good and great sales results.

Chapter 6 looks at the human aspect of the manufacturer/ Rep relationship, offering insights into the Rep's world and how manufacturers can go about becoming the Rep's "emotional favorite," a designation that is rooted in a relationship of trust and respect. Finally, Chapter 7 looks at taking that relationship to the next level—a long-term committed partnership that works much like a good marriage.

Our goal is simple: to help managers make good and informed decisions about how to go to market. This may be one of the most important decisions your company makes and should not be made lightly, nor should it be left solely to the sales management. We believe that this decision should go all the way up the chain of command, even to the CFO and CEO, who should be asking themselves whether selling could be done better and whether it is time to question the conventional strategy of vertically integrating (in-house) the selling function.

We invite you now to begin the process of reflecting on whether your field sales function is as lean, efficient, and effective as it can be.

Erin Anderson
Bob Trinkle

ABOUT THE AUTHORS

ERIN ANDERSON

Erin Anderson is the John H. Loudon Chaired Professor of International Management at INSEAD in Fontainebleau, France, which she joined in 1994 as professor of marketing.

Her research focuses on the problems of motivating, structuring, and controlling sales forces and channels of distribution. She emphasizes issues related to vertical integration, including modes of foreign market entry. She takes a field-data approach to these issues, which she structures using a blend of institutional economics, macrolevel organization theory, strategic management, and marketing theory.

Anderson has published articles, based primarily on original field research, in a number of journals, including the *Journal of Marketing Research; Management Science; Marketing Science; Rand Journal of Economics; Journal of Economic Behavior and Organization; Journal of Law, Economics, and Organization; Organization Science; Journal of International Business;* and the *Sloan Management Review.* In addition, she serves on the editorial boards of several journals, including *Journal of Marketing, Journal of Marketing Research,* and *International Journal of Research in Marketing.*

Anderson is co-author of a textbook that is widely viewed as the benchmark in distribution channel management and is the leading book in executive and MBA programs:

> Coughlan, Anne T., Erin Anderson, Louis W. Stern, and
> Adel I. El-Ansary (2001), *Marketing Channels,* 6th edition.
> Englewood Cliffs, NJ: Prentice-Hall. Website:
> http://www.mc6e.com.
> * Translation available in Portuguese (ISBN 85-7307-974-6) and Chinese Simplified (ISBN 7-5053-8258-6)
> * Translations in preparation in Russian and Chinese Traditional

Anderson has consulted or been involved in executive teaching for a range of industrial companies, including Dupont, Air Liquide, LaFarge, and Alcatel, as well as consumer goods companies such as Heuer Time and Electronics, Motorola Cellular Systems, and Phillips Lighting. She frequently lectures for executive audiences in England, France, Spain, and Belgium, as well as the United States and Canada.

Anderson received her Ph.D. in marketing in 1982 from the Anderson Graduate School of Management at the University of California, Los Angeles. Prior to joining INSEAD, she was associate professor of marketing at the Wharton School of the University of Pennsylvania, where she had been a faculty member since 1981. Anderson has taught at the Catholic University of Mons, Belgium and has been a visiting scholar at the European Institute for Advanced Studies in Management, Brussels. Erin currently directs an INSEAD-Wharton Alliance program for executives, *Leading the Effective Sales Force,* which focuses on the strategic issues around getting the most from field sales.

BOB TRINKLE

Bob Trinkle ("Trink") served as the third president of a large manufacturers' representative firm nationally known in the electronic component industry. In January of 2000, he sold his interest in that firm, which now continues with its fourth generation of management since being founded in 1924.

He began his career when he was eighteen years old. He attended Drexel University engineering classes at night and called on customers during the day. That was his routine until his father's untimely death, a year and a half later. Most principals cancelled their contracts within days, not trusting the talents of this untested, unknown twenty-year-old. That was his "fiery baptism" into the Rep business.

During his career as a manufacturers' representative, Trink became active in the Electronic Representatives Association (ERA) International. He served as an officer for eight years in his local chapter and later served eight years as a national officer, including two years as national president and two years as its chairman of the board. Trink was the youngest president that ERA has ever had and the only son of a past national president.

He was ERA's interface with the Marketing Department of the Wharton School of the University of Pennsylvania, which was one of the first major business schools to undertake a detailed study of the manufacturers' representative function. His service to ERA was recognized in many ways, and he has received all of its prestigious awards: Key Award, Honor Award, Educator's Award, and their Hall of Fame.

Since selling his Rep firm, he has been a featured speaker who has addressed thousands of Reps and manufacturers at many trade association conferences and manufacturer's sales meetings in a variety of industries. Trink has also served as a consultant to manufacturers concerning field sales issues as well as to Representative firms on a variety of subjects.

During his career he has published articles and spoken on such subjects as "Representing the Professionally Managed Principal," "Instincts," "Anatomy of a Disaster Plan," "Why Reps versus Direct," "Succession Planning," "Rep System on Trial," "How Reps Finance the Sale," and "The Rep Advantage." He is also an occasional lecturer at the certification courses offered by the Manufacturers Representatives Education & Research Foundation (MR-ERF) at Indiana University.

The True Costs of Field Selling Today: Why It Pays to Consider Outsourcing

To "outsource" a function is to pay someone else to do it for you. It's a simple concept; we do it all the time in our personal lives, in our businesses, and even in our governments. Individuals routinely outsource house maintenance, yard care, tax preparation, car repair, and a long list of other functions. Businesses routinely outsource advertising, accounting, and legal work—for starters. Many governments have taken to outsourcing ("privatizing" or "contracting") such vital functions as garbage collection, municipal bus services, and the building and management of prisons.

Historically, businesses outsourced what they deemed minor or peripheral functions. Outsourcing was considered "subcontracting" or "delegation"—terms that have a whiff of something pejorative about them (defeatism, laziness, incompetence, or simply indifference). In the 1950s, for a small firm to outsource was seen as an admission of its many limitations. Conversely, for a large firm to outsource was seen as a sign of failure, even financial distress.

How things have changed! Today, firms large and small outsource virtually anything. Indeed, large firms even *announce* they will outsource something in the hopes that this news will lift their stock price—which it often does. A time traveler from the 1950s would be stunned to discover that major firms now

- Outsource *production* to "contract manufacturers"
- Outsource *customer postsale support* to third-party specialists
- Outsource *entire logistical systems* to a third-party logistics provider (3PL) such as Federal Express or DHL
- Outsource *new-product development* to independent consortia, laboratories, and new product "boutiques"

- Outsource their *computer systems* to firms such as EDS
- Even outsource their *payrolls, after-sales service, finance, accounting, transaction processing, and other "back office" functions* to firms with names few people know.

As more functions become candidates for outsourcing, a new language, spoken by a generation of globally savvy business executives, is replacing the old pejorative labels. To these executives, outsourcing connotes strategic flexibility, a return to core competencies, focus, discipline, leverage, cost consciousness, nimbleness—in short, progressiveness, modernity, open-mindedness. The business press feeds these positive images of outsourcing, regularly exposing decision makers to success stories—and to their opposite (horror stories of bloated, inefficient, paralyzed firms that refuse to let go of their in-house functions and their treasured internal routines). What a difference a few decades make! Outsourcing has become downright fashionable.

This brings us to a curious phenomenon. Firms are exploring outsourcing functions that most people still consider sacred, such as human resource management, procurement, customer relationship management, finance and accounting, and after-sales service. Yet, there is still one function that has remained relatively untouched by the outsourcing boom: field selling in the business-to-business (B2B) arena. Yes, it can be done. *Outsourced sales professionals* (OSPs) are companies that are to the outsourcing of selling what Federal Express and its competitors are to the outsourcing of logistics. Outsourced sales professionals are highly specialized third-party providers of field selling services-only. They represent B2B producers, selling on their behalf to businesses for business use. Outsourced sales professionals not only exist, they thrive, along with their suppliers.

There are many success stories and proven formulas; when to outsource sales and how to manage a relationship with an OSP are not mysteries. So it's puzzling that the field sales function has been left out of the outsourcing revolution.

This hole in the market represents a real business opportunity. If you are not yet taking advantage of this kind of selling, you should begin by reflecting on some difficult questions: Could you be selling more? Selling on better terms? Selling to targeted customers on terms that allow you to capture a fair share of the value you create? And could you do all of this more productively, that is, at a lower ratio of sales spend to revenues?

The potential of the OSP, or representative (Rep), is enormous—if the circumstances are right and the relationship well managed. This book will help you identify the right circumstances in which to utilize an OSP (the answer is not always clear) and provide insights into how to manage and nourish the relationship should you choose to outsource the field sales function. For the remainder of this chapter, we will look at the typical reasons why companies outsource (all of which apply to outsourcing the field sales force) and review several major market trends that point to field sales as an ideal function to outsource. Finally, we will present a list of common misconceptions that tend to keep companies currently using an in-house sales team in a state of status quo. With these misconceptions dispelled, you will be more receptive to the idea of outsourcing the field sales function and to the arguments presented in the book.

REASONS WHY COMPANIES OUTSOURCE

Outsourcing is a trend that has gained increasing momentum in the past decade. Faced with mounting pressure to create value for their shareholders, companies are eager to free up scarce resources and apply them to the firm's most critical challenges (or "core competencies"). Outsourcing is one way to do it. In addition, better communication technology (e-mail, cell phones, BlackBerries®, PalmPilots®, etc.) make it much easier to coordinate across companies. But the decision to externalize rather than internalize a function generally comes down to "dollars and sense" arguments. The four major financial arguments are (1) cost reduction, (2) turning fixed costs into variable costs, (3) performing the function better, and (4) freeing up a firm to focus on its core competencies.

Cost Reduction

This is usually the first, second, and third reason given to turn to a third party. Cutting costs through efficiency is a compelling argument. Companies today often engage in activity-based costing (ABC) exercises that create a wake-up call. The idea of being able to reduce what ABC has shown to be a very big number has a universal appeal. Third parties work on a large scale by pooling (aggregating) demands for their services. Express delivery services are an excellent example, but the principle applies to any function.

A third party ought to be able to execute its specialty on a very large scale so as to move down the learning curve (finding a better way, thereby cutting out labor costs) or, more generally, the experience curve (finding a better way, thereby cutting out any and all costs).

Turning Fixed Costs into Variable Costs

There are two motives here. The first is to cut overhead (resources dedicated to doing a job, such as building costs and salaries) by using the infrastructure of the other organization. The second motive is to share risk with the supplier. Outsourcing contracts often specify that the supplier will be paid for performance. A variation is to cap payments, leaving the possibility of cost overruns to the supplier. As we will see, outsourcing field selling means extreme risk sharing: the Rep assumes all selling costs *and* is paid only for performance (sales).

Performing the Function Better

Third parties specialize in whatever service they offer (processing payrolls, creating computing infrastructure, maintaining buildings, and so on). Not only can they function on a larger scale (thereby cutting costs), but they can also function in a different way. *Specialization deepens competence.* In particular, a specialist can offer a career path to people with very particular competences (e.g., writing advertising copy). And by working across customers (e.g., advertisers), the specialist can learn a great deal and put the knowledge to the service of unrelated businesses. For example, an advertising agency can work on campaigns for computers, clothes, and cars. The result is a deep knowledge of how to create and deliver compelling messages about products that matter a great deal to people, or "high involvement" purchases.

One reason that outsourcing improves the performance of a function is that going outside gives companies a chance to reengineer the work. This means a zero-based approaching to defining and dividing what needs to be done.

Freedom to Focus

Here, there are really two motives. One is to turn resources (time, energy, buildings, equipment, space, money, and so forth) to alternative uses that are more pressing to the organization. Freeing up resources to work on a problem that is more vital or more amenable to being solved removes a major roadblock to breakthrough progress.

Lately, the business press is starting to examine another motive. Many top executives can see what they need to do but can't see how to break down organizational resistance to doing it. We're talking here about organizational politics, about a company's climate, culture, and paradigm. We're talking about people's hidden assumptions ("We don't do that sort of thing"), their taken-for-granted expectations ("All of us get to stay in the best hotels when we travel"), and their sense of what is inviolate ("Don't touch my compensation plan"). Company politics is a big issue, especially for big companies, and that's why many of them are turning to outsourcing. If you can't persuade people to change . . . you can change to another set of people.

Or you can change to the same set of people. In Europe, a solution is to combine the outsourced function and the outplaced people. European firms go this route because labor laws often make it difficult to shut down a division without finding alternative work for the displaced employees. An elegant solution is to contract with a third party to take on those employees while the third party takes on the function those employees were performing. Not all employees take the offer, but those who do are in a new organization, with a new culture and paradigm. Restarting the game in this way has been known to do what the former boss couldn't do: radically improve the way people do their job.[1]

In a series of white papers,[2] the Accenture Institute for Strategic Change argues that the future lies in business process outsourcing (BPO)—and that future is coming fast. Business process outsourcing means contracting out entire central organizational routines (e.g., benefits counseling, or learning and training) in a strategic way. Although the idea is radical, Accenture argues that big firms are experimenting with it on a scale that suggests that other firms will be copying them soon. The motives? Increasing capabilities, getting to market faster, and saving money. Big firms see BPO as a way to access capabilities they cannot grow, create, retain, or manage well. And a major reason for that is internal political resistance of the type that makes big companies famous for their bureaucracy. Outsourcing is a capability builder because it's a bureaucracy buster.

And this is truly curious: by giving up control over the people who carry out a function, big firms are discovering that they *gain control over how well the function is carried out.* The (outside) supplier is more responsive than the (inside) division was! Firms can hold the supplier accountable for results—without having to humor their own employees' explanations of why something can't be done.

Additional Market Trends Supporting Outsourcing the Sales Function

If these arguments don't convince you to consider outsourcing field sales, we'll give you a few more. These recent trends in sales channels are extremely specific to selling and make an even more salient argument for outsourcing field sales.

GENERAL BELT-TIGHTENING. The increasing costs of doing business cause everyone to look carefully at each item of expense to determine if there are economies that can be obtained or efficiencies that can be achieved. While labor costs continue to rise, the cost of maintaining quality sales people is rising even faster. Travel costs and other necessary supporting expenses become more necessary and more expensive. The ever-increasing growth of small (start-up) customers adds another dimension to the problem of achieving goals without blowing tons of money on unpredictable results. Who can afford to ignore tomorrow's potential blue chip customer who may be operating out of a garage today?

Meanwhile, customers are seeking the same economies by reducing vendors, analyzing and implementing centralized purchasing, establishing global suppliers, and reengineering smaller but more capable (and difficult to visit) purchasing departments. This means that yesterday's method of dealing with a customer—sitting in the lobby waiting to sell your product—is a thing of the past.

A major study by Cahners Research[3] shows that customers are making themselves more unavailable. In most industries, customers see only one or two salespersons a week (Figure 1-1). Customers use the phone to fill in, speaking to between three and five salespeople a week (Figure 1-2). That's not a lot of contact! From the seller's standpoint, this discouraging picture becomes even more so when you consider that in most industries, it takes four, five, or six calls to close a sale (Figure 1-3).

So customers are hard to see, yet they need to see salespeople before they make decisions. And when salespeople finally do get

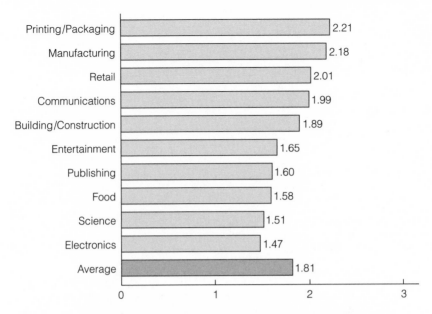

Figure 1-1. Average Number of Sales Representatives Customers See in Person per Week.
Adapted from Mulcahy (2002) (based on 23,341 businesses)

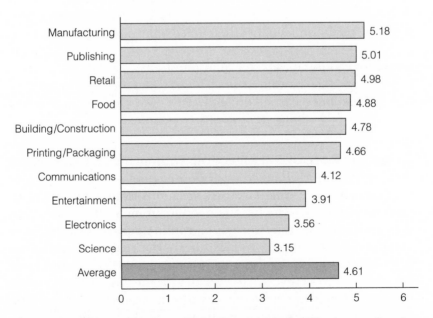

Figure 1-2. Average Number of Sales Representatives Customers Speak with on the Telephone per Week.
Adapted from Mulcahy (2002) (based on 23,341 businesses)

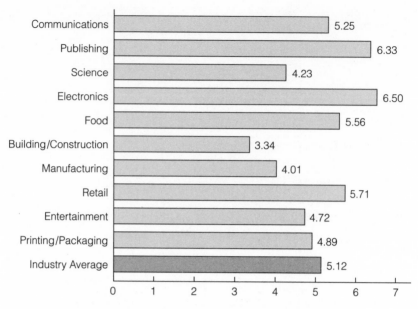

Figure 1-3. How Many Sales Calls Does It Take to Close a Sale?
Adapted from Mulcahy (2002) (based on 23,341 businesses)

an audience, the customer is often not impressed. Cahners finds that only 39 percent of customers think the company sales reps they see really understand their needs and aren't just trying to make a sale. Only 42 percent of customers consider that company sales reps can usually answer their questions.

In short, B2B customers see a lot of room for improvement in how field selling is carried on today. Part of this escalating demand is a result of the changing role of salespeople.

CHANGING ROLE OF SALESPEOPLE. Without question, the role of all salespeople has changed regardless of whether they are Rep or in-house. Today, elementary sales functions can be handled over the Internet, thus reducing the need for some of the more rudimentary functions that were once routinely performed by most salespeople. The biggest and most important sales are left to the field sales force, yet very little is ever said about the importance of the person who sits eyeball to eyeball with the customer: the salesperson. Salespeople are the folks who are closest to the scene; their customer awareness allows them to see the supplier of the future from the customer's point of view. The unskilled or uncaring salesperson who deals awkwardly with a customer can destroy important relationships in a heartbeat. Conversely, a competent salesperson can make up for problems that may arise.

INCREASED MERGER AND ACQUISITION ACTIVITY. The wave of merger and acquisition (M&A) activity that began in the 1980s has rearranged the business landscape. When two firms come together, they need to reconcile their brand names, product lines, and served markets. In "rationalizing" the two operations, the new consolidated firm very frequently is left with oddball products and oddball customers. These products and customers made sense in the old portfolio but not in the new one. And yet, these are products that have merit in themselves and are segments that deserved to be served. For example, a firm that specializes in office products acquires a company that makes office chairs as well as specialized chairs for use in dentistry. Without contacts in the dental field, the products will languish. Instead of dropping what might be a very successful product line because of lack of contacts in the marketplace, the firm could outsource to an OSP already well established in the market.

Also, M&A activity often produces large companies. This can create a real disadvantage if a company's size slows down the newly merged firm and prevents it from responding quickly to the market. Addressing this point, Bill Little, former chairman of the U.S. Chamber of Commerce, says, "The simplest and most predictable way for a larger company to capture the entrepreneurial spirit is to outsource. Outsourcing of field sales to independent sales representatives puts the producer in touch with the actual small businesses who are the essence of what makes the sector so dynamic." (See the case study at the end of the chapter for the full text.)

Outsourcing is an ideal way to hold onto and even profit from these oddball products and services. It is impossible to configure the consolidated company to fit the opportunity. But an OSP that already serves the oddball market, or that carries products and services that are complementary to the oddball product, can pursue the opportunity. Voilà, with the right Rep, there is instant coherence. Rather than being orphaned, the products and markets that don't fit after M&A can be placed with the right family.

THE ACCIDENTS OF RESEARCH AND DEVELOPMENT. In the same vein, many firms engage in research and development that generates inventions that are perfectly valid in themselves but just don't fit the parent company. For example, pharmaceutical firms tend to specialize in certain classes of disease. Routinely, their laboratories make discoveries that apply to a different problem. What to do if a cardiovascular company makes a dermatological discovery? The new product belongs with a dermatology sales force. One solution is to place it with an OSP (in pharmaceutical lingo, these are called CSOs, or contract sales organizations).

WHY IS FIELD SELLING SO OFTEN DONE BY EMPLOYEE SALESPEOPLE?

If outsourcing is becoming a tsunami, why is it that outsourcing field sales is still just ankle deep in the water? Surveys of what functions firms outsource—or are thinking about outsourcing—tend to put marketing and communication (of which field selling is the ultimate expression) at the bottom of the list. Even very small firms tend to keep sales in house.[4] As an Accenture partner involved in the firm's white papers put it, sales "is not a focus area for outsourcing in most industries."[5]

We have identified four major "objections" to outsourcing field sales. Some are misconceptions, while others are predicated on lack of awareness.

1. Misconception of Reps as "middlemen" who don't deserve to be paid when they succeed
2. Low awareness of the real costs associated with an in-house sales team
3. Not on the CFO or CEO radar screen
4. Concern about "losing" control over the people who sell your product

Misconception of Reps as "Middlemen" Who Don't Deserve to Be Paid When They Succeed

One of the biggest misperceptions of outsourced field sales (Reps) is that they are middlemen, and these days who wants to add another layer to the sales effort? The reality is that Rep firms are an *alternative* route to market, not a *duplicative* route to market. Manufacturers may choose to sell their products through the Internet, an in-house sales department, a distributor, or a Rep firm. If you pay a Rep to sell your product (which you do by paying a commission on sales), you are not paying for an in-house sales department and the costs associated with it. The fact that these costs (which we will address in depth) are not well understood makes it easy for manufacturers to look at a commission figure (which is quite clear and easy to track) and ask, "Why should I pay a Rep firm $2 million on that sale?" The number is so big that something must be wrong. It just can't be that such a huge check is fair pay for performance.

This flawed rationale (that the other firm doesn't deserve big pay for big results) has landed many a company in difficult straits. The question of whether to pay for performance (leveraged, or contingent, pay) is really the choice of whether to shift risk to another party. To see how this can play out, let's turn to Hollywood, where those involved in a movie (actors, directors, and producers) make a decision, one project at a time, whether to be paid a salary or to waive that safety net and instead commit to participate in the proceeds (if any) the movie generates.

The Walt Disney Company faced this choice early in the 1990s. Jeffrey Katzenberg, a Disney executive, agreed to produce an animated movie on a contract that was entirely variable pay. In return for 2 percent of the proceeds from the movie, Katzenberg agreed to waive any other compensation. At the time, Disney was happy to sign the contract because it didn't hold high expectations for the project, in spite of Katzenberg's superb track record. Disney considered the project risky because it was the first Disney film that had no human characters in it.

Katzenberg made the film for a relatively modest $50 million. To the industry's surprise, *The Lion King* became a runaway hit. A decade later, it remains one of the highest-grossing movies of all time. Disney made over a billion dollars *in profit* after recouping its investment. The merchandising alone paid back the film's costs many times over, beating all expectations. Recalls Roy Disney, "We all thought there wasn't much merchandise you could get out of the movie. We said, this is just a bunch of damn animals."

Such a brilliant result should have given Katzenberg a brilliant compensation. And that was the problem. The sum that Disney owed Katzenberg was so large that Chairman Michael Eisner became outraged. Eisner simply refused to pay Katzenberg, on grounds that nobody is worth that much money.

The results were catastrophic and long lasting. Katzenberg took Disney to court, holding up his signed contract as exhibit A. To the stupefaction of many observers, Disney refused to settle. Katzenberg quit Disney, in a move that is now regarded as a blow from which Disney has never recovered. Although the case was eventually settled, Disney lost Katzenberg's services and gained a powerful new competitor: Katzenberg went on to found Dream-Works LLC and to create more monumental hits (including *Shrek* and *Shrek 2*), while Disney has since stumbled in animation projects.

In short, pay for performance really does mean paying when performance is achieved. The winner does not get to revise the rules after the game is over. In 1994, Disney was fabulously successful, yet refused to pay the generator of that performance. The consequences are still accumulating a decade later.[6] In retrospect, honoring the pay-for-performance contract would have been a bargain.

And that is the nature of pay for performance—the apparent "bonanzas" can generate regret and envy, even though they give people a reason to risk getting through the not-so-apparent "lean years" when nothing works out and there is no pay. As Disney's case shows, pay for performance is a roller coaster and must be accepted as such. The big payoff is that contingent pay inspires people and organizations to stunning levels of performance. And the Rep often turns in a sterling sales performance.

Low Awareness of Real Costs Associated with an In-House Sales Team

The Disney case touches on a related concern: that Reps cost more than an in-house sales team. Of course, a big commission can look, well, big, if you compare it to say, the annual salaries of an in-house sales team. (We can liken it to "sticker shock" in the automotive industry.)

Almost always, a comparison of commission rate versus in-house sales salaries will come out in favor of the in-house team. But this is not an apples-to-apples comparison—and that's exactly the problem. Salaries are not the only thing you pay an in-house team—far from it. Major costs associated with an in-house sales team include not only compensation but

1. Employee benefits, including health and disability insurance and pension benefits
2. Vacation and sick time
3. Training
4. Support staff
5. Physical infrastructure, including office-related expenses

6. Cars and other travel expenses
7. Entertainment expenses
8. Other promotional expenses (such as advertising)
9. Insurance
10. Taxes, including payroll taxes
11. The opportunity cost of working capital

In short, your in-house field sales team may be costing you a lot more than you think. The Cost Calculator© that comes with this book offers a simulation that allows you to put in your real figures to find out just how much your in-house sales force is costing you.

Working out the real costs of performing any function is always difficult. This is especially true when firms perform a function in house. Typically, the associated costs are allocated over different activities and departments, which makes it hard to settle on a total figure. Worse, it creates a danger that the firm will fail to count up all the costs and will understate the true cost of performing a function. Among the most famous of cases is that of fashion and fabric maker Laura Ashley.

Founded by Laura and Bernard Ashley in 1953, the Laura Ashley brand name was a strong one in 1992. The British multinational was firmly positioned as synonymous with English country romanticism. Starting with flowery pastel prints on wallpaper and fabric, the company's strong brand name allowed it to grow rapidly, selling clothing and home decor around its proprietary designs. Laura Ashley had nearly 500 retail stores in 1990.

Yet, the growth was hollow. Laura Ashley's store network was largely made up of franchisees who worked hard to compensate for the many errors made by the franchisor. By 1992, the company was in crisis. Its supply chain was clearly the worst of both worlds: highly inefficient and highly ineffective. Laura Ashley knew it had large overheads tied up in logistics (personnel and infrastructure), although it was unable to ascertain the total sums. Yet, even though the firm had huge inventories, stores were frequently obliged to tell customers that their orders could not be filled—and this after months of saying the desired wallpaper or fabric was "on order." The reason: Laura Ashley had combined a poor information system with an ineffectual and bloated logistics function. The result: a customer could wait months before finally being informed of a "stockout"—and only later would Laura Ashley discover that it held thousands of yards of the ordered good in its warehouses. The accounting costs of running the supply chain were spiraling out of control, while the opportunity costs—lost business—reached alarming proportions.

In an atmosphere of crisis, Laura Ashley signed a sweeping contract turning all of its supply chain operations over to an organization eager to prove itself—Federal Express Business Logistics Service (BLS) in Europe. The concept of turning all one's logistics over to a 3PL was quite new and unproven in 1992, as was BLS, a new division of a firm that was not well established in Europe at that time.

Here was a reputable (and needy) client matched up with a capable (and hungry) supplier. It should have been a match made in heaven—and, to astonishment all around, it was, in spite of the open-ended vagueness of the contract. Result: Laura Ashley's outsourced supply chain hummed along nicely, and the old horror stories of frustration, stockouts, *and* huge inventories were a thing of the past. The much-scrutinized logistics alliance was a success, so much so that Federal Express could use it as a reference account to win new customers.

That, however, was the problem. Although Laura Ashley was never sure what it was spending in the old days, management now knew what the supply chain cost because it received a bill from a third party. What had been a largely fixed cost of unknown size, obscured by poor internal accounting, had turned into a precise figure, much of which was variable cost. And the bill was large. Remember, BLS was doing all of Laura Ashley's logistics worldwide for hundreds of stores and thousands of stock keeping units.

Apparently feeling gouged—a large bill had to be an unfair bill—Laura Ashley broke off the arrangement with Federal Express BLS and returned to doing its own logistics in-house. The details of the story are confidential, and both sides are quite discrete about their civilized business divorce. Nonetheless, the results were catastrophic. Laura Ashley went through five chairmen in five years. On the verge of bankruptcy, Laura Ashley was taken over by a Malaysian holding company in 1999. The new owner's first focus: get back on a sound financial footing by cutting costs, fixed and variable.

Laura Ashley discovered the hard way that it was spending far more than it realized to run its supply chain. In the same way, many manufacturers are spending far more than they realize to run their internal sales forces. Reps present a bill (on a pay-for-performance basis) to the manufacturer. That bill can look unreasonable (especially when performance is great), but it needs to be weighed against two costs: the opportunity costs of selling badly (the money that could have been made) and the accounting cost of selling in house (the resources devoted to an employee sales force).

Not on the CFO or CEO Radar Screen

You, the manufacturer, are at the decision crossroads. You have defined a sales role: somebody needs to sell *your products* to *your prospects* in order to meet *your expectations*. You need people to fill this role and managers to supervise the people. In other words, you need a sales infrastructure to fill your sales role. Who should own the sales infrastructure? Should it be you, the manufacturer? Or should it be an OSP? In the language of economists, should you vertically integrate forward (downstream in the value chain) to perform the field sales function yourself? Or should you go to the market for a solution, which means contracting with a third party, a specialist provider of the services you need?

This is a critical strategic decision that requires the involvement of high levels of management within the organization. Whichever way you go (make or buy) will have a huge impact on your sales and profits, on the success of your new products, and on your ability to enter new markets. Over time, how you perform the selling function will shape your capabilities and competencies as an organization. So the stakes are high. What is the right decision for each sales role?

This is a knotty problem, too important to be left to the vice president of sales to decide alone. Yet, that is exactly what many manufacturers do. They reason that nobody really understands selling anyway, so the logical solution is to just let the vice president of this mysterious function figure it out. When top managers duck their responsibility to work out critical strategic choices together, the inevitable happens. The vice president of sales argues a forceful case to build his or her own sales infrastructure and then proceeds to run it like an empire. Organization theorists note this pattern for any job: ask whether someone wants to be the boss of a division or to work with another organization, and the answer is always the same. So the head of sales becomes the head of a group of employees, and the manufacturer waits to see what sort of performance comes out of it. If overall results are satisfactory, vertically integrating "must have been" the right decision. If results are disappointing—well, it must be that the sales organization needs more resources.

Management needs to ask these critical questions: Even if results are good enough, *could we be doing better by outsourcing our field sales function?* Could our sales have been higher if we had utilized a network of OSPs? Could we have captured a larger market share? Could we have sold a better mix of our product range? And could we have obtained better sales *while operating at a lower, and a more predictable, cost of sales?*

Concern about "Losing" Control over the People Who Sell Your Product

Many manufacturers like the idea of having their sales force right where they can see them—all under the same roof. The word "outsourcing" confirms the conception that these people are *out*side of your physical location and, worse yet, *out*side of your control. "Who are these people whom I am going to let make or break my product?" many manufacturers worry.

It is true that OSPs are legally separate from the manufacturer, but in practice they are incredibly *interdependent* because the success of the Rep firm is inextricably tied to its principals' success and vice versa. A brief review of the Rep firm's business model explains this. These firms are independent companies that sell a portfolio of products to potential customers and tend to specialize in a certain industry so that they can meet the needs of their specific customers. Unlike distributors, Rep firms do *not* carry competing products but rather complementary products. For example, a Rep in the building industry may call on a contractor with a range of products from lighting fixtures to flooring to doors and windows. You, as the manufacturer, pay the Rep only a commission (the U.S. national average is 5.3 percent), and only on sales made. The Rep cannot make money unless your products sell. Thus, the idea of the freewheeling independent sales Rep has many holes in it. The Rep's success is highly dependent on your success.

SUMMARY

More firms are outsourcing more functions than ever before. Big firms, in particular, are experimenting with sending their "crown jewels" outside their boundaries. Yet, field selling remains a backwater. In spite of spiraling cost pressures and sea changes in the salesperson's role, many firms don't give much thought to selling through Reps (OSPs). They're trapped in their fixed ideas. Too many CFOs and CEOs don't have sales on their radar screen. Too many firms fear they will "lose control" over salespeople—and don't realize they might gain control over sales results. Or they don't really believe that Reps deserve to be paid well when they succeed, in the mistaken belief that the OSP is a "middleman" that doesn't do much. They don't understand the full costs of fielding their own sales force, let alone have an idea what it would cost to sell through a Rep.

The remainder of this book will break down even further the misconceptions we reviewed in this chapter and will help you to discern whether outsourcing field sales could be advantageous to your firm, and if so, how you can go about reaping the greatest benefits from this alternative way of selling.

CASE STUDY:
THE VITALITY OF THE ENTREPRENEURIAL SPIRIT

William Little is the former head of two major trade associations, the U.S. Chamber of Commerce and the Electronic Industries Association (EIA). In his decades of leadership, Little has seen companies of all sizes, in all industries. He has this to say about smaller companies.

The uniqueness of the American economy, what many feel is the strength of our economy and certainly what is the envy of the world, is our small business sector. For years studies have shown that the driver of our amazing growth and the source of almost all of our opportunity creation have been smaller, entrepreneurial organizations. They steadfastly avoid bureaucracy to compete with focus, flexibility, responsiveness and most of all high aspirations.

For these reasons and others, every company, but particularly larger ones, searches for ways to create or adopt an entrepreneurial spirit that is customer focused and fast to change and react. Perhaps speed is the real objective, the ability because management is so close to the issue to sense changes quickly and make course corrections with little or no hesitation.

Oddly, it may be that the simplest and most predictable way for a larger company to capture the entrepreneurial spirit is to outsource. Outsourcing of field sales to independent sales representatives puts the producer in touch with the actual small businesses who are the essence of what makes the sector so dynamic. The entrepreneurs who are the independent sales representative industry epitomize the spirit of enterprise that drives small business. They are quick on their feet, willing risk takers, customer centric, and most of all goal driven.

Many of the country's great large companies invigorate their sales activities by invoking the energy of small business by outsourcing field sales to independent reps. The great irony that I have seen regularly over the years is that shortly after hiring the independent they begin to bring the bureaucratic ways to the relationship with mindless reporting and the like, but that's a subject for another day.

Bill Little, President Quam-Nichols Co., Inc., Chicago, Illinois; Former Chairman, Electronic Industry Association; Former Chairman, U.S. Chamber of Commerce; Current Chairman, National Chamber Foundation, U.S. Chamber of Commerce

ENDNOTES

1. Linder, Jane C. (2004), "Transformational Outsourcing," *Sloan Management Review,* 45 (Winter), 52–58.

2. These include:

> Linder, Jane, Susan Cantrell, and Scott Crist (2002), *Business Process Outsourcing Big Bang: Creating Value in an Expanding Universe.* Cambridge, MA: Accenture Institute for Strategic Change.
> Linder, Jane, Alvin Jacobson, Matthew D. Breitfelder, and Mark Arnold (2001), *Business Transformation Outsourcing: Partnering for Radical Change.* Cambridge, MA: Accenture Institute for Strategic Change.

3. Mulcahy, Susan (2002), *Evaluating the Cost of Sales Calls in Business-to-Business Markets.* Newton, MA: Cahners Research.

4. Accenture (2003), "Control in the Manufacturing and Consumer Industries—Research Summary," in *Executive Survey Results: High-Performance Outsourcing: Gaining Control through Outsourcing.* Cambridge, MA: Accenture Institute for Strategic Change.

5. Personal communication with John D. Rollins and Adam Johnson, December 10, 2003.

6. This story is based on multiple press sources, including:

> Carvell, Tim (1997), "The Fox vs. the Mouse," *Fortune* (November 24), 119–124 (Roy Disney quote, p. 122).
> Corliss, Richard (1997), "There's Tumult in Toon Town," *Time Australia* (November 24), 80–82.
> ———. (1999), "Enough Is Enough!" *Time* (July 19), 76.
> Geier, Thomas (1997), "A Mickey Mouse Lawsuit Wraps Up," *U.S. News and World Report* (November 24), 1–3.
> Gunther, Marc (1999), "Eisner's Mouse Trap," *Fortune* (September 6), 106–115.
> ———. (2002), "Has Eisner Lost the Disney Magic?" *Fortune* (January 7), 62–47. Source of quotation from industry critic on pay package.
> Huey, John (1995), "Eisner Explains Everything," *Fortune* (April 14), 44–55.

2

Outsourced Sales Professionals: What They Are and How They Differ from Employee Sales Forces

So, we've got you intrigued! Chapter 1 triggered a few "aha!" moments, particularly with regard to some of the misperceptions that prevent manufacturers from outsourcing the field sales function. Maybe outsourcing field sales is an option you should consider, and now you want some more information about what they are and how they operate. This chapter answers these questions, specifically looking at how Rep firms differ from direct (in-house) field sales. But first, let's take a short detour to the topic of field sales in general.

In our view (both from the academic and business side), there is a tendency to underestimate the field sales role. Companies who are not using field sales to the fullest are missing out on a critical advantage in the market.

Consider field sales' proximity to the customer. While companies are making heavy investments in customer relationship management (CRM) tools in order to get "inside the heads" of their customers and anticipate their every need, the field sales force is already there, interacting with customers on a regular basis. Indeed, in the B2B arena, the only face-to-face contact customers generally have with a company is through the field sales staff, who have the ability to make a lasting impression (either good or bad) on a customer.

Consider, too, field sales' proximity to the market. By the very nature of their function, field sales staff are *in the field*—about as close to the market as you are going to get. They meet the competition while waiting to call on customers, and they see a trend as it's happening, not months later when it appears in a market report.

REPS AT A GLANCE

Facts and Figures

According to U.S. census data, Reps (broadly construed) account for 11 percent of U.S. wholesale sales volume; the other 89 percent is carried out by resellers (both independent and in-house).[1] About half of all producers in the United States use Reps,[2] though Reps account for only one-tenth of B2B sales in the United States. The average Rep commission rate in the United States is 5.3 percent.

Terminology

Salespeople working within an independent selling organization are generally referred to as "manufacturers' representatives" often shortened to "Rep." Some industries have their own labels for Reps, such as "agents," "commission agents," or "agencies" in insurance or electronic components, or "brokers" in financial services.

Business Model

Reps provide purely selling services on a contractual basis for makers (generally called "principals") of goods or services. They specialize in selling; unlike distributors they do not take title to what they sell, do not set their own prices, and do not handle merchandise. Reps sell a "portfolio" of complementary product categories, one brand per category, based on their customers' needs and buying patterns. Rep organizations share risk with the principal: typically, they absorb all selling expenses and are paid by commission on sales realized (at the principal's prices). The principal, not the Rep, is responsible for order settlement and fulfillment. Unlike most distributors, Reps usually accord *category exclusivity* to each principal (they do not sell competing products).

Keep these ideas in mind as you read through this chapter. The goal of this chapter (and the book for that matter) is not simply to help you understand the differences between Rep firms and direct sales forces, but to show you how to utilize the field sales function to its fullest to gain a significant competitive advantage.

The OSP (also known as the Rep) is *not* an employee sales force with a few differences. Reps generate revenue and create costs quite differently from an employee sales force. Thus, extrapolating directly from experience with employee salespeople is misleading. The OSP's different methods of operating have critical ramifications. Using an OSP will alter considerably your income statement and your balance sheet. Often, the OSP will improve your contribution to profit (that is, revenue after the cost of goods sold and the cost of selling them) and lower your fixed-asset requirements. Of course, the reverse can happen: sometimes the direct sales force offers the better income statement, even adjusted for the overhead it requires. Chapter 3 explains when and why this may occur.

To see how the Rep alters your income statement and balance sheet, it is critical to understand what Reps are—and what they are not. This chapter explains how the OSP operates and how selling through them can impact your costs and revenue.

As you read, keep two caveats in mind. First, remember that Reps, like employee sales forces, come in all shapes and sizes. Some organizations are well managed, competent, and worth your attention—and then there are the others. Second, no one would seriously argue that Reps always outperform employee sales forces. Chapter 3, as well as the Cost Calculator© (Chapter 8), reviews the costs and benefits of the Rep and direct sales force and helps you work through the complex tradeoffs you need to make when deciding your best route to market.

Earlier, we stated that OSPs alter the income statement (and, in most cases, the balance sheet as well). Specifically, they do so in four ways. First, the *nature of a Rep organization* is unique in the kind of people it attracts and the kind of organizational culture that flourishes. This impacts revenue. Second, selling your goods and services embedded in a portfolio of complementary goods and services (*portfolio selling*) is a dramatically different way to go to market, with many implications for both revenue and expenses. Third, the *cost of capital* is quite different. Less working capital is required when outsourcing selling, which reduces both expenses (interest expense on the income statement) and assets (the balance sheet). Further, the Rep operates much like a loan officer, extending, in effect, credit to each principal (thereby impacting expenses). Fourth, outsourcing selling will *reallocate risk* between the OSP and the producer. This influences both the income statement and the balance sheet, and alters the business's level of risk-adjusted return.

THE ORGANIZATIONAL NATURE OF THE OUTSOURCED SALES PROFESSIONAL

It is natural for a manufacturer to see a Rep in terms of "What do they do *for me?*" To answer this, we need to look at a broader question: what does a Rep do for its customers? For the Rep, everything

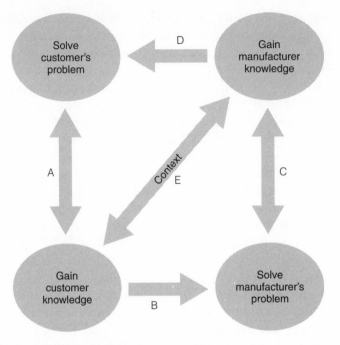

Figure 2-1. The Value Proposition of the OSP.
Adapted from Anderson, Philip, and Erin Anderson (2002), "The New
E-Commerce Intermediaries," *Sloan Management Review,* 43 (4), 53–62.

starts with customers—literally. Figure 2-1 shows the business proposition of the OSP.

The overriding goal is to solve a problem faced by a customer ("How can I do something reliably, effectively, and economically?"). To propose a good or service that will solve the problem, the Rep needs to gain knowledge of the customer—its installation, procedures, needs, constraints, and plans. In the process of trying to solve the customer's problem, the Rep will learn quite a bit about the customer. This sets up a virtuous cycle—the opposite of a vicious cycle—of problem solving and learning on the customer side (arrow A). Reps are rewarded for their problem-solving ability with orders (or punished with no sales and, therefore, no income).

But this is only part of the proposition. The OSP then uses its customer knowledge to offer value to the manufacturer. By understanding the customer, the Rep can solve the manufacturer's problem—how to get to market effectively and at a reasonable cost of sales (arrow B). In solving the manufacturer's market problem, the Rep gains knowledge of the manufacturer's capabilities, processes, needs, constraints, and plans (arrow C). For the Rep, that manufacturer knowledge has two main purposes. One is to do an even better job of solving the customer's current problem (arrow D). The other purpose is to accelerate learning about the customer (arrow E). The Rep leverages its knowledge of the producer to deepen its knowledge of the customer—which in turn kicks off another virtuous cycle. This cycle increases the Rep's knowledge of how well the customers and the producers fit each other. While the Rep is motivated to know as much as possible about the principal, its highest priority is the customer (thus the one-way arrow), and more specifically, the *overlap* between the customer and the producer.[3] This is *context,* shared by the two parties (producer and customer). Recognizing contexts in which the manufacturer's capabilities and the customer's needs match up is a big part of the Rep's value proposition. By creating a match and convincing customer and producer that the match is valid, the OSP makes a profit—or disappears.

From this business model we can see that OSPs are motivated (and therefore behave) quite differently than their direct sales counterparts. For example, given their interdependence with customers, OSPs are generally a stable force in a specific geographic region; because they are paid after a sale occurs, OSPs are extremely outcome oriented; and because they are already in a marketplace, OSPs are nimble enough to enter a market quickly. We will look at how each of these implications translates to benefits to the manufacturer.

Reps Are Stable

An important feature of a Rep is its permanence in the market. *The OSP is immobile.* Why? Outsourced sales professionals are built on ties to a given set of needs of a given customer base in a given geography. They are small business enterprises that are wedded to their market. If they can't keep satisfying the needs of that market, they cannot divert their resources elsewhere. There is no "elsewhere"!

In practical terms, this means the OSP must create local recognition and local position. The OSP is driven to focus on building long-term relationships, on forging strong interpersonal bonds at all organizational levels. Seldom is the direct salesperson in a position to develop long-term relationships; they are more likely to seek advancement within the company—onward and upward.

BUSINESSPEOPLE IN SALES

Sit in on a sales meeting at an OSP, and you will find a distinctive ambience. This is a community of cohesive, like-minded people. They are clear on what they are doing and why they are here. They have a sense of shared vision, a powerful and compelling organizational culture. This climate of can-do permeates the building and envelops everyone there, from the receptionist to the top producers and the owners (often, these are one and the same people). These are business-people in sales, *not* salespeople in business.

Specialization means that everyone celebrates the one and only thing the OSP does: make markets. There are no distractions from the task of solving customer problems by making markets for producers, a task more commonly known as "selling." Inside an OSP, this is a noble function. Of course it is—there *is* no other function! Inside a Rep, everyone celebrates selling done well. There is no question that selling is a profession, a service, a skill, a value-adding activity. No one need apologize for being a salesperson. It's a badge of honor inside the OSP.

Of course, in the larger world, not everyone is so enlightened. As we discussed in Chapter 1, the status of selling is more ambiguous and less positive in most societies and inside many companies. Not everyone considers selling a noble function. In French, for example, there are a number of derogatory ways to say "salesperson": a common term means "peddler." In Germany, it's even worse, to the point that German firms are notorious for calling all their sales-people "engineers" simply to avoid giving them a title that suggests they make transactions happen.

Because of this cultural-status bias, inside the manufacturer, the in-house sales force is often of depressingly low prestige. In many manufacturers, the status belongs to those who work in some other part of the company—operations, marketing, finance, accounting, and so forth. Many salespeople leave producer sales forces and join an OSP to get away from what they experience as constant jealousy, politicking, and backbiting directed at sales from the rest of the company.

Indeed, few salespeople start out working inside an OSP. Most Reps get their employees from in-house sales forces. Why would a direct salesperson quit a producer to work for a Rep? We've mentioned one reason: to be celebrated for being a great salesperson, with no reservations. But there are other reasons. Everyone has their private motives, of course, but two stand out. First, the very immobility of the OSP is attractive because it means salespeople can settle down in a community and stop worrying about what will happen to their careers the day they refuse a transfer. The OSP is part of a community's fabric. A manufac-turer's employee salespeople join Reps if and when they decide to settle down where they are. In this day of two-career families and growing concerns about the effects of frequent moving on family life, more and more employees are re-sisting transfers, even at some cost to their career.[4] Reps are able to recruit and hold some great salespeople simply by offering geographical stability. Great sales-people are the keystone of a great sales organization. Being able to attract, de-velop, and hold the best is a powerful business asset.

In short, the very nature of the OSP elevates and glorifies selling as a career as well as a profession. The OSP is a vehicle to build motivation. For their part, in-house sales forces need to devise their own ways to elevate the sales job within an organization that performs many other functions (of which production is usually the driver).

For the producer who uses a Rep, this means that there is a bench of strength behind the owner (or owners). A group of high-caliber, motivated salespeople is carrying the product. However, as any sales manager knows, some of these people are, frankly, quite difficult to manage. Top producers are often prima donnas, as temperamental and ill mannered as the worst operatic divas. And many have an aversion to being managed, which they are quick to dismiss as "bureaucracy." The management of the OSP firm learns how to handle high-strung top producers, simply because they have to. In contrast, many a manufacturer cannot absorb such people and is forced to let them go.

Net, the OSP is a place that brings out the best in its personnel, who are proud to call themselves professional career salespeople and who are unapologetic about betting their futures on one community. Indeed, they are civic boosters, unabashedly affectionate for Cherry Hill, Missoula, Twin Falls, and other cities that the reader may be hard pressed to locate on a map. Skilled, motivated salespeople and sales managers who aren't looking for a transfer or a promotion, who are proud of what they do and gain personal satisfaction from making markets—this is the nature of the people who work in an OSP.

This is understandable given that promotion (and often relocation) is a means to higher earnings for a solid performer.

Often, but not always, this change in sales coverage dislocates the salesperson/customer relationship, with the new salesperson having to begin the relationship and trust-building all over again. Rep firms' permanence in a geographical area gives them an advantage in retaining long-term relationships with customers. (For more on the Rep culture, see the "Businesspeople in Sales" sidebar.)

The rewards are great for those who have developed these kinds of relationships. They have established what author Dr. Stephen Covey refers to as an emotional bank account. They have consistently made deposits into this metaphorical bank account by treating people fairly. Because they have done so over a period of time, they can ask for special favors (making withdrawals from the account) and nobody gives it a second thought because they know that future deposits are a sure thing. The salesperson that has always gone to bat for the customer and has a long record of helping them solve *their* problems will have a substantial balance in the customer's emotional bank account. Creative problem solvers who can make things happen become integral parts of the *customer's team,* and at no additional cost to them. These types of salespeople will be given opportunities that others will never see or even hear about.

This is a major reason why good Rep firms, who have done their homework, are generally able to introduce new products and services or new principals faster than a company salesperson. In fact, new research of a broad range of manufacturers in B2B markets has shown that the most profitable accounts are the ones where the salespeople (whether direct or outsourced) have been in place the longest![5] Given time, salespeople build the credibility and relationships that get them a higher share of the customer's wallet. They've paid their dues in the form of service, developed their relationships, and have done so over a long period of time. The customer is more receptive to the introduction of new things from a long-trusted and reliable advocate who will be around in the future to stand behind their statements and commitments.

The OSP is also motivated to have the same close links on the principal side, as illustrated in Figure 2-1. Without something to sell and the context in which to sell it, the OSP's business model fails. This is why we don't refer to Reps as "independent agents." They are *not* independent. OSPs are highly *inter*dependent with their principals because their business model runs on context. The Rep's operations are necessarily intertwined with those of its principals, insofar as the customer's needs are concerned.

Necessity is the mother of invention; Reps need to reinvent themselves continuously. The OSP is quick to adapt to market changes, not because its personnel like change (after all, they are human, and humans like stability), but because it cannot escape. Those who don't adapt to market change ultimately fail. The Rep is interdependent with its customers as well as with its principals.

Reps Are Outcome Oriented

A Rep firm is going to earn money only when it performs for both parties: the customer and principal. (Later in this chapter we will discuss in greater detail Rep firms' economics and payment structures.) The key message here is that Reps must understand these two groups well enough to solve their problems. On this basis, Reps prosper when they turn their customer assets to the service of a manufacturer by making markets for the producer. In the process, Reps must come to know their producers, focusing on the context in which they can align customer needs and producer capabilities. For most producers, building a market-oriented culture is a challenge.[6] But for the OSP, being customer-centric is like breathing.

In dealing with a customer over a period of time and having worked through many different business issues, a Rep gains an in-depth awareness of the culture of the customer and their business environment. They make a determined effort to know who *their customers* are and who *their customer's competition* is, as well as the business conditions of the markets that their customers serve. Good Reps anticipate the customer's needs, often determined from another principal's opportunities or solutions to a requirement or a project. Reps make sure that they are always promoting the entire capability and services offered by their principals in order to sell the total partner value to the customer. It's more than just selling the product. It's selling them on the entire package of the principal's capabilities and then keeping it sold.

In turn, the principal expects that a strong customer/Rep relationship will produce a substantial amount of feedback concerning the customer's product direction. Communicating this intelligence—suggestions for new products, new technologies that they may use in future processes, and an analysis of the customer's views of competing vendors—back to the principal is considered essential in today's impatient business world where the shortest time to market is of the essence.

Indeed, Reps must sell in both directions: to the principal and to the customer. This means that Reps are in an ideal position to be an advocate for both sides, negotiating solutions that are good for all parties involved.

Reps Are Nimble

The fact that the OSP is typically a smaller organization is an advantage: smaller firms are nimble. This, combined with the fact that they are stable within a geography and are focused solely on selling means that they tend to be quick and adaptable, able to adjust efficiently to market shifts.

Often producers turn to the OSP when they become impatient with waiting for products and services to take off and expenses to come down. They want market share now, *and* they want cost containment now. They don't want a long period of converting a prospect to an account, investing in market foundations, and waiting for the return on that investment. They seek results—and on this quarter's income statement, not next quarter's.

HONEYWELL USES OSPS TO GROW FASTER

Tom Dalton is vice president of worldwide sales for Honeywell Sensing and Control. In later chapters, Dalton tells us in detail how Honeywell moved from a direct sales force to the OSP model. Here, Dalton tells us why Honeywell executives were open to this strategic change in organizational structure.

I'm a bit surprised that the top management was as receptive to quick/dramatic changes (after all, we revamped everything within 90 days of my arrival, which is amazing). There was a recognition by all that the current structure wasn't suitable to scale our business beyond its current level. I think what made it "easy" for me is that the execs I reported to wanted to make growth happen fast, and were willing to put their chips on the table immediately versus agonizing over decisions. It was a refreshing and healthy process, not one you'd typically observe in a $20B+ organization.

Tom Dalton, Vice President, Worldwide Sales, Honeywell Sensing and Control, Freeport, Illinois

Honeywell Sensing and Control, a world leader in sensors and controls, is a large firm that can certainly afford employee salespeople. The sidebar above explains how Honeywell instead used Reps to grow fast. In a nutshell, the OSP's stability, specialization, nimbleness, results-oriented approach, and market ties give the producer a way to get to market, to penetrate the market quickly, and to enjoy cost containment now, not after a long set-up period. These benefits are often reflected in the reasons manufacturers give for outsourcing the field sales role. Steve Haynes, senior vice president of worldwide sales and services for Xilinx, Inc., San Jose, California, touches on several of them when explaining his company's decision to work with OSPs. "Xilinx embraced the concept of outsourcing its sales force from the beginning. We made the decision to partner with a very strong North American network of Rep firms, and even moved that decision into Europe. The reasons were around variable cost of sales, market focus, engineering focus, and long-term account relationships. These are the same things that continue to drive those partnerships today."

MEANS OF SELLING

So far, we have focused on the nature of the OSP. At first glance, it looks a lot like a freelance version of a direct sales force, but as we have already shown, the Rep has its own properties: it is customer-focused, stable geographically, and nimble. The differences become even more pronounced when we look at how the OSP sells.

The direct sales force sells some or all of what a manufacturer makes. The manufacturer responds to market needs as best it can, but in the last analysis, it is the manufacturer's capabilities that drive the product and service assortment. The job of the employee sales force is to try to match what comes out of the firm with what customers need. If customers need something the firm doesn't make . . . well, life is like that. Salespeople struggle to make do.

Conversely, the OSP is *unconstrained* by what the manufacturer can make. If customers want to buy a gidget and a widget in a bundle, and the producer only makes gidgets, the Rep takes on a widget maker and then presents the widget-and-gidget bundle to the customer. This is *portfolio selling*. The Rep compiles each brand in a portfolio, composed of complementary (not competing) products and services. What makes them complementary are the customer's needs. The customer sees a connection among them, based on application, and is interested in being presented with a set, or assortment. Customers want a *scope* of products and services.

Readers who live in an advanced economy take assortments for granted in their daily lives. You expect to be presented with bundles of goods and services that make sense to you. For example, if you are creating a garden, you are interested in everything from soil, plants, and fertilizer to motorized equipment, statuary, and outdoor paint. From a manufacturing standpoint, these items are utterly unrelated: the scope of products and services is too great. But, as a customer, *you don't care about their problem.* As far as you are concerned, the fact that you need them for your project makes them related. Indeed, they are complements: one helps to sell another (now that the lawn is planted, it's time for a lawn mower . . .). A garden center with scope (variety, assortment) that can meet all your needs will win your business. That's why, in advanced economies, garden centers drive out the series of shops that sell only what some producer can make.[7]

This retail logic is even more powerful in business-to-business markets. Why? The net present value (NPV) of a business customer is much greater than the NPV of an individual (even someone who is creating a garden from scratch). Business-to-business sales efforts generally turn into a revenue stream that continues, year in and year out.

The beauty of the OSP is that it can compose whatever assortment fits the customer base. *Portfolio selling* opens doors for the Rep.

USING A BROAD LINE TO MEET CUSTOMER NEEDS
FOR ELECTRONIC COMPONENTS

Mike Swenson is the president of Mel Foster Company, a highly respected OSP of electronic components, based in Minnesota. Swenson describes how the breadth of the offering that Mel Foster has put together enables this OSP to meet customer needs.

A primary advantage of a manufacturer's representative is the ability to leverage multiple product lines into a customer's product design. The representative model entails working with customers closely to gain an in-depth knowledge of the programs and key personnel involved within engineering design and marketing teams. The best selling scenario is to get into an account as early as possible in the new product cycle. The salesperson tries to time the initial contact when engineering or marketing are conceptualizing a product. The focus for the manufacturers' representative is to follow key architectural platform shifts within their account base.

The goal of the sales team at this point is to understand the key program requirements at a high level and to evangelize and enable technology direction across the product lines represented. This gives the manufacturers' representative more opportunities for engagement with the customer due to the product breadth offered than the direct model, which offers a more limited product offering. Adding value to the customer at this stage is key to selling success. Typical requirements can start with a microprocessor, application-specific semiconductor product or another key design component. The customer normally will make device selections surrounding their initial architectural decision. In many cases we will start with the microprocessor. After that selection is completed, typically we will look then for memory, power, display, application-specific semiconductor devices, and passive component requirements in the design. Thorough knowledge of product areas that the design team is reviewing can enable a manufacturers' representative to go in with multiple product lines that would add value to the design. Typically we can get four or more different lines into an application. Once you have added value by assisting in selection and support within the design, your credibility and trust are raised. The salespeople in the manufacturers' rep firm are tasked with selling as much of their line card into the design as it warrants.

In effect the manufacturers' representative is able to add more value to the customer due to more products than the direct model. The customer's time is spent more efficiently by using Reps with more lines offered, and thus having to work with fewer salespeople. It is becoming more common that most customers are running leaner than ever: hence the time to spend with salespeople is limited. In many cases some of the product selections of the commodity-type components are made without the salesperson or with minimal time spent on the selection. The opportunity to influence these selections is greater when you have more products to offer in the design. The multiple-line selling approach is a compelling reason to have a manufacturers' representative over the direct selling model.

Mike Swenson, President, Mel Foster Company, Edina, Minnesota, www.melfoster.com

Consider a Rep that serves the building trade. The Rep can call on architects and contractors and can discuss any element of the proposed building (heating, ventilation, air conditioning, pipes, electricity, roofing, paint, wallboard, lighting, security systems, etc.). The Rep has the scope to do this because it is irrelevant that each product category is a separate industry and that different manufacturers operate in each industry.

Why does portfolio selling matter? It gives the OSP *economies of scope* and *economies of scale.*

Economies of Scope

Economies of scope are advantages that accrue from variety. Selling "synergy" is another name for this concept. The idea is that two products each sell better when presented together (by one sales force) than when presented separately (which requires two different sales forces). There are three reasons for this.

1. The customer is more likely to accord an appointment to a multiple-line salesperson, and will give that salesperson more time per call, because the salesperson offers one-stop shopping, which reduces the customer's transaction costs. (Consider that you are the architect or contractor mentioned in the example above. Would you rather meet with one person who can meet all of your buying needs or take appointments from six different people, each selling just one product that you need? Logic gives us the answer.)
2. The salesperson with a portfolio can ask more questions about the project without appearing to waste the customer's time. The customer will accept the questions as legitimate. Thus, portfolio salespeople can learn more about the customer's current and future needs, which means they can solve the customer's problems better and present their solutions more persuasively. And that means higher sales.
3. Buying spurs buying. Even the toughest, most seasoned buyers tend to accelerate their decision making after they settle on the first item. They move more rapidly to the second, then the third, then throw in the fourth, and so on. Momentum builds. A selling encounter becomes a chain. Salespeople call this "getting to yes." Skilled salespeople sequence their presentation so that the most likely item for that customer is first, simply to start the chain. Most Rep

salespeople organize their sales calls in advance by utilizing some form of a "call organizer" to plan their customer presentation so as to accomplish this very result.[8]

In short, selling synergy is real and part of the reason that multiple-line selling is effective. There are powerful reasons for it, both economic (transaction costs) and psychological (legitimate questions, getting to yes). Of course, there are limitations to economies of scope. We will address those a little later.

Economies of Scale

Economies of scale are advantages that accrue from sheer size. Economies of scale work for any sales, but the OSP can exploit scale economies particularly well for a simple reason: *the Rep pyramids economies of scope into economies of scale that surpass the potential of any single principal in a territory*. Let us explain.

A given manufacturer is constrained by the potential a territory holds for its brand of the product category. That potential hits a ceiling, limited by the size and needs of the customer base and by the strength of the competition.[9] If that potential supports no more than three people, a direct sales force must forego economies of scale and operate at a higher cost/sales ratio—or forego the market entirely. By pooling the demand for representation from several complementary manufacturers, the OSP circumvents this problem. Economies of scale can be fully exploited because the Rep taps into the potential of all the products on its line card. The OSP can be thought of as an aggregation machine. Aggregation, or pooling, is the key to justifying a sales force large enough to reap operating efficiencies. Put differently, the Rep amortizes the cost of each call over multiple principals. *Scope gives rise to scale.*

The notion of an aggregation machine is perfectly general and is a central concept in applied economics. Pooling demand to gain economies of scale is the single most important reason why outsourcing is so often more efficient than vertical integration—*of any function whatsoever*.[10] In Chapter 1, we referred to the outsourcing boom that is sweeping up business and transforming almost every business function. A major reason is that firms are discovering the power of the aggregation machine.

Why didn't they discover it before? The power of pooling has always existed in every area—human resources, procurement, manufacturing, research and development, and so on. What is new is the intensity of competitive pressure as business has globalized, combined with the way that new technologies permit managers to coordinate activities from afar.[11] Competitive pressure has obliged firms to dig deeper than ever for efficiency gains, while better coordination has removed a barrier to dealing with other firms. Outsourcing to a pooling machine in order to reap economies of scale is a fast way to realize much greater efficiency.

Putting It All Together: Gains from Portfolio Selling

It all comes down to this: *economies of scope create selling synergy and feed economies of scale*. Scope and scale together give the OSP the ability to

- *Cover a territory heavily.* The OSP calls on more customers in greater depth, more influences within each customer, and more often. This is economically justified by the market potential of all the (complementary) products taken together.
- *Learn about their customers.* Reps sell products and services that are adjacent to each other in terms of the customer's needs. The competencies and constraints of the producer are irrelevant: the OSP can sell anything the customer considers part of a need, ignoring the technical and organizational challenges that make it difficult for one producer to manufacture to all these needs. Thus, the OSP can legitimately inquire about needs and applications that a given manufacturer does not currently meet. The OSP is a storehouse of market intelligence.
- *Solve customer problems.* The OSP parlays its understanding of the customer and its ability to propose a portfolio of complementary goods and services to provide comprehensive solutions. In turn, the ability to solve customer problems gives the Rep a level of customer leverage, particularly with key accounts—the accounts that permit the most in-depth learning. (Chapter 3 expands on sources, uses, and limits of customer leverage.)

Sales synergy, a lower cost/sales ratio, customer loyalty, market intelligence—these are the principal benefits of portfolio selling by the outsourced sales professional. The implications for the income statement cut across all categories of sales-related expense, as well as the level of revenue.

In short, the Rep is an organization of a different nature than a direct sales force, even though it performs the same function (making markets). The OSP has a different organizational culture, and, via portfolio selling, different methods of achieving a cost/sales ratio. Clearly, the OSP and the direct sales force will generate different income statements and balance sheets selling the same product to the same market.

Earlier we mentioned that there are limitations to economies of scope. Although outsourced sales professionals do reap economies of scope, there is a limit to this due to exclusivity. Reps carry one and only one brand in each product category. This means they can offer breadth of assortment (many categories) but can't offer depth of assortment (choice within each category). The downside is obvious: if the one brand the Rep carries doesn't connect, the Rep has no fallback position. (This makes the Rep especially interdependent with its principals.) The upside is that it is feasible for the Rep to master each line and be knowledgeable of all competitors. And that is essential: the Rep must create markets and build demand. To do this, product expertise is essential.

If a customer wants greater economies of scope, the place to turn to is a distributor. Distributors seldom offer exclusivity to a supplier. Instead, they offer the maximum assortment, breadth, *and* depth. The customer who wants to compare three competing brands would have to take a call from three OSPs (or three employee sales forces) but would only need to see one distributor. Of course, the customer pays a price for the convenience. Because it is well nigh impossible for a distributor salesperson to master the product portfolio, it is difficult for the distributor to create demand. Knowing this, manufacturers tend to reserve demand creation for their sales forces (employee or outsourced) and look to their distributors for demand fulfilment.

In other words, field selling and distribution are two different synergistic functions: one is not a substitute for the other. The question of whether to outsource your field sales force is separate from the question of whether to use distributors. Because distributors are separate organizations, it is easy to confuse them with OSPs. But the counterpart to the OSP is the employee sales force. The counterpart to the distribution is a distribution division. Field selling and distribution play different roles in the marketplace. Figure 2-2 shows the persistent myth that Reps are an additional mem-

Wrong!

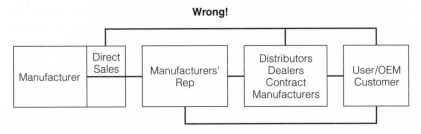

Figure 2-2. The "Additional" Channel Member Myth.
Adapted from Tim Coakley, President, Coakley, Boyd & Abbett, Inc.,
Framingham, MA.

The Real World!

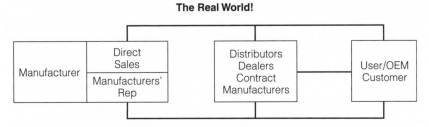

Figure 2-3. The Channel Member Reality.
Adapted from Tim Coakley, President, Coakley, Boyd & Abbett, Inc.,
Framingham, MA.

ber of the distribution channel. The reality, the true picture, is shown in Figure 2-3. We now turn to two other features of the OSP, features of particular interest to the corporate financial officer.

THE COST OF CAPITAL

So far, we have presented two images of the OSP: one as a market maker, another as an aggregation machine. Now let's add a third: banker. Yes, banker, because the OSP is a source of financing.

To see this, let's go to cash flows. When you operate a direct sales organization, all cash outlays are your responsibility as soon as they come due. Salaries, payroll costs, entertainment, transportation, support staff—these expenses arise regularly and require steady cash disbursements. Eventually, revenues are booked, then converted to cash. Outflows lead inflows, creating a working capital requirement. Every business has its hurdle rate, its cost of capital that must be factored into the net present value of every project. A large part of that hurdle rate is the foregone interest on the working capital that is locked up in a sales force.

Let's replay this story, this time using the OSP. The owners and managers of the Rep worry about cash flows. The producer no longer needs to worry. Why? Because it is now the Rep's problem. The manufacturer does not pay for sales expenses. These are on-going costs which the OSP pays and which the principal does not see. Instead, the manufacturer pays a commission on sales realized—if and only if they are realized and *after* sales are realized. Indeed, commissions are paid well after sales are realized. A typical contract in many industries calls for payment of commissions thirty days after shipment!

In other words, the OSP provides float between when an expense is paid and when a commission falls due. *Reps finance the sales effort*. And the longer the elapsed time from expense to shipment plus thirty days, the more float the Rep provides—automatically, and without even notifying the principal. Few bankers are this accommodating!

The foregone interest on the capital deployed by the Rep can be substantial, particularly if the OSP is penetrating a new customer or is working to replace an established vendor. These are break-in situations that require considerable effort up front and take months or even years before the effort converts to sales. The time between the first call (the beginning of cash outlays) and shipment plus thirty days is a significant cost consideration often overlooked and under valued.

Bankers don't make interest-free loans, and neither do Reps. The OSP factors in the cost of capital and expects to recoup it, just as does the corporate financial officer. Commission rates are negotiated accordingly. This is important in evaluating whether a commission paid to an OSP is at the correct level. The commission paid to the Rep should not be compared directly to the commission paid to an employee salesperson because the employee does not provide float.

SHARING THE RISKS BETWEEN
PRINCIPAL AND AGENT

The fourth and final image of the OSP we will present is as a partner in risk taking. Not only do Reps finance the sales effort, but they bear the risk of failure as well. Indeed, Reps provide float for sales that occur and for sales that don't occur.

The Failed Sales Effort

What is the nature of this risk? It comes in two forms. The first is the risk of customer default. Reps don't extend credit—the manufacturer does. But credit risk is transferred to the OSP via commission deduction. The Rep is paid commission after shipment. If the customer subsequently fails to pay because of credit issues or quality problems, the Rep's commission is deducted from future commissions. In this way, manufacturer and Rep share credit risk: the manufacturer loses the value of the shipment, and the Rep loses commission. This arrangement mirrors common practice when in-house salespeople are paid commission on paid shipments. (There is no formal equivalent for employee salespeople on salary.) The idea is to give salespeople an economic incentive to screen prospects for credit-worthiness and to use their influence within their accounts to make good on debts.

The second form of risk is the opportunity cost of the time. Opportunity cost is the profit that would have been realized had the effort been devoted to the next best application (for example, spending time with customer X, who ends up not buying anything, instead of customer Y, who might have bought something). Sometimes the opportunity cost is zero: the next best use would have turned out no better. But on average, the opportunity cost is positive: a positive contribution margin (revenue less the costs of goods and the cost of selling the goods) would have been generated elsewhere.

Opportunity costs are "might have been." They can be quite large, but oddly they are easy to overlook. Why? Because an opportunity cost is the money we could have made, and since we never really know what that is, we forget about it. This is particularly the case when markets are growing, and the seller is struggling to expand along with the market. Here, betting on the wrong purchase and losing it to someone else puts the firm farther behind in the race to establish position before the market stabilizes and the inevitable shake-out occurs.[12]

Shifting the risk of failed sales effort to the OSP, however, doesn't mean the manufacturer is relieved of all risk. The manufacturer is relieved only of the accounting costs of failure. However, both the OSP and the manufacturer suffer opportunity costs, although not the same ones. For the manufacturer, the opportunity cost is the foregone profit on the sale that could have been made to another customer: this is revenue minus delivered cost of goods and Rep commission. For the OSP, it's a foregone contribution, that is, commission (from this product or from another) less out-of-pocket selling cost. Both upstream and downstream lose when a sales effort goes nowhere. Once again, the OSP and the manufacturer are *interdependent*.

The Risk of an Excessive Cost/Sales Ratio

Another risk that can be reallocated to the Rep is that of spiraling sales costs. These costs—compensation, information systems, entertainment, group medical and other insurance, transportation, payroll, training, and so on—quite frequently, and without warning, spiral out of control. (Sales forces are inherently difficult to manage, and this creates volatility in the key performance indicator: cost/sales ratio.) This risk applies to any sales force and can emerge surprisingly fast. But the direct sales force that fails to produce continues to rack up expenses and earn a salary.

Outsourcing the field sales force is a way for the manufacturer to contain the risk that its sales costs will spiral out of alignment with its sales. *The cost/sales ratio when using a Rep will be the same as the OSP's commission rate,* because virtually all the actual sales costs belong to the Rep and therefore become irrelevant (even invisible) to the manufacturer. Instead, the costs the manufacturer incurs are its commissions—which arise only when a sale is made and in lockstep with those sales at a predetermined rate of commission.

In the United States, averaging across all industries, the average commission rate paid to Reps is 5.3 percent.[13] Let us underscore that 5.3 percent is the national *average*. The true rate varies considerably from product/brand to product/brand and from industry to industry. Actual commission rates can go very close to zero percent for product/brands that are easy to sell and that enjoy huge market potential. The actual commission rate will go far higher than 5.3 percent for hard-to-sell product/brands facing small markets.

Let's use the average for illustration. When selling through an OSP, producers know in advance that no matter how the market turns out, their cost/sales ratio will be 5.3 percent. Using an OSP removes the risk that the rate would turn out to be a much higher figure (the downside risk, or risk of negative outcome). Of course, it also removes the upside risk (of positive outcome), which is that the rate might have been lower than 5.3 percent. In Chapter 4, we show how to calculate whether your in-house sales force is one of those that can beat the cost/sales ratio of the OSP.

In short, outsourcing field selling is rather like hedging currency: the objective is to reduce the variability of a critical number, to create stability in a critical and inherently unstable outcome.

We don't want to suggest that outsourcing field selling removes the entire "S" from your SG&A (selling, general, and administrative expense). The manufacturer still has "S" because they have, at minimum, a sales manager and/or regional manager and their staff, who works with the OSP. Further, many companies support their OSPs, for example, with technical staff and internal information systems. Some firms even pay fees to their OSP (for example, to cover product development or to share the risk of failure in a long and arduous sales task). These are enlightened ideas. Manufacturers who take on some sales overhead in order to back up their Reps view the sales effort as a win-win. They project an attitude of partnership, flexibility, and willingness to share risks and tend to get the most from their Reps. Chapters 6 and 7 detail how they do it.

For the sake of completeness, we note that it is actually technically possible to have zero sales expense when outsourcing field selling. How? By outsourcing the management of the OSP! Yes, it can be done. And why not? *Anything* can be outsourced. All you need to know is the name of the institution that does the job. If you are looking to outsource your national sales manager, try searching for a "master rep." [14] This is an (admittedly obscure) term for a freelance sales manager who will recruit OSPs and act as the producer's liaison with them. Start-up firms that need their first big break especially favor master reps. The master rep aggregates demand from tiny firms for sales management, and in a sense functions like an investment banker, helping OSPs to spot embryonic firms that deserve a chance at the marketplace. If the manufacturer takes off, it may well ask the master rep to accept employment as its national sales manager.

THE REP ADVANTAGE: MORE THAN SELLING

Throughout this chapter we have reviewed a number of ways that Rep organizations differ from in-house field sales departments. All of these differences relate to the process of selling (i.e., portfolio selling vs. single products, commission vs. salary). Indeed, the *way* Reps sell is quite different from the way a direct field sales team

Figure 2-4. The Field Sales Hierarchy of Value

does. But if you look further, you will see that these differences have an impact on more than just the selling process. Let us explain.

The fact that Reps are in the field working for both sides (the customer and the principal) means that Reps see the big picture, putting them in a unique position to perform additional functions *beyond selling.* Instead of looking at Reps as another optional route to market, many manufacturers see them as a partner in market development and a source of business intelligence (insights into the customer and competition). In fact, good Rep firms already perform these value-added services as part of their everyday functions. As they move toward "peak performance" (see Figure 2-4) these high-performing Rep firms, well aware of the value of customer and market information, have made significant investments in data management tools.

Off-the-shelf software exists for such data management, but many Rep firms invest in their own proprietary software in order to gain even greater value for their information. Making such an investment, according to Craig T. Anderson, president of Sumer Inc., Rolling Meadows, Illinois, is often a clear distinction between an average and a great Rep firm. For an OSP to "efficiently and effectively manage and grow business in a territory," their database should include

- A contact management module to manage information on customer, distributor, and principal contacts
- A new business opportunity tracking module to track opportunities from discovery through a customer's product end of life
- An order entry/backlog tracking module to track customer purchase orders, shipments, POS (point of sales), and commissions
- A reporting module to allow the dissemination of any information collected. Reports could include monthly new business opportunity reports for principals, management reports for the Rep ownership to track territory performance and growth, and salesperson reports to allow salespeople within the Rep firm to receive feedback and monitor their own progress

(A complete copy of the Craig Anderson case study is available at the end of this chapter.)

Good Rep firms know that the data they collect on customers and the market over a long period of time is priceless information. Accumulating and applying knowledge on customers throughout their territory is a form of "geographic competence" that manufacturers hope will be a big advantage when utilizing a national network of Reps. This knowledge provides a Rep firm with a perspective of many more customers and their potential than an in-house salesperson will ever see or even know about. (This is both scope and scale.)

Indeed, this expanded role for Rep firms is a trend that will continue. With many manufacturers cutting back on costs, Reps are stepping in to fill needs formerly considered out of their domain. Robert Terwall of Cherry Electrical Products, Waukegan, Illinois, believes that Rep firms can leverage their infrastructure, experience, and service offerings beyond traditional selling. He points to many possibilities: doing supplier audits for principals, providing first-line quality services including on-site root cause analysis (saving the manufacturer the initial trip), maintaining safety stock (on certain key components), customer service, and marketing support. (See complete copy of the Robert Terwall case study at the end of this chapter.)

The trend here is clear: Rep firms are moving beyond the realm of sales and becoming long-term business partners with manufacturing firms. This progression is illustrated in Figure 2-4, the Field Sales Hierarchy Pyramid. Manufacturers want their field sales force to be at the top of the pyramid. In this chapter we talked about how OSPs are in an ideal position to get to that point on the pyramid. Later in the book we will discuss what role you, the manufacturer, can play in ensuring that your field sales force is performing at peak levels.

SUMMARY

How is a well-managed outsourced sales professional different from a prototypical direct sales force? The two have much in common. Both exist to generate demand, to make markets. Neither offers the breadth and depth of assortment of a distributor, and neither is well suited to meeting needs for small lots right away (that is the undisputed province of the distribution function).

Beyond these similarities are numerous differences. The Rep is an extreme specialist that does only one thing: translating a family of latent needs into demand, in a delimited territory, by matching producer capabilities and customer needs (the matchmaker role). The Rep is immobile geographically and extremely focused in terms of tasks (demand generation with no distractions). These features come together to foster an organizational climate that celebrates professional selling, with no apologies. The Rep firm is permanent, market focused, small (compared to many producers), and nimble. Out of necessity, the Rep adapts to market changes. The people who work in a Rep firm are customer focused, like minded, and proud to live in one community, working for the OSP of which they feel a part. Stability, specialization, market ties, nimbleness—these boost revenue, contain costs, and get results fast.

Selling a portfolio *composed to customer desires* from *multiple noncompeting* manufacturers further differentiates the OSP from the direct sales force. Portfolio selling generates economies of scope, or selling synergy, three ways: gaining customer entrée, providing legitimate opportunity to probe deeply, and getting the customer to yes. These properties give the OSP customer leverage and market intelligence. But perhaps the best virtue of economies of scope is that the OSP can use them to overcome the size limitations of any brand or product's market in a limited geography. The OSP is an aggregation machine, a mechanism for pooling demand for market building from multiple complementary suppliers. This enables the OSP to achieve economies of scale. Overhead is easier to justify, variable costs go down, and sales levels go up because size creates a host of advantages: negotiating power, amortization, and capability.

The corporate controller should be particularly interested in two other advantages of the OSP. One is a reduced cost of capital: Reps finance the sales effort and buy their own equipment and supplies. The other is that OSPs shoulder some of the risk inherent in selling by bearing expenses and accepting to be paid on commission, which fixes the ratio of costs to sales.

Finally, manufacturers looking to streamline activities are turning to OSPs to do more than traditional selling. New trends see OSPs providing services such as customer service, quality control, and marketing. Indeed, the OSP is looking more like a long-term business partner than an outsourced supplier.

You might ask, "So where's the hitch? If the OSP really has all the features you claim it does, why don't more producers use them?" First, OSPs do have limitations, and we will address them in Chapter 3. Second, and perhaps more important, is that outsourcing has not yet become "the mode" in selling. Herein lies the opportunity. Business is conservative: few companies are comfortable being contrarians and pioneers. In order to change the business culture and convince companies to take risks, people need examples they can hold up and show around of others who are doing it—and succeeding. Good new ideas need innovators to show the way. Years later, everybody claims they knew it all along.

- In 1983, a strategic alliance was suspiciously viewed as a uniquely Japanese practice. Today, firms feel social pressure to form "alliances" to do almost anything, from snow removal to research and development.
- In 1993, outsourcing entire factories was unthinkable. Today, contract manufacturing is part of every businessperson's lexicon.
- In 2001, human resources was considered the core of a firm's identity. Today, consulting firms are putting out reports that are finding their way into the business press: outsourcing HR is the next big thing.[15]

- In 2002, customer technical service was the bastion of people who lived near their customers and sounded just like them. Today, fiber-optic cables permit technicians in India to solve problems for customers in Boston. (This has created a side market in India to teach regional linguistic mannerisms and baseball chatter to the men and women who answer the telephone.)

The trend is clear: yesterday's radical idea is today's obvious must-do. Businesses today are thinking about outsourcing every-thing. Firms are outsourcing to entities we couldn't name a few years ago ("offshore call centers" anyone?). Unlike these strange new institutions, OSPs have existed for decades. But now that top-level management is viewing all available alternatives in order to keep their companies focused on their core competencies, the OSP option is being viewed in a new light.

In the next chapter, we will look at some of the innovators in outsourcing field sales forces and find out why they took the risk and what they gained as a result.

CASE STUDY:
DO MORE AND EXPECT TO BE COMPENSATED

Beyond doing what you do (selling) well, I believe that representative organizations are in a unique position to do more and with an adequate return on their investment. We are well into the age of outsourcing, witness the fabless semiconductor model, or the proliferation of contract manufacturers, or the growth of service providers like ADP (for payroll). Manufacturers, in their own survival mode, have "skinnied" down their organizations on many fronts and have a natural affinity for variable cost solutions. I encourage representatives to leverage their infrastructure and expand their service offerings beyond traditional selling.

There are many possibilities. Do supplier audits for your principals. Provide first line quality services including on-site root cause analysis, saving your manufacturers the initial trip. Maintaining safety stock on key components might make sense in certain instances. These and others can raise your value (and compensation).

To me the two most obvious extensions from the current selling activity are to offer customer service and marketing support. To the former, take the function over so it isn't duplicated at the Rep and the manufacturer's office. This will require support, notably IT support, from your manufacturers but seems a real opportunity to optimize the supply chain.

As to marketing, this function has been pared back by many companies. I'm not talking about general information on competitors or customer initiatives—that should be a part of normal business and included for the commission. Rather, I'd encourage a service whereby you are deeply entrenched at a few major customers and can accurately merge the technology roadmaps of these key accounts and your lines.

Compensation is an issue, but must be jointly resolved via increased commission rates, fee for services, some model. In the end, if you can deliver the marketing function effectively and efficiently (for less cost than the manufacturer can do it for themselves), you have a golden opportunity to grow income and strengthen relationships with customers and principals.

Robert Terwall, President, Cherry Electrical Products, Waukegan, Illinois

CUSTOMER AND MARKET RESEARCH

For a manufacturers' representative to efficiently and effectively manage and grow business in a territory, the ultimate information tool would include the following:

1. A contact management module to manage information on customer, distributor, and principal contacts.
2. A new business opportunity tracking module to track opportunities from discovery through a customer's product end of life.
3. An order entry/backlog tracking module to track customer purchase orders, shipments, POS, and commissions.
4. A reporting module to allow the dissemination of any information collected. Reports could include monthly new business opportunity reports for principals, management reports for the Rep ownership to track territory performance and growth, and salesperson reports to allow sales individuals within the Rep firm feedback to monitor their progress.

Ideally this tool would operate on a single database platform to allow for easy implementation using a minimum amount of software and operating systems. Additionally, the database needs to allow for remote clients and easy replication to the master database to allow outside salespeople to work while not attached to the Rep's local area network or the Internet to input data or obtain reports.

For many years, manufacturers' representatives undertook the task of creating and writing their own software systems because the commercially available Rep software systems only filled one or two of the above criteria. These Rep-written systems track a great wealth of territory knowledge and often differentiate the Reps that have made the investment in information management apart from their territory peers.

During the dot com era, a number of new software companies began promoting sales information management tools to manufacturers that included contact management modules, new business opportunity tracking modules, and limited reporting. Unfortunately, these systems reduce the efficiency of the Rep on a number of levels by requiring the Rep's sales staff to input data on

---

Craig T. Anderson, President, Sumer Incorporated, Rolling Meadows, Illinois

multiple systems. A similar situation occurred in the 1980s as manufacturers began adopting proprietary e-mail systems and requiring the Reps to utilize their e-mail systems. It was not unusual for an electronic component manufacturers' representative to be using five or more proprietary e-mail systems. Imagine the inefficiency for an outside salesperson to check five or more e-mail systems three or more times a day! Fortunately, the Internet became widely adopted, which created e-mail clients utilizing industry standard formats.

The next step in the sales information management evolution is for the adoption of industry standard formats. Once accomplished Reps, manufacturers, and distributors could utilize their own systems but efficiently exchange a wide array of information including sample requests, quote requests, opportunity reports, and sales data.

ENDNOTES

1. Fein, Adam J. (1999), "2000 U.S. Industry and Trade Outlook," *Modern Distribution Management* (July 10).

2. Dishman, Paul (1996), "Exploring Strategies for Companies That Use Manufacturers' Representatives as Their Sales Force," *Industrial Marketing Management* 25 (5): 453–461.

3. If you have been wondering why arrow A goes in both directions and arrow C goes only in one direction, here's why: what is most important for Reps to know about their producers is context (arrow E). However, *all* customer learning is valuable because it feeds into diagnosing the customer's problem, which is step one to crafting and selling a solution.

4. Green, Anne E., and Angela Canny (2003), *Geographic Mobility: Family Impacts*. Bristol, UK: The Policy Press.

5. Bowman, Douglas, and Das Narayandas (2004), "Customer Profitability in Industrial Markets," *Journal of Marketing Research,* 41 (November), 333–355.

6. For more on building customer-centric organizations, see Day, George S. (1999), *Market-Driven Strategy: Processes for Creating Value*. London: Free Press.

7. In emerging economies, producers dominate resellers, in part because producers provide credit where capital markets are inefficient. Producers tend to use their influence to oblige resellers to specialize in whatever the producer makes. This creates transaction costs for buyers, who must visit a series of outlets to compose their own assortment. A leading indicator of economic transformation is the rise of resellers who are sufficiently well funded to ignore producer displeasure and compose assortments that appeal to customers. This transformation is gaining ground in India, China, and parts of Eastern Europe.

8. This idea was first popularized by Jack Berman in the electronic components industry. It has become standard practice, on the theory that a call worth making is a call worth planning.

9. Ryans, Adrian B., and Charles B. Weinberg (1987), "Territory Sales Response Models: Stability over Time," *Journal of Marketing Research,* 24 (May), 229–233.

10. Williamson, Oliver E. (1996), *The Mechanisms of Governance*. New York: Oxford University Press.

11. Gatignon, Hubert, and John Kimberly, Eds. (2003), *The INSEAD-Wharton Alliance on Globalizing: Strategies for Building Successful Global Businesses*. Cambridge, UK: Cambridge University Press.

12. The importance of this point is underscored in these paired works:

    Moore, Geoffrey A. (1991), *Crossing the Chasm: Marketing and Selling High-Tech Products to Mainstream Consumers*. New York: Harper Business.
    ———. (1995), *Inside the Tornado: Marketing Strategies from Silicon Valley's Cutting Edge*. New York: Harper Business.

13. United States Census Bureau (2001), *1997 Economic Census: Wholesale Trade-Subject Series*. Washington, DC: U.S. Department of Commerce Economics and Statistics Administration.

14. DuBois, Lois C., and Roger H. Grace (1987), "Master Reps: Value-Added Distribution," *Business Marketing,* 15 (December), 62–63.

15. Anonymous (2001), "Out of the Back Room," *The Economist* (December 1), 59–60.

3

Outsource or Direct?

You, the manufacturer, are at the decision crossroads. You have defined a sales role: somebody needs to sell *your products* to *your prospects* in order to meet *your expectations*. You need people to fill this role and managers to supervise the people. In other words, you need a *sales infrastructure* to fill your sales role. Who should own the sales infrastructure? Will you keep this function in-house or outsource to a third party?

This is a critical *strategic decision*, which requires the involvement of high levels of management within the organization. Whichever way you go (make or buy) will have a huge impact on your sales and profits, on the success of your new products, and on your ability to enter new markets.

Indeed, even if your current sales results are "good enough," management needs to ask some critical questions: Could we be doing even *better* by using a different path to market? Could our sales have been higher? Could we have captured a larger market share? Could we have sold a better mix of our product range? Could we have obtained better sales *while operating at a lower, and a more predictable, cost of sales*? These are all opportunity costs—the results you would have achieved if you had made a better decision. And the opportunity costs of the wrong choice (which your accountant can never tell you) are very high.

This chapter focuses on working out the answers to these questions *before* choosing between the OSP option and the employee field sales force. While there are no simple answers or guarantees, the chapter will help you to forecast which sales infrastructure (in-house or outsourcing) will give you better results for your unique sales situation.[1]

THE MAKE-OR-BUY DECISION

Unfortunately, the make-or-buy decision is not a constant: it wholly depends on your products and the prevailing market conditions. You have to work it out, one sales role at a time. This chapter explains the best way to do that. The key is to think like a trial lawyer, following a template that is hammered into students in law school. It's odd and counterintuitive, but it works whenever a decision is binary (two choices, such as "guilty" or "not guilty"). We will follow this template in order to simplify the outsource/don't outsource decision. First, we begin with a "conclusion" and build a case illustrating all the reasons why this conclusion is right. Next, we will reverse the exercise and attack the conclusion, going through all the holes and reasons why the conclusion is wrong. The final step is to become the judge by assessing the damage to the initial conclusion. If badly damaged, the conclusion falls and its opposite stands. Otherwise, the first conclusion holds.

This "devil's advocate" style of reasoning works because it cuts through confusion and detail, helping the lawyer to be methodical, orderly, thorough, and balanced. (In contrast, listing pros and cons quickly degenerates into complexity and double counting and encourages leaping to conclusions.) The key is to start with a conclusion that, when in doubt, is the best one (the "default option"). Western traditions argue that "not guilty" should be the default option, and lawyers should start with that conclusion, then see if they can overturn it.

The "default option" we are starting with is in favor of outsourcing the selling function. In step 1, we walk you through seven reasons why you should outsource the field selling function and illustrate with a success story from Intel and other companies. Here, we single-mindedly praise selling via the OSP.

Then in step 2 we attack the "outsource selling" conclusion. We go through four circumstances that create problems and discuss how vertical integration (employee salespeople) can solve them. Here, we single-mindedly praise direct selling.

We finish with step 3, judging whether the arguments against the OSP carry the day. We ask you to consider each sales role in light of both arguments to determine which route to market is best for your specific situation. Finally, we finish with the good news—you don't have to choose between the two. There is a way to have both through a hybrid sales structure. This is addressed in depth in Chapter 4.

STEP 1: THE DEFAULT OPTION—USE THE OSP

We start with a brief review of the Rep advantages, which we presented in Chapter 2, and follow with case studies.

Advantages of the OSP

Economists argue that when in doubt, markets (outsourcing) prevail over hierarchies (in-house operations). That's the economist's default option.[2] The general line of reasoning is that third-party specialists perform or disappear. The "invisible hand of the marketplace" does an excellent job of encouraging high performance and "correcting" anything else. Either management learns how to perform or the company goes out of business. Behind this stark Darwinian logic is the idea that specialization is itself advantageous. Specialists focus on one thing, pooling demands for whatever they do (logistics, processing payrolls, running information technology systems, and so forth) and getting very good at it by dint of practice and focus. Aggregating demand (pooling) in turn creates economies of scope and scale. Discipline, competence, scope, scale—these reasons undergird outsourcing as the default option.

This rationale fits the selling function, as it fits any function. As discussed in Chapter 2, the OSP will approach the role with these seven advantages:

1. *Motivation and entrepreneurship.* These advantages spring from the opportunity costs of a lost sale and the lost entrée to sell something else, and the failure to meet the need of a customer that the company will face over and over again. That's because the OSP never gets transferred! As a double penalty, the OSP bears the expenses, finances the entire cost of the sale, and buys its own equipment. You pay only for performance.
2. *Geographical stability and territorial competence.* These enable salespeople to control where they live (a growing concern to many people) and give them an advantage in forging and keeping bonds with segments of customers who value personal relationships.
3. *Survival of the fittest.* Poorly managed or underfinanced OSPs eventually succumb to market pressures.
4. *Specialization.* By virtue of doing one thing—selling—the OSP develops a deep core competence in running a sales infrastructure and remains a student of this craft.

5. *Economies of scope and scale.* A full product portfolio creates the ability to obtain an appointment and get to yes (scope). The costs of the sales force infrastructure are then spread over many lines, not only yours, so that the OSP can run a sales infrastructure on a bigger scale.

6. *Heavier coverage.* This means more calls, more often, on more decision influences, in more prospects, and more different *types* of prospects. There is no such thing as a small customer—for the entire portfolio.

7. *It's their balance sheet.* The OSP is another company. You can use them as an intellectual sparring partner to help you work out your marketing and sales strategy. Also, the OSP's people are not burdened by your traditions—the way your company thinks and operates. This means the OSP brings a fresh, unfiltered, outside perspective and different ways of operating. This is healthy for a business relationship.

The OSP as the Default Option: Examples

If the OSP is a good starting point, we should see companies that can easily afford to run a direct sales force yet choose Reps instead—and indeed we do. These companies don't merely copy what other companies are doing ("mimetic isomorphism"), on the idea that the others must be onto something. Rather, they analyze their situation carefully and come to realize that outsourcing is in vogue for good reasons.

Notice that all of our cases are of big businesses. The OSP's ability to allow smaller firms to "put up" a sales force without having to pay the heavy costs of developing an in-house team (physical infrastructure, computers, printers, cell phones, cars, sales managers, etc.) is already well documented. But their relevance to big businesses is less known. Indeed, the perception that OSPs are only for the "little guys" ("big guys" go direct) needs to be corrected. Let's start with Intel.

One of the most successful firms on the planet and the world's largest maker of semiconductors, Intel broke decades of tradition and upended its own corporate culture in 1999 by studying and committing a segment of its market to OSPs.[3] Until then, Intel had operated using exclusively employee salespeople. Widely admired and consistently profitable, Intel epitomized the big firm that had no use for the OSP. Indeed, Intel's corporate culture was one of self-sufficiency in sales: it was taken for granted that Reps were not an option.

By 2003, Intel was using 25 Rep firms to generate over $800 million in sales on four continents. Why the change?

Intel began working with OSPs after purchasing the Digital Semiconductor business unit from Digital Equipment Corporation in 1998. Given that the newly acquired products had a wide variety of uses—from cell phones to Internet data processing— Intel faced the possibility of selling into multiple and varied markets in which it had little experience. (Heretofore, Intel had focused primarily on the PC market.) Management wanted fast results with these new customers and did not want to wait for investments in relationship building to pay off.

The worldwide director of Intel's program of selling through OSPs, George Langer, says that Intel became convinced after seeing the ability to shift the heavy payroll costs of high-paid, salaried semiconductor sales professionals to the OSP, making for an extremely cost-effective way to sell. Senior managers were particularly impressed because they liked the simplicity of packing most of their sales cost into a commission, which falls when results do.

The results were so compelling that within *90 days* Intel was recruiting more Reps. The $800 million in revenue the OSPs generate for Intel is all new business: no direct salespeople lost their jobs. Today, Intel's network of Reps (which they call their "extended sales force") works closely with Intel staff, is trained alongside Intel's employee salespeople, and functions as a supplement to their efforts.

Clearly, OSPs have been a means of fast growth *and* operating efficiency for Intel. Says Langer, "We've shown that a large company can outsource sales and be flexible, cost-effective, and efficient." (Langer tells the Intel story in his own words later in the chapter.)

Intel is not alone among large firms using OSPs. Table 3-1 lists other large, well-known firms in the electronics industry who outsource field sales, countering the image of OSPs being suitable mainly for small firms. The advantages of the OSP apply to any business. Table 3-2 shows the variety of industries that use OSPs. Indeed, size often creates new motives to use the OSP, as a way to reengineer fragmented product lines, a problem faced by many large firms.

Table 3-1. Some Large Firms Using the OSP in the Electronic Components Industry

- Advanced Microdevices
- Fairchild Semiconductor
- Motorola
- Altera
- Intel
- IBM
- LSI Logic
- ON Semiconductor
- Texas Instruments

Source: The Electronic Representatives Association, reported in Elliott (2003).

WHY SHOULD BIG COMPANIES CARE?

The OSP is frequently viewed as well suited to represent small manufacturers. The (often unspoken) assumption is that small companies, being resource constrained, can't really mount a proper in-house operation. Large companies, the reasoning continues, can duplicate the OSP's economies of scope and scale, because a large company probably got that way by making multiple, related product lines. Therefore, rather than embed its products in a line composed by the OSP, a large manufacturer can compose its own portfolio of what it makes. Ergo, the OSP is for small firms. When they grow up and become big firms, they can shed the OSP and vertically integrate.

There is something to be said for this argument. A large, multiproduct maker probably can muster the resources needed to field a sales force and can provide a portfolio of products for it to sell. But does that make in-house selling a good idea? Not necessarily. The manufacturer may have better uses for the resources. Most important, manufacturers compose portfolios of what they can make. Almost invariably, these portfolios are not entirely coherent *from the customer's perspective*. Remember, the customer is uninterested in technical exigencies and organizational constraints. The customer wants what it wants, regardless of how unrelated the products are from the factory's standpoint.

Holes in the producer's portfolio occur in three ways. The first and most obvious way is the sheer absence of a category. The customer doesn't care why the producer doesn't make it yet or never will make it or doesn't make it anymore. The second and subtler way to have a hole in the portfolio is to have the "wrong" level of value. The customer may consider a particular item to be overpriced, or to be too low in quality, or even too high in quality (bells and whistles). Or the customer may want some feature that the producer doesn't provide (here, the list is very long—design, weight, size, shelf life).

The third (and very common) way that big companies generate incoherent portfolios is invention. Big manufacturers tend to run R&D operations that create many new products. Quite a few of these don't fit the existing product line very well. Yet, they deserve a chance at the market. In the right portfolio, they would do well.

The net of these arguments is simple: big companies *do* have many uses for the OSP!

Table 3-2. Multiple Industries: Large Firms with Substantial OSP Representation

FIRM	SPECIALTY
Federal Signal Corporation	Supplier of safety, signaling, and communications equipment
Hoffman Enclosures, Inc.	Producer of industrial enclosures that protect sensitive controls and components
Ingersoll-Rand	Provider of air and electronic power tools, material-handling equipment, fluid-handling products, and dispensing systems
Energizer	Manufacturer of dry-cell batteries and flashlights
Delta-Therm	Manufacturer of innovative faucet designs and safety features
Avery Dennison	Manufacturer of pressure-sensitive adhesives and materials, office products, labels, and tags
3M Company	Provider of innovative and practical solutions through diversified technology
Intel Corporation	Manufacturer of innovative technology for the computer and Internet industry
Fabri-Kal Corporation	Manufacturer of custom and stock thermoformed plastic products
Delta Faucet Company	Manufacturer and innovator of faucets and faucet-related products
Humanicare International, Inc.	Maker of protective garments and protective features for the incontinent
Tennant Company	Manufacturer of systems to assess supplier performance
Fiskars, Inc.	Manufacturer of value-added, branded consumer and commercial products serving the needs of volume purchasers worldwide
Master Lock Company	Maker of padlocks and security products
Rust-Oleum Corporation	Manufacturer of protective paints and coatings for home and industry
Jacuzzi Whirlpool Bath	Leader in innovative jet technology, air controls, and product design

Continued

Table 3-2. Continued

FIRM	SPECIALTY
Danfoss Controls	Manufacturer of controls for water application needs: analyzing process and pump performance
Tyco Adhesives	Diversified manufacturing conglomerate
Pass & Seymour Legrand	Conglomerate manufacturer of low-voltage electrical products
Elkay Manufacturing Company	Conglomerate manufacturer of faucets, water coolers, and fountains
Hunt-Wesson Foods	Manufacturer of a variety of food products
Kraft Foods	Manufacturer of snacks, beverages, cheese, grocery items, and convenience foods
Carl Zeiss, Inc.	Technological innovator of optical and opto-electronic industries
Kimberly-Clark Corporation	Manufacturer of health and hygiene products

Based on information provided by the Manufacturers' Representatives Educational and Research Foundation (MRERF).

This was the case for Honeywell Sensing and Control of Freeport, Illinois. Tom Dalton, vice president of worldwide sales, tells us that his firm decided to add OSPs because of the fragmented nature of their business. "We added Reps to leverage existing relationships in accounts and have additional resources on the ground in key territories. A Rep writing 5 or 10 lines into a customer already is a rather compelling value proposition to a principal. Additionally, the 'variable cost' aspect of Reps in this environment is obvious—they are hungry and driven to grow our business."

You might think, "But these are specific cases, where companies had some very special needs. Surely Reps can't *still* be the default option for large companies working in large territories packed with market potential." Actually, more often than not, they are. Indeed, the economics often favor the Rep model *even for large companies operating in large territories.*

Robert Terwall, President of Cherry Electrical Products in Waukegan, Illinois, conducted an economic analysis in 2003. Cherry faces a mix of inherently small territories and a few large territories. Although Cherry, as a large company, could have subsidized money-losing operations in the small territories, the idea was to work out the economics of each sales force operation in each part of the market. Therefore, Cherry did its analysis one sales territory at a time. The study looked at payroll and fringe benefits (including automobiles and expense reimbursement), as well as costs associated with office locations and staffing, both selling and support. An exhaustive pro forma expense budget for each of the 16 territories in which they sell through Reps showed that *even their largest marketplace* still favored the Representative model by 8 percent. That advantage became extremely pronounced in the smaller territories that make up the bulk of the marketplace. Observed Terwall, "In the end, we found that as territory sales get smaller, the scale tipped more dramatically to the variable costs of Reps, typically two to four times premium to staff a direct office. In aggregate, we estimated our costs to cover the United States and Canada would more than double, an estimated 122 percent premium over commissions expense, to staff a direct versus representative field sales organization." (See the full case study in Chapter 8.)

These success stories show the reason why outsourcing is the default option. The simplistic logic of "big firms go direct" is the default option of the conformist. Unfortunately, it leaves money on the table. The opportunity cost of conformity is high.

STEP 2: ATTACK THE DEFAULT OPTION OF USING THE OSP

Like a trial lawyer, we have single-mindedly argued the case for using an OSP for your sales role. Now we reverse gears and attack this idea: What situations create problems that erode the reasons to outsource field sales? Enough erosion means that creating the infrastructure of an employee sales force will work out to give you a lower cost/sales ratio. We cover three conditions that create strong arguments for an in-house sales team.

Conditions Favoring an In-House Solution: Company Idiosyncrasies

A major reason to outsource (anything, not just the sales force) is to focus on performance. If your OSP is not performing, you can work with that organization to fix it—or change to a different OSP. An OSP can thrive only by understanding this dynamic, which means that the OSP is motivated to be highly effective, efficient, and responsive—and will go out of business if it doesn't deliver.

But what happens when your company's products or processes are highly unusual? Economists prefer to use the term "idiosyncratic," but the idea is the same: there is a distinctive or peculiar feature of something within your company that will require the salespeople to master an intricate, idiosyncratic role. Role mastery is the good news. The bad news is that now you badly need these salespeople and will find them very difficult to replace. *You depend on salespeople once they acquire your company-specific capabilities.* And you are now dealing with monopolists—they are the one source of what you need.

Economics teaches that dealing with monopolists is very delicate. If their performance falls unreasonably low, your usual remedy (threaten to replace them) is useless. *They* know it, and *you* know it. This is an instance where absolute control is not only ineffective but also completely useless. So what can you do?

You can vertically integrate, or, in other words, become the monopolist's employer.

What does that buy you? First, you are in a better position to detect poor performance: your ability to demand and get information is probably higher. Second, you have a certain legitimate authority as an employer. Most people accept that they owe their employer a reasonable degree of cooperation and will accept the constraints imposed by a supervisor (also employed by you). Third, you monopolize their time. This means that it is harder for them to replace you: you are balancing your dependence against theirs. Fourth, you have a variety of ways to pay them and influence them: this gives you motivational leverage. Fifth, you can build a corporate culture that enhances employee loyalty (and retention). These are five compelling advantages of employing your sales force.

Of course, there are disadvantages. You give up the economies of *scope* that are inherent to the OSP: your employees can only sell what you make. The customer may prefer the customer focus and one-stop shopping of the OSP. You may find it difficult to recoup the OSP's economies of *scale,* some of which are due to specialization (their focus on selling only). Economies of scope and scale increase your coverage, so by vertically integrating the sales force, you may underserve your market. Because it's hard to manage employees, it's easy to end up with an underperforming sales force, too expensive for the sales they generate. And it's easy for an internal sales force to become an empire, accountable to no one. In short, you give up the benefits of the default option.

However, for highly idiosyncratic companies, there is much to be said in favor of vertical integration of the sales force.

Determining if Your Company Is Highly Idiosyncratic

Idiosyncrasies within companies tend to emerge on two levels: products and processes.

IDIOSYNCRATIC PRODUCTS. Idiosyncratic products are not only quite different from the competitors' products: they are highly unconventional *for their industry*. That's why even an industry-experienced salesperson needs time and training to master them, to acquire the capability of understanding what these products do and how your customers use them. For these products, industry experience is very far from doing the job and may not even be very helpful.

Of course, one goal of selling is to convince the customer that every product is unique (even if the differences are not critical). We go beyond that. The acid test is how hard it is to master *your* products/applications from a good base of knowledge about what your *industry* makes. The more fundamentally unusual your product happens to be, the more the salesperson must learn that is specific to you, and to your company.

This is not just a matter of how technical the product is. For example, a semiconductor is a highly technical product, sold by people with training in engineering. But most brands of semiconductors are not idiosyncratic: if you know how to sell one brand, you don't have to adapt much to sell another brand. What you know can be redeployed from one brand to another. *This is the key to idiosyncrasy.* Knowledge that is easy to redeploy is *not* idiosyncratic.

What kinds of products (and services) are likely to require company-specific capabilities? Ask yourself if your brands are sophisticated *and* customized *and* unique *and* complex *and* fast changing *and* technical? That's a lot of "ands." If your brand fits, the odds are good that it is idiosyncratic.

Here's a good test. You have come to depend on a salesperson who over time has come to learn your product, processes, and so forth. If your salesperson leaves you and joins the competition, can he or she slip into a new sales role and learn another set of brands—using his/her knowledge of *your* brands and how *your* customers use them? If your brand is idiosyncratic, the answer is "no." Your brand knowledge doesn't transfer because your products/applications are unlike any of your competitor's products/applications. Like good wine, idiosyncrasy does not travel well. Your salespeople must pick it up directly from your company, either by formal training or by on-the-job experience. And since much idiosyncratic knowledge is tacit, on-the-job training (learning by watching and doing) will be more effective than formal training.

Brands like this tend to have another feature: the salesperson is privy to a good deal of confidential information. So here's another test: how much do you worry about the damage that your salesperson's inside information could do to you? Do you take security measures (locking the files, blocking and cleaning out the computers), and do you do it as soon as your salespeople leave? When legally feasible, do you make them sign contracts pledging not to compete and not to reveal? If you take these steps, chances are you are selling something that is truly idiosyncratic.

Now, many brands are somewhat idiosyncratic but not completely so. It's good for the ego to think that what you make and sell are truly "distinctive" or idiosyncratic. But to get the real flavor of what we mean, ask yourself if *these* adjectives fit what you sell: peculiar, eccentric, weird, bizarre, odd, quirky, and unconventional. Now that's idiosyncratic. Remember, base this against other brands in your industry. (Of course, if you *are* the industry, you are unquestionably idiosyncratic.)

IDIOSYNCRATIC INTERNAL PROCESSES. There are three principal ways of being idiosyncratic in your internal processes. The first way concerns your operating methods that affect the salesperson (for example, procedures for getting approval of a sale, getting a quotation, or arranging delivery). If your methods are unusual, complex, slow, or bureaucratic, your internal routines are probably idiosyncratic. Here are some symptoms:

- Your salespeople need to learn many "ins and outs" of your company to be effective.
- Your firm has a long list of nonstandard, written rules.
- Your firm has an even longer list of nonstandard, unwritten rules—but that the salesperson had better learn.
- Industry-experienced salespeople aren't sure what to do to get anything done for your customer.

- Your firm has its own "language," its own words that the new-comer needs to master. If industry veterans need a glossary, your firm fits here.

Second, it may not suffice to spend enough time on the job to come to know your company's proprietary methods. Your sales-people might also need to form a myriad of close relationships *within your firm* (we're not discussing the customer here). These relationships are needed to get something—anything—done and include relationships with people in shipping, on the factory floor, in the credit department, and in customer service. This, too, is characteristic of a bureaucratic company: relationships are needed to cut through the red tape.

In short, company-specific capabilities include knowledge and relationships that an industry veteran does not have but will need to acquire when joining your firm. They are not redeployable. They cannot be acquired from the outside—a salesperson has to work for you to develop these capabilities. In addition, many of them are tacit: you could not turn them into a classroom presentation, and even if you could, you would not expect people to really master them that way. Salespeople, even industry veterans, must learn by doing.

If this description fits your company, you may realize a lower cost/sales ratio by vertically integrating field selling. The rationale is the same: you will be doing business with a monopolist once your salespeople have acquired these idiosyncratic assets that revolve around your internal processes. If you must do business with a monopolist, you may need the leverage that vertical integration gives you.

A word of caution is in order here. If you must have internal processes that are idiosyncratic, you probably need an employee sales force. But do you really *need* to be idiosyncratic in how you do things internally? The reader, going through the list of what makes internal processes unusual, cannot fail to notice the downside. These are places where it is hard to get things done. Rules, regulations, protocol, etiquette, complicated procedures, administration, officialdom—sounds like big government! These can be stifling places in which to work. Many companies like this want to change, to become more nimble, flexible, and responsive—in short, more entrepreneurial. Ironically, a direct sales force actually perpetuates the bureaucracy rather than helps a company to become leaner. This is because employees can be made to master the system, and they will. So if you need the system, an OSP may not be appropriate. However, if you merely tolerate this system, and wish you could change it, hiring an OSP may help accomplish this shift.

Intel once again provides a good example. George Langer explains in a sidebar on page 65 how Intel went about finding and hiring the highly technical sales operations they needed, despite company idiosyncrasies. Several points are critical here. First, high-order technical skills are utterly critical. Second, there are many third parties that possess those skills. Third, it wasn't difficult to verify which OSPs really had the right technical expertise and which merely appeared to have them. Fourth, Intel made a conscious tradeoff. There *were* idiosyncrasies to the Intel version of the product category and to the manufacturer itself. That's why Intel was not convinced that an outside company could do the job as well as Intel employees—and why Langer judges that "This thinking was probably accurate with respect to knowledge of Intel culture and Intel product." Nonetheless, Intel traded off the benefits of mastering these idiosyncrasies against the cost of the time it would take to penetrate new market segments with an in-house sales force. Several years later, Intel is satisfied with its decision and "very impressed with the technical capability and results" of their OSPs. Contrary to a popular myth, an OSP can be deeply technical. Chapter 2 explains how an OSP can attract, motivate, and retain highly trained, highly capable people.

IDIOSYNCRASY AND A VOLATILE ENVIRONMENT. The argument is that there is an advantage to going direct when you are idiosyncratic in your products/applications or in your internal processes. This is particularly true when you operate in a highly volatile market environment, which is extremely hard to predict. In such environments, forecasting is a particularly frustrating exercise, and no one should have much confidence in the predictions anyway. Organization theorists call these "high-velocity" or "high clock-speed" settings, in which change happens so fast that the only safe expectation is that things will change fast. Not surprisingly, many decision-makers do not put much effort into forecasting: they focus instead on quickly sensing developments and moving to adapt to them. Managers in these markets describe them as highly complicated, volatile, difficult to monitor, and uncertain. Firms often face environments like this when they put a heavy strategic emphasis on new products.

INTEL ON FINDING AND HIRING TECHNICAL SELLING SERVICES

As Intel considered an outsourced sales force to penetrate new market segments, it was quickly apparent there was a wide range of selling services available for hire. It was important for Intel to describe and document the work to be done before beginning the recruiting process.

Intel management was not convinced that an outside company could do as good a job selling Intel as Intel itself. This thinking was probably accurate with respect to knowledge of Intel culture and product. However, penetration of new market segments, where the value of the Intel brand was not yet established, required customer relationships and familiarity with technical silicon socket design cycles. Intel could do both well, but it would take time, and Intel was characteristically impatient.

Intel's mission statement for several years had centered on being "the preeminent building block supplier." Intel's core competencies included semiconductor design and manufacturing. Intel customers were historically OEMs, which incorporated Intel "building blocks" into finished goods. Selling Intel products required being able to read and understand product design specifications, often down to individual sockets on a circuit board layout. If Intel was to hire selling services to "escort" customers through a technical silicon socket design process, then those salespeople would have to be comfortable working at that level of detail.

Intel solicited feedback from local distributors, customers, and industry organizations. There were technical electronic Representative firms available for hire. Intel inspected Representative line cards to judge whether these firms routinely sold active electronic semiconductor parts. Intel found that approximately 65 percent of employees (in these Rep firms) were trained as electrical engineers with industry design experience, who during their career came to realize that they preferred, and were skillful at, working with customers to design in semiconductors parts. Intel could confirm credentials through required "quick" interviews with sales employees of each Representative firm, which was a final candidate to represent the Intel line.

Intel was also clear that there were services typically offered by Representatives, which Intel would *not* utilize or hire. Intel had sophisticated "in-house" capabilities around demand forecasting and order fulfillment (for direct relationships with larger customers), which were augmented by our network of distributors (for indirect relationships with smaller customers).

The local Intel sales team was responsible for recruiting local Representative firms. This was accomplished through a series of first and second round interviews, which resulted in two or three candidates. An Intel decision team was formed for each territory to conduct final interviews across two or three days. There was an Intel-only "debriefing" session after each final interview where the Intel decision team would discuss the merits of and the impressions left by the Representative candidate. Intel evaluated depth and breadth of customer relationships (and customer feedback) and recounted first impressions made by the quick interviews with individual salespeople. Intel considered Representative market knowledge and strength of local distributor relationships (and feedback).

In the end, Intel was able to recruit and hire Representative firms, which offered the required technical selling skills. And, after several years, Intel management has been very impressed with the technical capability and results of the Representatives hired for the communications, embedded and networking market segments.

George Langer, Intel's Worldwide Representative Program Manager

Regarding volatility, Intel is a case in point. The first Intel sidebar in this chapter describes an "emerging customer base" and success tied to a "broad base" of small firms whose "engineering ideas had not been adopted as standards, and it was well known that many would fail in their efforts to become market leaders."

In an environment like this, the advantages of the OSP are obvious. The manufacturer is placing risky bets. Working with an OSP is one way to hedge one's bet—and that's exactly what Intel did. As the situation changes, the manufacturer can adapt its relationship with its OSP—or switch to a different OSP. And if the manufacturer can forge a good working relationship with its outsourced field sales force, the OSP's market-sensing capabilities are particularly helpful. In economic jargon, the manufacturer enjoys the flexibility of market contracting and relies on the market mechanism to create incentives for both parties to adapt. In business English, the manufacturer does not carry high overhead, and it *does* need to invest in an employee sales force that might turn out to be inappropriate as things keep changing. Or, as most people would put it, it is easy to shift your bet if it turns out that you bet wrongly.

But what happens when we put together high idiosyncrasy (*not* Intel's case) *and* a volatile environment? The combination is exceptionally difficult to manage. Now, the manufacturer depends on a monopolist (thanks to the necessary idiosyncratic knowledge and relationships) *and* needs to adapt fast and frequently. The market mechanism breaks down because there is no equivalent alternative supplier of selling services. (There are plenty of alternative suppliers, but they do not have the company-specific capabilities.) The manufacturer has no leverage. Managing in a volatile environment but with no leverage is not a viable business proposition.

In short, the combination of high idiosyncrasy and environmental volatility tilts the forecast of the cost/sales ratio in the direction of the company sales force. Note that this ratio will be high.

On average, though, it will be even higher when outsourcing the selling function.

How can the manufacturer get a low cost/sales ratio under the combination of high idiosyncrasy and high environmental volatility? The answer is that this is impossible. Unless the manufacturer can earn a very high return, entering a market like this is unwise. High returns are necessary to offset the high cost of entry and high risk of failure. It is safe to say that the most common reaction to this situation is not to enter the market vertically integrated—it is not to enter at all. This is synonymous to walking away from the market. Those few who do enter will need very high returns to offset the high cost/sales ratio they are certain to incur.

So far, we have focused on idiosyncrasy. The general principle is that when you are extremely unconventional in what you sell and how you operate, vertical integration will frequently give you a lower cost/sales ratio. Let us turn to other arguments that bear on the cost/sales ratio you will realize for your sales role.

Conditions Favoring an In-House Solution: When Performance Is Difficult to Evaluate from the Results

This argument is about messy sells, of the sort that are a sales manager's nightmare when the time comes to evaluate performance. Assume (imagine) that you do not have good, accurate, individual records of who sold what to whom and of how much each salesperson costs. Or assume that even if you *do* have a good information system like this (and many companies don't!), you still cannot evaluate a salesperson's performance without the feeling that you are being very unfair about it. Economists call this situation "performance ambiguity" or "internal uncertainty." This means that you can't really figure out who the good and bad performers are.

Compared to other professional occupations, selling suffers less from performance ambiguity than most. That's why there is much more performance-based pay in selling than in almost any other managerial job, apart from that of the CEO.[4] Still, some sales roles are fiendishly difficult to evaluate in performance terms. There are many reasons for this.

- Sales might be made by teams rather than by individuals.
- Sales might come in from one place while decisions are made in another. For example, detailers (pharmaceutical salespeople) call on doctors because they decide what drugs we take, but orders come from pharmacists.

- Being able to verify what the salesperson says may be much more important than how much the salesperson sells. For example, salespeople selling hazardous chemicals or pharmaceuticals expose their companies to heavy legal liabilities if they say anything that might appear misleading. In the face of such risks, the manufacturer may be more interested in being able to monitor how salespeople present the product than in whether they make a sale.
- A sale may be long and complex, with so many decision influences that it is hard to figure out how much credit (or blame) a salesperson deserves.
- A market may be poorly developed, so that it's difficult to tell whether a given sales level is high or low—no one knows what to expect from this brand in this territory.
- A firm may simply have a slow, inaccurate information system that makes it hard to tell how anybody is doing in time for management to make decisions based on the information.

Whatever the reason, the result is the same: a manufacturer cannot say with much confidence how well a salesperson is doing. Performance is hard to evaluate from the outside, using the sort of data (such as orders, sales, or costs) that can be pieced together to show what a salesperson is achieving. Thus, it is hard to evaluate performance—even from the inside. This is an extremely difficult situation to manage—it's rather like sailing through choppy seas without a good navigation system. It's easy to give salespeople the wrong rewards, with damaging consequences: rewarding too much is not economically viable, rewarding the wrong things sends everyone on the wrong course, and rewarding too little is demotivating.

There is no really satisfactory solution to this problem. However, when performance ambiguity is very high, an employee sales force is frequently the better solution. The reason is that an employer can work around the issue of how to motivate salespeople to do the right thing (even if it's hard to tell if they're really achieving anything). Salespeople can be supervised closely and be paid a salary for exhibiting the right behavior (if you know what that is) and avoiding the wrong behavior (if you know what that is). Also, the manufacturer can take steps to build loyalty and raise morale. For example, the firm can create a participative, supportive atmosphere and offer job security, with a view to creating a loyal workforce that will do the right thing—even if you cannot enforce it or prove that it *is* the right thing!

Why not pay the OSP to do the same thing? Why not contract with an organization that is run like this, and let them worry about ensuring that your brand performs well (even if you can't be sure about whatever that means)? You can, and many firms do. Indeed, the OSP often has developed better ways of dealing with this problem than most manufacturers. But you are left with a nagging problem. Remember, when dealing with an OSP, you are paying for results. Lacking the ability to manage the results, you will find yourself wondering whether your OSP is doing the best possible job for you. We focus on situations where the numbers, if they exist, are not reliable or interpretable. The fallback, then, is to closely manage what *individuals* are doing day to day and to inspire their loyalty to your firm alone. This is not the nature of a relationship with another organization.

Put into jargon, vertically integrating in the face of high performance ambiguity allows you to monitor inputs as a substitute for assessing outputs. In contrast, outsourcing allows you to focus on rewarding results—which is difficult to do under high internal uncertainty about what constitutes a good result and a good measure of results.

Note, however, the underlying logic. Performance ambiguity means you cannot tie rewards to results. Therefore, you substitute a supervisor (a sales manager) for performance pay, and you substitute your own sales organization for that of the OSP. Logically, once you do this, you need to supervise salespeople closely and pay them essentially on salary, rewarding them for doing the right things and/or showing the right spirit. *This means overhead.* Your managers need to be in close touch with salespeople. This implies that they must have a low span of control. Having a dozen people report to a manager, for example, makes this impossible. Having a "manager" who also services accounts has the same effect. And paying employee salespeople for results (commissions, performance-based bonuses and contests) is logically inconsistent.[5] If you are going to manage your employee salespeople lightly and pay them for results, you might as well outsource and reap the benefits of the default option.

If you *do* outsource, do not despair. A complex sell can be managed with an OSP structure. The scenario of convoluted hard-to-attribute sales is very typical in the electronics industry. For example, design is done in Philadelphia, purchasing is done in

San José, manufacturing is done in China. As confusing as this can be, OSPs in all areas *do* get paid! It's not pretty, nor is it always done fairly, but it is typical and frequent. Some of these projects take years before anybody gets paid. Reps finance the entire cost of the sale for the entire period.

Conditions Favoring an In-House Solution: Heavy Nonselling Responsibilities

Most sales roles demand the salesperson perform activities that are not selling per se. These activities are related to selling and help to get selling done, but they do not cover time spent securing an order. An exhaustive multiyear study detailed 150 things salespeople do, a startling number of which are nonselling activities.[6] Some of these activities include

- Following up on sales and service with the customer (e.g., maintenance, installation, training of customer personnel)
- Meeting with other people from your company (e.g., marketing)
- Participating in the formulation of marketing strategy
- Serving on company task forces
- Mentoring and training other salespeople
- Drawing up call reports and other forms of inputting and processing data (this category has grown massively since the mid-1980s)
- Gathering market intelligence (in general, responding to requests for information from your own company). For example, there are some sales roles that require salespeople to count and report the number of machines in a factory or cars in a parking lot in order to provide data for marketing to do customer segmentation studies.

Now, all salespeople do some of this, and some do most of it, and different industries have different levels of demands. However, some sales roles take this to an extreme, demanding very heavy nonselling activities that crowd out the selling function. These sales roles are often better suited to an employee sales force, which will create a lower cost/sales ratio than if the same role is filled by an OSP. The reason is that outsourcing rests on the principle of pay for performance. In contrast, these jobs demand pay for behavior or activity. There are no clear, outward indicators of whether the activity is being done. Therefore, there are no "results" to reward the OSP for achieving. Vertical integration, compensation via salary, and close supervision are usually appropriate to these jobs.

This said, there are OSPs that have more detailed customer and market data than any principals expect. Although there are many industries that do not ask for much feedback, some industries, such as the electronics industry, expect a high level of non-selling activities from their OSPs—and get it. Those who don't or won't supply detailed information have their contracts terminated.

STEP 3: PUTTING IT ALL TOGETHER

Notice what does *not* matter. The issue is *not* how big your company is. Big firms might be better off outsourcing a field sales force, while small firms might be better off integrating it. It's *not* what other firms in your industry are doing. Their situation may be different from yours—or they may be leaving money on the table by making the less efficient choice (thereby running a higher cost/sales ratio than they could be getting). It's *not* what your firm prefers or is used to using. The real issue is what creates the right cost structure and performance standard, given what you sell, how you sell it, and how you operate, *one sales role at a time.* Outsourcing has seven compelling reasons supporting it. Companies large and small can reap great benefits from outsourcing. Yet there are cases when direct can override the outsourcing default option.

If the sales role is so idiosyncratic that it requires substantial company-specific skills (especially in a volatile environment), if performance in the sales role is inherently ambiguous, or if your salespeople have extremely significant nonselling responsibilities, you may achieve a lower cost/sales ratio by going with an employee sales force. A word of warning: to do better with an employee sales force than you will with an OSP, you will need to pay a substantial salary component, invest in sales management and the tools managers need, and build employee commitment. Otherwise, you will lose much of the leverage you need to manage the individuals who carry out your sales role.

The good news is that you don't have to choose between an OSP and direct: you can have your cake and eat it too! Many companies—in an effort to reap the benefits of both systems— use a hybrid approach. We will discuss this in greater detail in Chapter 4.

SUMMARY

Approaching the make (direct)/buy (outsourcing) decision requires the foresight to understand which infrastructure will give the best results for your unique situation. Instead of comparing the two choices side by side, we started with outsourcing as the default position and then attacked the position, offering scenarios where outsourcing might not make sense.

To start the process, we reviewed the major advantages of OSPs outlined in Chapter 2. We showed that household names like Intel and Honeywell Sensing and Controls use OSPs, dispelling the myth that OSPs are the domain of smaller companies that cannot afford their own in-house field sales force. Intel has been extremely successful in blending OSPs with their direct sales forces (an example of a "hybrid solution," which we will discuss in Chapter 4). The Intel, Honeywell, and Cherry Electric cases also serve to dispel another myth: that OSPs cannot provide the same level of technical expertise that an in-house team can. In fact, Intel found that a majority (65 percent) of the employees of the Rep firms it interviewed were electrical engineers with industry design experience, who during their career came to realize that they preferred and were skillful at working with customers to design in complex semiconductors devices.

This is not to say that outsourcing is always the right choice. The second half of the chapter attacks the "default position": looking at scenarios where the advantages of the OSP fall short. This is the case when companies have very specific or unique products or processes. These idiosyncrasies mean that a company must invest a great deal in training and educating its field sales force. The good news is that these sales representatives will master a role; the bad news is they will be extremely hard to replace. Economics teaches that dealing with monopolists is very delicate. In this case, it may actually be better to become the monopolist's employer. This gives you the upper hand—most people acknowledge the fact that they owe their employer cooperation. Also, by monopolizing their time it is harder for them to replace you: their skills will be completely tailored to your specific products or processes, making it difficult for them to find a job with a different company.

Another scenario that lends itself to an in-house field selling team is when the role has many nonselling responsibilities such as mentoring or managing other employees, sitting on special task forces, or helping develop marketing strategy. Outsourced sales professionals are paid to sell; many will offer additional services (we address these in Chapters 6 and 7), but their main focus is selling. If you need a salesperson to do more, you might consider an in-house solution.

The final scenario that turns the tide toward away from an OSP is when you have "performance ambiguity." This can occur when sales are made by teams rather than by individuals or when sales may come in from one place while decisions are made in another (for example, pharmaceutical salespeople call on doctors because they decide what drugs we take, but orders come from pharmacists). This also occurs when a sale is long and complex, with so many decision influences that it is hard to figure out how much credit (or blame) a salesperson deserves. In scenarios when a manufacturer cannot say with much confidence how well a salesperson is doing, it's easy to give salespeople the wrong rewards, with damaging consequences. Rewarding too much is not economically viable, rewarding the wrong things sends everyone on the wrong course, and rewarding too little is demotivating. Thus, when performance ambiguity is very high, an employee sales force is frequently the better solution. The reason is that in-house salespeople can be supervised more closely and be paid a salary for exhibiting the right behavior and avoiding the wrong behavior. Also, the manufacturer can take steps to build loyalty and raise morale. For example, the firm can create a participative, supportive atmosphere and offer job security, with a view to creating a loyal workforce that will do the right thing.

Finally, we conclude with the news that you don't actually have to choose between a direct and outsourced field selling force. A hybrid solution allows you to combine both systems and apply to your specific situation.

CASE STUDY:
GEORGE LANGER ON WHY INTEL USES REPS

When Intel purchased the Digital Semiconductor business unit from Digital Equipment Corporation in 1998, the acquisition included a fabrication facility and several product lines with promising market potential. Each of these product lines incorporated onto semiconductors or silicon chips the latest solutions to some of the problems facing the computer industry as it continued its march along the path of Moore's Law (which argues transistor density doubles every 18 months) and new application requirements (Internet usage was increasing exponentially).

One product line was an implementation of PCI (Peripheral Component Interconnect), an emerging standard addressing the need for higher performance in the electronic connections within and between chips. Another product line was based on the ARM™ architecture and emphasized low-power, high-performance processing so critical to handheld computer and communication devices. A third product line used this low-power high-performance architecture to confront the overhead of the packet processing associated with transporting data over Internet protocol. A fourth product line, where Intel already had considerable experience, was Ethernet chips, which formed the physical connection between a device and the network.

Intel quickly realized that these small product lines were growth opportunities, especially in networking and communications. Further, Intel was aware that business and market analysts were predicting flattened growth in the PC market segment, which had fueled Intel's own growth in recent years. The timing appeared correct, and Intel was ready to invest in new high-growth market segments. Within Intel it was argued that the go-to-market sales strategies that had proved so successful for Intel in the PC market segment were not suitable in developing the customers, original equipment manufacturers (OEMs), who would be the leaders in the high-growth communications businesses of the future.

So the important question was how to gain immediate sales traction with an emerging customer base, in a market segment where Intel was *not* necessarily a household name, nor a recognized silicon supplier. Success seemed to be tied to a broad base of small, often venture capital funded OEMs, whose engineering

---

George Langer, Intel's Worldwide Representative Program Manager

ideas had not been adopted as standards, and it was well known many would fail in their efforts to become market leaders. This was the landscape of networking and communications OEMs in the late 1990s.

While Intel viewed these newly acquired (i.e., Digital Semiconductor) product lines as suitable for communications and networking, Intel also recognized their potential in the more mature but still profitable embedded applications market segments. Embedded applications included industrial computing, medical equipment, and point-of-sale terminals, where products were not considered "computers" yet proper application function was based on microprocessors and network connections. Years ago, Intel had many design wins among embedded OEMs; however, in recent years Intel had focused almost entirely on the higher growth and more profitable PC market segment. Most of these early embedded OEM customer relationships faded and probably more than one of these customers had feelings of being ignored or abandoned by Intel.

In summary, Intel's product portfolio was expanded through acquisition, and these new product lines showed great potential outside the PC market segment. However, there was no sales organization, few established customer relationships, and more than a few OEMs who questioned Intel's renewed interest in the embedded market segments. Intel did not have existing capability to get these new product lines in front of the appropriate customers. The customer base was broad and diverse. (This was not the PC OEM customer base where Intel had nurtured strong business relationships over time.) And finally the value of the Intel brand was not yet clearly associated with communications, embedded, and networking market segments.

Intel turned to outsourced selling.

ENDNOTES

1. This research includes:

> Anderson, Erin (1985), "The Salesperson as Outside Agent or Employee: A Transaction-Cost Analysis," *Marketing Science,* 4 (Summer), 234–254.
> ———. (1988), "Selling Efficiency and Choice of Integrated or Independent Sales Forces: A Test of Darwinian Economics," *Management Science,* 34 (May), 599–618.
> Anderson, Erin, and David C. Schmittlein (1984), "Integration of the Sales Force: An Empirical Examination," *Rand Journal of Economics,* 15 (3), 385–395.
> Anderson, Erin, and Barton A. Weitz (1986), "Make or Buy Decisions: Vertical Integration and Marketing Productivity," *Sloan Management Review,* 27 (Spring), 3–20.

2. Williamson, Oliver E. (1996), *The Mechanisms of Governance.* New York: Oxford University Press.

3. This story is based on Elliott, Heidi (2003), "Building a Big Rep with Reps," *Electronic Business,* 20 (April 15), 1–2. We have supplemented this story with our own information from industry sources.

4. Gomez-Mejia, Luis R., and David B. Balkin (1992), *Compensation, Organizational Strategy, and Firm Performance.* Cincinnati, OH: South-Western Publishing.

5. For more on the trade-off between variable and fixed pay, and low and high overhead structures, see:

> Anderson, Erin, and Richard L. Oliver (1987), "Perspectives on Behavior-Based versus Outcome-Based Salesforce Control Systems," *Journal of Marketing,* 51 (October), 76–88.
> Oliver, Richard L., and Erin Anderson (1994), "An Empirical Test of the Consequences of Behavior-Based versus Outcome-Based Sales Control Systems," *Journal of Marketing,* 58 (October), 53–67.
> Cravens, David W., Thomas N. Ingram, Raymond W. LaForge, and Clifford E. Young (1993), "Behavior-Based and Outcome-Based Salesforce Control Systems," *Journal of Marketing,* 57 (4), 47–59.

6. Moncrief, William C., III (1986), "Selling Activity and Sales Position Taxonomies for Industrial Salesforces," *Journal of Marketing Research,* 23 (August), 261–270.

> Moncrief, William C., Greg W. Marshall, and Felicia G. Lassk (1999), "The Current State of Sales Force Activities," *Industrial Marketing Management,* 28 (1), 87–98.

4

When to Use Reps in Addition to Other Channels: The Hybrid Question

Botanists practice the ancient art of improving the plants that occur in nature. One of their techniques is hybridization, or cross-breeding two unlike plants to create a third plant. The botanist's dream is that the new plant will have the best properties of both parents and bypass their defects. Many of the plants we enjoy today are the result of crossbreeding. Some strains of roses, for example, have been bred to enhance their size, shape, or scent. Indeed, hybrids are not just a recombination of the parent plants' properties. Hybrids fuse the parents' features to create new properties, such as novel colors.

Can manufacturers create field sales networks that combine two unlike institutions (in-house sales forces and OSPs) in the same way that botanists create plants? Yes and no! *Yes,* in that there are several excellent examples of hybrid sales organizations that have thrived and been successful for all parties. *No,* in that there are more failures than successes in attempting to blend these two different types of sales organizations. We aren't dealing with plants here; we're dealing with people, money, and structure, and all of the emotions and trepidation that such associations can create.

In principle, the hybrid solution can be an excellent idea when done for the right reasons and with the deft touch of talented management. The manufacturer needs to eliminate the chance of failure by planning and executing a hybrid sales strategy that is viewed as nonthreatening and long lasting. We will talk about some of the pitfalls that need to be avoided as well as the

LUTRON ELECTRONICS: REP *AND* DIRECT

Lutron Electronics is a global leading manufacturer of lighting controls, such as dimmers and lighting controls systems, and serves the United States and Canada with a network of 70 direct salespeople *and* 65 manufacturers' representative organizations. Because the Reps employ 550 salespeople, every day 620 individuals meet prospective customers for Lutron products. Lutron senior vice president Richard Angel explains the fundamental driver of the sales structure: both sales forces are essential. Lutron lighting controls increase the user's ability to control the lighting environment (and its costs). A residential or commercial builder can light a structure without using Lutron's products: for example, a simple light switch is all that is functionally necessary. Someone (for example, an architect or interior designer) needs to explain the usages of lighting controls to the decision maker. The sales forces need to explain it to all parties!

Angel sees Rep and direct sales forces as having different skill sets. Reps excel at anything that is shorter term and based on relationships. This includes managing channels (distributors), managing customer relationships, closing orders, and understanding the intricacies of a market. But Reps face constant sales pressure from multitudes of principals; they need a shorter sales cycle and must be compensated reasonably quickly. In contrast, direct salespeople excel at market development, which means developing business that could take as long as 1.5 years to materialize. Direct salespeople are excellent at taking the long view, the strategic view, with selected architects, designers, builders, and other customers when selling products/solutions that the customer is unlikely to include in the building without a good deal of manufacturer support.

Lutron therefore assigns its 70 direct salespeople to those product/markets that require a long-term perspective and demand very deep knowledge of Lutron products, coupled with extensive technical expertise in lighting controls and deep knowledge of a product application. Typically, the salesperson needs to figure out how Lutron fits into the customers' application. For example, "green buildings" are a hot new market. Among other demands, salespeople need to work out how Lutron products help building owners, for each building, earn certification under new design standards (LEED) that encourage environmentally responsible construction. This requires a salesperson technically adept in the intricacies and nuances of how Lutron fits in the commercial market.

Angel views the direct sales force as playing an essential marketing role: helping Lutron determine its value proposition. How do you sell a product for which the need is subjective and highly dependent on the builder's vision of the building? The answers change constantly. Lutron's direct salespeople help the manufacturer listen to the market, spotting trends, new markets, and new product opportunities. In contrast, according to Angel, the Rep excels when the customer already understands the principle of what Lutron lighting controls can do for the building or its occupants.

If direct salespeople must think strategically and perform a marketing function, how does Lutron give them incentives them to do it? One element is the management system: salespeople are paid on salary plus bonus and are managed with the expectation that they will give extensive feedback to business unit managers. Another element is the company culture of stability and investment in human resources. Says Angel, "We continually invest and develop our people. If they come out of sales, we put them in another position, and we value the real-world experience they received in sales. In our 41 years, we have never laid off anyone." Knowing this, direct salespeople are more loyal and flexible. So how does Lutron deal with downturns? The company views its mission to be expanding the market (remember, nobody has to buy their product category). So when times get tough, Lutron focuses on growing revenue by convincing more prospects that controlling light, not just turning it off and on, has a host of advantages.

How does Lutron split up the responsibilities? The guiding principle is that the customer is at the root of the design. Customer preferences drive who does what. The 65 Rep organizations serve a multitude of customer types. One Rep model type sells all kinds of lighting products, but only lighting. The other Rep model serves a broader construction need, not just for lighting but for other construction products (e.g., pipe, wire, smoke detectors, and so on). Lutron looks for the best possible Rep organization and Rep principal (owner) whose vision is aligned with its corporate goals. Both models are successful for Lutron. A Rep's territory is defined as a combination of U.S. counties and Lutron product lines, which in turn roughly corresponds to customer segments. As for direct salespeople, they are assigned to the market influencers, following the principle of market development. Further, direct salespeople need to perform some functions to back up the Rep.

Flexibility is the key to the arrangement. Flexibility begins with what each Rep does. Each one proposes a list of functions it will take on. The more value the Rep brings, the higher the commission Lutron offers. Angel calls this an "activity-based commission." Lutron direct salespeople and support personnel fill in what the Rep leaves and that creates occasional tension. To defuse it, Lutron gives each Rep the "opportunity to upgrade" by submitting business and market plans. If the Rep presents a convincing "how we will do it" plan and has been performing on its existing areas of responsibility, Lutron adapts. And if Reps can show they can assume the roles of Lutron salespeople, Lutron will "redeploy" their employees, typically to corporate positions or other sales positions. Salespeople view this as Rep and career development.

Another way to defuse tension has to do with how Lutron's direct salespeople are compensated. Part of their pay is a bonus that is tied to the sales growth of their region. Therefore, the better the Rep does, the better the direct salespeople do.

Invest, build, think long term, be customer oriented, grow the market, keep your people—Lutron has a distinctive corporate culture. Not surprisingly, their relationships with their Reps are relatively stable. Of the 65 Rep organizations, on average, only two Reps change per year. Some terminated Reps come back later and are welcomed back if they propose and execute a plan to make the arrangement more effective next time around.

Lutron's use of Rep and direct sales systems is about a dozen years old. Lutron regularly modifies the way the system works. Says Angel, "If you always stick to last year's methods, you'll probably get last year's results." Like most firms, Lutron periodically reorganizes. When it does, the Reps' input is sought—and used.

So far, Lutron follows closely the rules we suggest in this book. But there is one exception: a common reporting structure. Those who work with Reps report to the same sales manager as do direct salespeople. Lutron makes this work by having a matrix reporting structure built around three groupings: commercial, residential, and distributor. The Rep organizations effectively have three points of contact, not just one. This helps keep checks and balances in place. Ultimately, Angel and his senior sales managers are the final point of contact. When things need to be worked out, Angel relies on his senior managers, a stable, experienced group.

Says Angel, "The Reps really are our sales force." Part of the job of the direct people is to keep good communication with Reps and make sure they are successful executing Lutron initiatives.

Fairness, flexibility, and loyalty (both to Reps and employees)—these are three hallmarks of the Lutron hybrid sales system.

reasons for considering such a strategy in the first place. But, in addition, we will cite several excellent case histories of companies who have utilized this concept with great success and whose management skills have demonstrated a capacity to make things work well for all parties! For openers, see the sidebar on Lutron Electronics.

Start with the Sales Role

A good analysis of the need for a hybrid sales organization always begins with a definition of the manufacturer's *potential* sales roles. A sales role is a job description that includes the products carried, the target market, and the appropriate sales strategy. The objective should be to create sales roles that are coherent and feasible. *Feasibility* means the role is physically and financially viable (example: the territory is compact enough to cover and has enough brand sales potential to justify a salesperson's efforts). *Coherence* means that the role is not internally contradictory. For example, a role is full of contradiction when most of the products the salesperson is responsible for need a consultative sell (long calls, many decision makers, drawn-out process, needs-based selling, minor price sensitivity), but other products in the same portfolio are on a short sales cycle, are hard to differentiate, and essentially demand a price appeal and frequent short calls.

The key is to ask which organizational form—an employee or an OSP—is better suited to *each sales role.*

Getting Stuck in Sales Role Inertia

Field evidence indicates that firms tend to pick the organizational form that they used for the first products they brought to a market. Then they add on subsequent products, probably to fully utilize the structure they put into place. If the later products have different needs than the earlier products, the manufacturer ends up with an organizational form that doesn't fit the bulk of what it sells. For example, a firm might enter the market with a well-known brand—easy to sell, aimed at a well-defined segment—and set up a sales team that lives on customer pull. Later products might require more skill and effort to sell (sales push), and the segment might be difficult to spot. This requires a different type of sales force. Firms might go on like this quite a while (loading more products onto the original structure) before things get so bad that managers finally break their inertia and reorganize.[1]

The beauty of hybrid selling is that it frees managers to get creative, to really start all over again to devise *potential* sales jobs. This means reengineering the sales job. An all-Rep sales organization might have roles that could be carved out for direct salespeople. An all-direct sales organization might have roles that could be carved out for Reps.

This latter possibility is particularly appealing because a direct salesperson needs a role big enough to occupy him or her (or them) completely. A potential sales role that doesn't support an individual *could* fit into the activities of a Rep organization. This strategy, for example, can be used when selling in areas too thinly populated to support a direct field sales force. Another example would be to use a Rep to sell to the military post-exchange (PX) system. Since a PX does not procure in the same way as civilian organizations do, adding the PX to a salesperson's other accounts would create an *incoherent* role.

Firms that see these opportunities and creatively reengineer their sales roles are often pleasantly surprised at how much good business is to be done in these markets. Corner markets like these can be stunningly lucrative.[2]

Benefits of Redefining a Sales Role

One of the very best, most effective ways to boost sales force productivity is to improve the way that salespeople allocate their time over their customer base (that is, improve their call planning).[3] Good call planning creates breathtaking increases in results.[4] Experience with hundreds of sales forces shows that one of the very best ways to improve a salesperson's call planning is to redraw the sales territories and rebalance the product loads.[5] Creating coherent, feasible sales roles has a tremendous impact on the productivity of each salesperson.

There is a curious knock-on effect here. When managers redefine sales roles, they usually make them smaller, more delineated. Managers assign these new "mini" roles with fear and trembling. They worry that there won't be enough to do, not enough potential, and that they will not be able to justify assigning people to these delimited roles. In all likelihood, however, the reverse will happen. Those "mini" roles get to look "maxi" quickly. Freed to tackle a coherent, feasible job, salespeople typically exploit their markets far better than management expected, leading to upward revisions of estimated market potential.[6]

A word of caution is in order here. Some products don't suit *any* market, and they should be terminated. This is, of course, unpleasant and can be bad for the sales manager's career. Adding inferior products to a salesperson's role, knowing that the role is large enough to allow the salespeople to avoid actually trying to sell them, is a form of passive resistance. It is a way to "kill" the product without appearing to do so. But these losing products are harder to bury when the manager starts to streamline the sales roles. An unsaleable product stands out much more in a delimited role than in a sprawling, unmanageable role. There are fewer excuses for not selling it. There are fewer places for the salesperson to hide. This means that redefining sales roles will force an organization into moments of truth about its products/markets.

In short, hybrid sales organizations fit many circumstances. *But they should be created around specific sales roles and for specific reasons—not just for the heck of it.* Indeed, putting two different organizational forms into the field can create tension, duplication of costs, and inefficient, silent competition. We will now look at some of the hidden costs that should be considered before deciding to create a hybrid sales organization.

THE HIDDEN COSTS OF A HYBRID
SALES ORGANIZATION

In principle, is a hybrid a good idea? Some firms say "no" on principle. They insist on using only one organizational form (outsourced or vertically integrated) in the name of consistency, unified decision making, policy, "streamlining," or "rationalization of strategy." Their managers simplify their lives by imposing needless rules ("We must have one strategy everywhere"). But they suboptimize, sometimes grossly. Such firms are the stuff of many a business-school case study. They are candidates to be taken over. The acquirers break the firms up or overhaul the monolithic strategy, installing management that is more tolerant of complexity.

That said, firms should not run headlong into creating a hybrid sales organization before seriously considering the decision. The fact is, *hybrids are not free* because there are hidden costs to consider.

Hidden Cost 1: Hybrid Managers Are High-Grade Resources

Fundamentally, vertical integration (employee salespeople) and outsourcing (Reps) are two very different ways of going to market. They cannot be managed the same way—managing people who work *for* you is quite different from managing people who work *with* you. Working *for* you means you are in the role of the boss. Working *with* you means you are in the role of a diplomat, enlisting and persuading a partner.

These demand two very different skill sets.[7] The boss of a sales force needs key skills, interests, and other characteristics (KSIOs) such as recruiting, training, motivating, deploying, and evaluating employees (all involving subordinates). Further, the boss needs desk-based KSIOs such as forecasting, budgeting, and quota setting. The focus here is on attending to his or her salespeople. These KSIOs are *inward looking*, based on superior position in the hierarchy.

Now consider the person who interfaces with the OSP. This is typically a senior sales manager or senior salesperson. This manager must attend to another company, with its own income statement, balance sheet, operating methods, and portfolio of suppliers. This manager must understand the Rep and its economics. She or he must negotiate, build trust, and forge long-term relationships. The needed KSIOs are *outward looking,* based on persuasion, not rank. The person who manages the relationship with the OSP needs a different leadership style than the person who manages an employee sales force.

Thus, hybrid sales organizations need to have two kinds of managers operating under two different mental orientations. This in turn calls for different systems for supporting, measuring, evaluating, and rewarding these managers.

In short, hybrid sales organizations demand high-grade resources, which means high overhead. Even worse, hybrids may lock up scarce personnel who could be more productive doing something else. For example, most direct sales forces are short of competent key-account salespeople. It is not worth it to assign this caliber of person to get the most out of a partnership with an OSP. It's worth it only if the manager can get more out of the Rep (by assigning a skilled manager) than out of the key account (by assigning that manager to the key account instead).

Hidden Cost 2: Letting Them Fight It Out

We know of a company with a huge product line, broken up into multiple divisions and subgroups. Sometimes a division sends its OSPs and its employees after the same market, selling the same product. One corporate executive told us, "I don't know why this works, but it really does. It's synergistic. Our sales go up whenever we have two sales forces." But a product manager in the same company told us he has a different idea. He wonders:

- Why costs of sales are out of control
- Why each sales force cherry-picks the line (i.e., they won't sell the whole line)
- Why unit volume is high but dollar volume is not
- Why neither sales force is very good at penetrating new markets or selling new products
- Why the direct sales force has high turnover of personnel
- Why the OSP has a calculative, transactional attitude toward this principal.

There is more than one reason for all of this, but the way this company executes its hybrid strategy has a lot to do with it. "Let the best one win" is an invitation to combat. Of course, you *can* combat other brands, but someone selling the same thing to the same market is going to end up meeting you in the lobby of the same prospective customer. The prospect forces you to address their presence. So what are you going to do? There are only two possibilities. First, you can argue that your organization is better than theirs. Second, you can propose to give them a better price. Now you aren't capturing value, and you may be diminishing your image of quality.[8]

The result of this "let the best one win" attitude is that the competition wins more often than it should. Yes, it can happen that two sales forces will sell more than one. That's a sign that the market merits sales calls and other investments. But the hybrid sales organization won't get all the sales they should for all the efforts they make. Costs will be duplicated. Prices will be cut. "Whatever works will get attention from people desperate to make their numbers—forget about representing the whole line. Service will be given away. Unrealistic promises will be made, creating unrealistic customer expectations. The direct sales force will be demoralized because it has nowhere else to turn. The outsourced sales force will be calculative because it doesn't trust this principal.

Yes, two sales forces could possibly sell more than one. But it's often a Pyrrhic victory—market share at the price of profitability. This means you need to pick the one best sales force for a segment of customers and then put only that sales force in front of them. *If it's one set of needs and one set of products, a hybrid sales organization cannot be made to work well.* The principle is simple: only heterogeneous markets need a hybrid. Homogeneous markets don't.

MARKETS THAT FAVOR HYBRID SALES

We've argued that the best reason to create a hybrid sales force is to exploit a heterogeneous market that is full of opportunity. In these markets, both sales types are likely to find lucrative market segments that they can dominate, and there is enough opportunity that each sales type is too busy chasing prospects to spend their time chasing each other.

Field research[9] uncovers five types of markets where this works, markets that are sufficiently heterogeneous that the two sales organizations each have at least one segment where they hold the advantage. Given the opportunity, each organization will be too busy serving its own group of customers to play gladiator with each other in the same arena.

Feature 1: Customer Perception of Differentiation

A key feature of markets that support hybrids is that the product category is not a *commodity*. A category is a commodity when customers believe (rightly or wrongly) that there are no meaningful differences among the brands. Very mature markets tend to suffer from the perception of commodity status. In commodity markets, there is barely enough grass to feed one cow, let alone two. The two sales forces have no natural basis of differentiation from each other, will be unable to create a perception of differentiation, and will be forced to fight toe to toe.

How do you know if a market is a commodity? Contrary to what most people think, this is not a question of fact but of perception, and perception is often wrong.[10] Markets exist where the real differences are very small, but buyers believe they are meaningful. Buyers *believe* the product category is differentiated. Therefore, it makes a difference what brand they buy, and they don't consider the brands to be ready substitutes for one another. We know this is true in consumer markets, but many of us don't realize that it's often true in business-to-business markets. Conversely, there are markets where the brands have genuine and meaningful differences, but customers fail to recognize that they matter.

The point is that customers decide whether a product category is differentiated or is a commodity. If their verdict is "commodity," stop the analysis here and don't use a hybrid. Pick whichever organizational form fits your circumstances, outsourcing or vertical integration, and don't worry about whether you are missing a good bet by not using both.

Feature 2: Growing Markets

Hybrid sales organizations work when markets are growing. There is room for everybody here. Opportunities are plentiful enough that each organization can target its best prospects, but be sure those prospects fall into different segments. If buyers all have the same needs and buy the same way (i.e., there is only one market segment), the two sales forces will both target the most promising prospects. Fortunately, growing markets usually do have multiple market segments.[11]

Feature 3: Consistent Decision-Making Style

In markets that can support hybrids, customers have a consistent decision-making style. They don't need a consultative sell on

Tuesday and a price/no-frills sell on Thursday. A consistent decision-making style means customers will have a finite set of preferred vendors who fit what the buyer needs. In contrast, customers who have multiple purchasing styles have relationships with many different types of vendors to suit their many styles of buying. Naturally, they will set their vendors to bid against each other, and two sellers of the same brand will be caught up in the customer's trap.

How can the buyer have multiple decision-making styles? Customer behavior depends on the needs that motivate each purchase, and those needs depend on the purchase occasion. In France, for example, consumers keep two types of cognac in their home bars. One is a prestigious brand in an attractive bottle. The other is a little-known brand in a plain bottle with an unpretentious label. One cognac goes on the table when entertaining guests, the other is what the family drinks. Each cognac meets the same family's needs, but the needs depend on the occasion.

Here is the key. When the *same decision-making unit is charged with procurement* in an organization that has *many different purchase occasions,* the customer will buy one way on Tuesday and another way on Thursday. Such customers will go to the effort to establish relations with multiple vendors, which could include both of the manufacturer's sales organizations. *This is when hybrid sales organizations are difficult to sustain.* In contrast, customers that use *different decision-making units* to purchase for different occasions are *good candidates* for hybrid sales organizations. Each unit will operate in accord with its needs. The two elements (OSP and direct) will gravitate to different units, and the customer won't bring them together in the lobby.

Table 4-1 gives an example: a company selling information technology to the medical market in the United Kingdom.[12] On the surface, each hospital is a prospect. Underneath the surface, a hospital is merely an originator of checks. Each hospital has multiple occasions to use information technology. Each occasion demands its own application. Many hospitals don't put one purchasing group in charge of buying for all applications. Instead, they entrust purchasing to each group shown in Table 4-1. Hospitals like this are good candidates for a hybrid sales organization. In contrast, hospitals that centralize all the buying are more likely to set an organization's two sales types into competition with each other, making it difficult to sustain a hybrid.

Table 4-1. A Hospital Is Not a Prospect

A British hospital, on the surface, is a prospect for a seller of medical information technology. But on closer examination, the hospital is not the prospect. Each buying center is a prospect. A buying center is the group of individuals who influence the purchase decision, directly or indirectly. Salespeople target buying centers: *these* are the prospects. A typical British hospital has these buying centers:

- Reception
- Patient records
- Purchasing
- Hotel services
- Pathology
- Surgery
- Outpatients
- Personnel management
- Financial accounting
- Payroll

Feature 4: Stand-Alone versus Bundle Buying

Many customers buy products or services separately, in stand-alone fashion. This means each sales force has a clean chance at some targets. In contrast, if all customers buy a group of products/services together in a bundle, a direct sales force will have difficulty competing with a Rep (or a distributor, if the customer wants a deep assortment). In bundle buying, there isn't room for two sales force types.

Feature 5: The Absence of Buying Groups

The more customers do their own buying, the more hospitable the environment for a hybrid sales organization. When each customer does its own buying there are many decision-making units offering many opportunities to sellers. In contrast, when customers buy through a buying group that negotiates on their behalf, the buying group is likely to call in both sales organizations and pit them against each other to fight for one big order. In markets dominated by buying groups, hybrid sales forces become gladiators.

In short, the most hospitable environments for hybrids are growing markets in which customers see differentiation in the category, have consistent purchase styles, buy products in stand-alone fashion, and don't turn their procurement over to buying groups. The principles here are simple. Each sales force can attack a market segment it is well suited to serve. Each sales force has an advantage somewhere. There is enough opportunity for both, and customers won't force the two sales forces to battle it out.

OTHER MOTIVES TO CREATE A HYBRID: BENCHMARKING AND LEVERAGING

The major reason to use Rep and employee sales forces is to match each sales role to the form that best suits the role. However, there are other reasons to field a hybrid sales organization. One of them is to *benchmark*.

There are selling situations in which it is very hard to tell whether the sales force (*any* sales force, OSP or direct) is doing a good job. These are situations of "performance ambiguity," meaning that the principal has no real way to tell if the results being generated are good. Ambiguous situations tend to be ones where no one quite knows what to expect. The potential of the market is anybody's guess. The competitive superiority of a brand is difficult to establish, perhaps because buyer behavior and requirements are not well understood. In ambiguous situations, sellers always wonder if they could have done better, and if their sales representatives (Rep or direct) are giving it their best efforts. They wonder whether they are hearing the truth ("This is the best anybody can expect to do") or excuses. Of course, manufacturers always wonder about this, but there are situations that are particularly opaque.

Field research reveals[13] that many manufacturers respond to performance ambiguity by creating a hybrid sales force. Each form acts as a reference, or benchmark, for the other. By using direct sales forces, the manufacturer learns about the market. Thus, it can ask better questions of its Reps, as well as have more sophisticated conversations with its Rep partners. Simultaneously, the manufacturer can hold up the Rep's results to its direct sales force and, once again, ask better questions and engage in a better dialogue. Of course, this benchmarking benefit should be weighed against the cost of significant rivalry between the two sales forces and the risk of duplication of effort.

A second reason to launch a hybrid sales organization is as *leverage*. In Chapter 3, we discussed the idea that a manufacturer and Rep will need to make significant investments in each other if the manufacturer's products or processes are idiosyncratic. These investments create assets (principally knowledge, relationships,

WHAT ABOUT CUSTOMER PREFERENCES?

Shouldn't a customer's preference have something to do with what institutional form your sales force takes? On the face of it, yes. Customers (and prospects) sometimes have very strong opinions about how a manufacturer should go to market. And it's always risky to ignore a buyer's opinion.

AT&T recently learned this lesson the hard way.[14] AT&T sold and distributed via its own divisions, as well as via third parties. For years, management of the giant manufacturer of capital equipment related to telephony was convinced that customers and prospects preferred dealing with AT&T employees, the only people who could service and sell AT&T's sophisticated products and services "properly." AT&T was regularly accused of favoring its internal divisions in pricing and terms of trade, as well as withholding selected products from resellers. Customers did indeed like AT&T products, but many wanted to buy them through other vendors, in particular, their preferred resellers. Why? Because these resellers used their economies of scope and scale to learn about important customers and to serve them well. Customer pressure on AT&T management to stop favoring in-house people was ineffective. Therefore, customers took their arguments to the board of directors. Under board pressure, management launched an initiative to level the playing field between third parties and AT&T employees.

The point is that customers may have very strong ideas about how the manufacturer goes to market, and they want the manufacturer to respect their preferences. The AT&T example involves preferring third-party resellers, not the field sales force, for their learning, scope, scale, and service. It can go the other way, too. For field selling, some customers prefer being served by the manufacturer's employees rather than by an OSP. They reason that employee salespeople are "closer to the factory" and, therefore, customers can expect better service.

Should you adapt to this preference? This is a decision to be negotiated, like anything else involving customer preference.

But wouldn't a good marketer just do what the customer wants? Absolutely not! Firms that just do what the customer wants go bankrupt, because customers want everything, and they want it "perfect, free, and now."[15] A good marketer doesn't give in. A good marketer *does* create value for the customer—but also makes sure to capture a fair share of it! Creating value is not enough; capturing value is essential.[16] This is equitable—why should a supplier work for free?

When manufacturers that use Reps agree to a customer's demand to be served directly instead of by Reps, they assume they will create value for this customer *and* that they will capture a fair share of it for themselves. Therefore, manufacturers carve out house accounts (key accounts) and create a direct sales force to serve them. For some customers, this makes sense, because they need the supplier to make substantial investments in them, investments that are hard to redeploy to other customers. They don't need economies of scope as much as they need dedicated brand-specific knowledge.

However, the manufacturer must be on guard for what happens next. A hidden motive of many key accounts is to draw the manufacturer into an important relationship, then demand steep and steady price cuts—often accompanied by steep and steady increases in service provided. These accounts are a headache and a resource sink.[17] They force the manufacturer to create lots of value for them, but it is the customer that captures all of it—and then some. Many suppliers actually lose money on their key accounts.[18]

This is the customer's path to getting what the supplier can provide, for free, perfect, and now. The first step of this path is the argument made by many a customer: "You won't have to pay the Rep's commission." True. Instead, you will pay the costs of your direct sales force. The customer doesn't know what that is and doesn't care. But the customer does know the Rep's commission—and will demand to see it in a price cut as soon as the direct sales force is in place. So, beware of this argument. Selling is a function. If you shift that function to someone else, you don't eliminate the costs—you merely move them.[19] The only way to eliminate selling costs is to eliminate selling.

This said, a major motive to have a hybrid sales force is to accommodate customers that are worth having and that want to be served by whatever route to market the supplier does not use.[20] For this reason, firms going direct add Reps, and firms going Rep add direct. (In the same way, firms with in-house distribution add resellers, and firms with resellers add in-house distribution.) This reason to become a hybrid sales organization makes sense if the customers have good reasons to need whatever you don't have—on the condition that these customers will permit you to capture a fair share of the value you will create for them.

---

and routines) that are tailored to the manufacturer. The good side of these investments is that they make the Rep more effective in selling the manufacturer's products. The potential downside is that the manufacturer cannot find another Rep with these idiosyncratic assets in place. Therefore, the manufacturer is locked in and would find it very difficult to switch to another Rep. Thus the manufacturer loses some leverage in the relationship.

In Chapters 6 and 7 we will cover how to rebalance the situation. Here, we note that one way to do so is to use a hybrid sales organization. Manufacturers that are locked into their Reps because heavy idiosyncratic assets are in place often use a small direct sales force to sell selected accounts.[21] This gives the manufacturer a way to tell if its Reps are selling well or not (the benchmarking argument again). More important, the manufacturer can more credibly threaten to terminate a Rep that is abusing the lock-in position. How? By threatening to divert the Rep's sales to the direct sales force that is already in place. That sales force has made idiosyncratic investments and stands ready to use them. (The astute reader will have noted that the OSP that possesses an idiosyncratic asset also gives the manufacturer some leverage against employee salespeople who decide to behave like prima donnas.)

A caveat exists here. Manufacturers use this strategy (direct sales to provide a credible threat of termination of a locked-in Rep) when their products sell reasonably well by themselves. Manufacturers tend not to supplement Reps with a direct sales force if their products benefit greatly from being part of a product portfolio. The reason is that the direct sales force will be unable to sell effectively: the product needs to be embedded in a portfolio of complementary products if it is to thrive.

FOUR KEYS TO MAKING A HYBRID SALES ORGANIZATION WORK

The botanists who created modern roses by hybridizing also created uniquely awful strains as an accidental by-product of their efforts to make something superior. They created Frankenstein roses: prickly, misshapen, with a repelling scent and an ugly color. They created feeble roses: prone to insects and disease, slow growing, overly sensitive to poor soil or drought. Rose botanists took such failures in stride. They simply eliminated these roses—after taking note of how they had produced them. Botanists used their failures to learn what *not* to do and kept crossbreeding roses until they found what worked.

Hybrid sales organizations have been put together so many ways, by so many companies, that today's managers don't need to experiment about how to implement the concept. The experience of other firms is very clear: four key factors determine whether a hybrid will be superior or inferior to a unitary sales force (all Rep or all direct). Superior hybrids offer better results (sales, market share, growth, customer satisfaction, contribution to profit) and at a lower ratio of costs to sales. Inferior hybrids—feeble Frankenstein sales organizations—not only fail to generate results but spend too much and lock up too many assets. These organizations are full of conflict and politics. They spend their efforts on pointing fingers and assigning blame.

Many manufacturers have experienced a hybrid failure that leaves a sour taste for all parties (Reps, the direct sales force, and the manufacturer). "We tried that once and it was a miserable failure" becomes the refrain. It's not easy to make a hybrid work. That's why some companies make it a policy not to use hybrids.

WHY ZERO ZONE AVOIDS HYBRIDS

Our company has always recognized that outsourcing can be extended to almost any function within a company, and I am proud to say that Zero Zone has made an art of this practice. In many cases there may be a slight sacrifice in margin, but the avoidance of capital expenditures along with other related costs make the practice very palatable.

Nowhere within the corporation is outsourcing more visible than in the sales function utilizing Independent Factory Representatives. Our estimate is that direct sales costs would be two to three times greater than using Representatives. That being said, one must always be mindful that there are costs associated with selling in this fashion. These costs are associated with such intangibles as "control," "reporting," "ego," sometimes "flexibility," and most important "communication."

There is no such thing, in our minds, as a combination direct and Representative sales force. When this does occur, and many companies try to do it by having "house accounts" or "house territories," the above intangibles became more severe. The terms *fair, honest,* and *equitable* become obsolete, eventually leading to a greater breakdown in communication and trust.

Zero Zone, 18 years ago, turned all of their house accounts back to the representatives, took the territory surrounding their plant sites and assigned it to a new representative, and made the decision that a representative had to be paid a commission for every sale made in his assigned territory. We then turned around and appointed regional sales managers to help the representatives work his territory, perform missionary work for the representative, and open new accounts on the representatives' behalf. The representative gets credit for *all* sales made by the sales manager.

Jack Van Der Ploeg, President, Zero Zone, Inc., North Prairie, Wisconsin

Hybrids are difficult, but they are not impossible. Being able to harness the energies of two different sales organizations can be effective and enduring. There are four ways to make this happen. They have to do with the way the hybrid is conceived and implemented. Done right, they make the idea work. Done wrong, they are traps.

Trap 1: The Wrong Business Proposition

The business proposition that is put to the Reps must make sense and be definable. If it looks like an experiment or a short-term proposition, good Reps will not be interested. They will not be inclined to invest their resources (selling time, money, management time, and above all, the goodwill of their customers) on a short-lived project. Outsourced sales professionals are cautious about any initiative that has the feel of trial and error because most of them have had experience with hybrid selling. They know how easy it is to crossbreed an inferior sales organization by accident.

To avoid the trap of appearing to propose an unstable, poorly defined business proposition, manufacturers need to craft a program that they know in advance will attract the right kind of OSP. To do this, they need to think like the management of the Rep. This means being explicit and detailed. Intel provides an excellent example here. When Intel added OSPs to their direct sales force, management anticipated every objection the OSP might have. The business plan Intel proposed to prospective Reps explained in detail why they should become part of Intel's "extended sales force." The plan covered:

- The rationale for enacting hybrid coverage
- The reasons Intel believed it would succeed, both for the Reps and Intel (win-win)
- Intel's goals and expectations, in detail
- The products to be carried
- The markets to be served, with dollar estimates of market potential (enough potential to attract good Reps)
- The sales history, in actual dollars, of the assigned accounts
- The reporting structure, with names in the organization charts
- Intel's plans to avoid conflict with the direct sales force
- Intel's desire for a long-term relationship

This example belies a common belief, which is that being specific and working out objections in advance poisons the relationship. This idea is commonly cited in the literature on organizational alliances as a reason to leave things open.[22] The argument is that anticipating and working through nasty possibilities actually raises the likelihood that they will happen. In contrast, leaving things "fluid" encourages both parties to build trust and use that trust to work things through as issues arise.

It sounds good, doesn't it? Unfortunately, it doesn't work that way.[23] Anticipating and working through problems in advance is not a sign of mistrust but of experience, expertise, and preparation. Put differently, "leaving things fluid" is a euphemism for failure to anticipate and to make necessary decisions. Business relationships need to be built on detailed planning and communication, particularly when it comes to expectations and obligations.[24] Otherwise, it is not trust that grows but disappointment and recrimination. And, ironically, the relationship that starts out on the basis of full and frank communication (including communication about possible negative outcomes) is the one that is more likely to develop trust.[25]

Another way to project that the proposed hybrid sales force is not merely an experiment or a short-term proposition is to assume some risk. Some manufacturers offer monthly income guarantees to their Reps for specified periods in order to demonstrate their commitment to the program. Others, such as Intel, actually remove large accounts with well-known potential from their direct sales force, turning them over to Reps. Manufacturers cannot afford to disappoint such accounts. Their willingness to turn them over is a powerful demonstration of their confidence that the hybrid model will work.

It's important that manufacturers explain why the hybrid is a good business proposition to all parties involved, including the direct sales force. Management needs to explain to its own employees why part of the sales function is being outsourced. If there is no good explanation, direct salespeople will interpret the hybrid organization as a rebuke and as a sign that management considers them somehow deficient. These fears must be addressed, frankly, fully, and up front.

Trap 2: Bundling the "Garbage"

Most manufacturers become hybrid by starting out with one kind of sales force and then adding the other kind. It's rare to start out with both forms. The issue then becomes how to divide up accounts and prospects that are already assigned to somebody else. Too many manufacturers approach this by giving the most desirable targets to the in-house sales force and leaving the rest to the OSP. Obviously, this "bundling the garbage" strategy will destroy whatever trust the Rep might have toward the manufacturer. The message behind the manufacturer's rhetoric is clear: the OSP is not a valued partner and the "hybrid strategy" is merely a convenient way to offload small, difficult, or hard-to-serve customers. Giving the worst customers to Reps signals that the manufacturer is taking these accounts off the organization's to-do list, without going so far as to refuse to fill the occasional order from them. And the customer can read the signal, along with the OSP and the in-house sales force.

In short, the manufacturer should have a compelling reason why one customer is best served by a Rep and another customer by a direct salesperson. If few existing accounts are assigned to Reps, or if only small customers are assigned to Reps, the message can be read as "We reserve all the good business for our employees." The implication is clear: the manufacturer is not truly interested in a win-win partnership with its OSPs. Also, there is the ugly specter of appropriation in the background. A manufacturer that will not let its Reps have good business at the outset may not let its Reps keep whatever good business they eventually create. Lest the reader think this concern is paranoid, consider how often manufacturers take the Rep's major customers as house accounts, arguing that a customer that has grown large "has special needs." This argument flies in the face of logic: how did this customer get to be large if the OSP wasn't meeting its needs? Nonetheless, appropriation of the Rep's large customers as house accounts, reserved to employee salespeople, is a common event.

This does not mean that the manufacturer should not assign small accounts to Reps. But if only small accounts are involved, it is critical that they represent substantial dollar *potential*. This does not mean that no one should hold house accounts, but the manufacturer should be aware that excluding large accounts often makes it difficult to recruit quality OSPs. (It should also be noted that the OSP is more than likely still calling on your "house accounts" on behalf of their other principals.)

Reserving house accounts is easier to explain if excluded accounts represent extremely high sales dollars, particularly if the principal's overall size is very large relative to the Rep firm. The match of extreme size (customer) and extreme size (principal) has a logic that doesn't appear to the OSP to be simply "keeping the good accounts." On this basis, Intel, a very large principal, has maintained many of its biggest customers. This decision doesn't strike Reps as unprincipled or as an indicator of bad faith because the world's largest maker of semiconductors *has* turned over other worthwhile customers with known potential to its Reps. The result is impressive: Intel's extended sales force accounts for $800 million in annual sales.[26]

In dividing up accounts and prospects, the easiest and smoothest scenario is to assign clearly defined market segments. Here, there are no overlapping customer segments and no conflict with other selling groups. To the Rep, dealing with this hybrid principal is like dealing with a principal that has no other sales force, or a principal that has only Reps. The existence of the direct sales force, which is usually a sensitive issue, becomes a nonissue.

In practice, these clean-segment situations are often handled with not just one OSP (and one direct sales force), but with multiple Rep organizations. The reason goes back to an essential difference between OSP and direct sales forces (Chapter 2): unlike direct sales forces (which are often built around product lines), Reps build their business around customer needs. As a result, Reps tend to focus on a segment. Therefore, when market segments are distinctly different, multiple OSPs will be needed to serve each one. (One example is a manufacturer of uninterruptible power supplies that used multiple Reps to reach multiple segments—same product, different buying needs—in the same territory. See the sidebar later in the chapter.)

Trap 3: Picking the Wrong Champion

The decision to utilize a hybrid sales organization structure should have the blessing and support of top management. If it is conceived and exercised only at the sales management level, Reps will be wary of its permanence. The choice of outsourcing, especially a function as important and as integral to the firm's identity as field sales, should be a major strategic decision. Any other major outsourcing decision (production, purchasing, human resources, information technology, R&D, etc.) generally involves top management. If field selling is outsourced without the visible backing of top management, the decision has the air of expedience and transience, a clear red flag for a seasoned OSP.

One of the responsibilities of top management is to send a very clear signal that the OSP and employee sales forces are *not* expected to fight it out. Honeywell uses a hybrid sales force but takes pains to make sure that Rep and direct salespeople are not fighting for the same business. According to Tom Dalton, the company's vice president of worldwide sales, "The definition of roles and responsibilities are crucial to proper coexistence of direct and Rep personnel. In cases where it is appropriate to assign direct resources to the account, it is imperative that the business is either segregated from the Rep channel, or compensated on a reduced basis to avoid channel conflict." He finds that Rep organizations are very willing to coexist with direct folks "as long as the 'rules of engagement' are defined and understood."

This kind of interventionist approach is not easy to create and enforce, but it beats letting two sales forces play gladiator with each other.

Trap 4: The Wrong Reporting Structure and Style

Perhaps the most critical element in establishing a hybrid organization is to establish how it will be managed and by whom. It is no accident that Intel, Honeywell, and Lutron worked this out and presented it to prospective Reps up front. If the management and reporting structure of the hybrid is not worked out with care, a firm risks the negative effects of ineffective management, or worse, management facing conflicts of interest. Let's look at these in turn.

INEFFECTIVE MANAGEMENT. George Langer, head of Intel's "extended sales force" (network of OSPs), has a standard opening line when he talks to other Intel executives: "How much do you know about Reps?" Usually, they don't know much, which gives them something in common with the executives of most manufacturers. Hence, Langer briefs his colleagues about outsourcing the field sales function before he presents his initiatives.

Langer is distinctively knowledgeable about Reps (he learned about them in a prior position with a division of Digital Equipment Corporation that was acquired by Intel). However, because few sales managers have substantial exposure to the OSP concept, the Reps in a hybrid organization are likely to report to someone who knows very little about them.

People do what they know how to do. The manager of a direct sales force knows how to use authority to manage employees in a superior/subordinate relationship. This is quite different from managing a relationship with another business. Many well-intentioned sales managers try to micromanage their Reps, which is akin to barging onto the factory floor and giving orders. And managers inexperienced in dealing with Reps tend to establish programs that are good for their direct sales force but not well suited to their OSPs. In Chapters 6 and 7, we will look at the types of skills necessary to maximize the performance of and relationship with an OSP.

CONFLICTS OF INTEREST. Imagine the position of the sales manager in a manufacturer that is going hybrid. If the producer is adding Reps to a direct sales force, the sales manager may be under pressure to produce better results. If the Rep succeeds, upper management is in position to rebuke the sales manager: "I told you the business was there!" In short, Rep performance can be embarrassing to the sales manager in a hybrid sales organization.

Now visualize the reverse: the manufacturer is adding a direct sales force to an all-Rep structure. The sales manager is now under pressure to get results fast to justify the setup and operating costs of employees. Since the firm has used exclusively OSPs, top management may be unaware of the many and varied costs of a field sales force (see the Cost Calculator© that comes with this book). Even a skilled, experienced sales manager needs time to move a sales force along the learning curve, mastering the products, customers, and competition and building relationships. Result: the cost/sales ratio will be high for a while, and management expectations (which might well be unreasonable) will not be met in the near term. Meanwhile, the OSP continues to sell, providing a potentially embarrassing benchmark for the direct operation. Once again, the sales manager of the hybrid organization is in an uncomfortable position.

DODGING THE TRAP OF THE WRONG REPORTING STRUCTURE. Having separate management (with equal status within the organization) for the OSP side and the direct side of the hybrid sales organization is by far the best way to go. The results will be more than worth the additional overhead and expense. By separating the roles of Rep manager and direct manager, the manufacturer eliminates the conflict of interest, the mixed-motive scenario. Managers can be judged by the success of their group, and their group alone. It's like coaching one football team instead of two: the coach doesn't need to worry that one team's success embarrasses the other team. Further, having separate management means the manufacturer can hire the skill set that matches each sales force. The profile of the direct manager corresponds to hands-on people management and internally oriented forecasting and reporting tasks. The profile of the OSP manager corresponds to the diplomat, externally oriented, who understands another business and can argue management-to-management. Chapters 5 (economic arguments) and 6 (the people factor) cover what the OSP manager needs to do to be successful.

Of course, having a separate management structure means overhead, and a manufacturer may well ask if there is enough business there to be worth it. At the outset, the answer is probably "no." The key is that a separate structure will *grow the business.* Intel is an excellent example, having created $800 million of largely incremental business in four years. Such growth occurs when a hybrid strategy is well conceived in the first place. Having separate management doesn't make a hybrid strategy successful in and of itself. Having separate management is an implementation decision that allows the beauty of the original conception to shine through.

A compromise used by many companies is to create a position of senior salesperson with two responsibilities: managing third parties (such as Reps) and selling to key accounts.[27] This is like holding two part-time jobs, and there is something to be said for it. Selling to key accounts and managing relationships with other firms call for many of the same skills, but the two sets of results are harder to compare, since one is selling and the other is managing. This person should be well informed about the Rep function and how it differs from an in-house sales organization.

SUMMARY

Hybrid sales (Rep and direct) make economic sense when the manufacturer has many different potential sales roles, some of which are better suited to one organizational form than to the other. Creating the infrastructure to have both employee sales forces and OSPs gives the manufacturer flexibility. Managers gain the ability to create delimited sales roles that are coherent (job demands don't contradict each other), which enables the salesperson to plan calls better. The result is that salespeople exploit their product/markets much better than management expected. A Rep can be a good solution to the problem of indivisibility (having to create sales roles that justify creating a job for someone). A sales role that doesn't add up nicely to a direct sales force may fit well within the Rep's portfolio. However, products that don't match market needs should not be given a sales role at all. Good Reps won't take them, and good employees can't make a living out of them.

A supplier that is all one form or all the other (Rep or direct) might justify creating a hybrid sales organization for other good reasons. Worthwhile prospects, firms that will let the supplier earn a fair profit, may have strong, well-grounded reasons why they prefer whatever route to market you don't have. Some may prefer the learning, scope, and scale of a third party. Other firms may prefer the deep, dedicated supplier product knowledge of an employee. Within limits, these preferences are worth honoring.

Suppliers that sell predominantly through OSPs sometimes add house accounts for two purposes. One is to benchmark each sales force against the other. This is particularly useful when performance is extremely difficult to evaluate. The other arises if the manufacturer makes heavy idiosyncratic investments in its Reps. Then the manufacturer may hold house accounts as a credible threat of termination if the OSP were to abuse its leverage over the manufacturer. However, this strategy is used when the products and services can stand alone, without losing much from being outside the economies of scope that come from portfolio selling. Brands that benefit from being presented alongside complementary products use house accounts much less.

Heterogeneous circumstances are the best reason to have a hybrid sales organization. Creating a hybrid is a choice. In contrast, a poor reason for a hybrid is to avoid making a choice. Some firms have a hybrid structure because management can't decide whether they should go Rep or direct, so they do both. It's rather like having two desserts because you can't pick one—you might regret it later.

The reason is that hybrids have hidden costs. One is the need to tie up two sets of managers with two different sets of skills. Good internal sales managers have inward-looking skills based on their legitimate authority as the boss. Good external sales managers have outward-looking skills based on their ability to understand and influence another business. The other hidden cost of a hybrid is the consequences of setting up two sales forces in the same market, selling the same products, and letting them fight it out like gladiators.

Some managers actually like this idea. They reason that the prospect will be getting more sales attention, which is good. They believe their two sales forces will bring out the best in each other, and the most deserving one will win. Implicitly, these managers assume that one of their two sales forces will win.

Rivalry is one thing; warfare is another. Unbridled, undirected competition between in-house and outsourced sales forces does more harm than good. Very frequently, the real winner is a competitor. The loser is the manufacturer, which ends up with fruitless duplication of efforts and therefore duplication of costs, plus a demoralized employee sales force *and* an alienated outsourced sales force. The victim of the inevitable collateral damage is the brand's reputation.

The key is to find markets where customer needs are different enough that employee and outsourced sales forces will *not* meet each other in the same lobby. Each type of sales force will focus on its own market, where it has the advantage. The most promising and heterogeneous markets are ones in which customers think the brands in the product category are differentiated and markets that are growing, in which customers exhibit consistent purchasing styles, buy products unbundled, and don't turn their procurement over to a buying group. The worst markets for hybrids are commodities and low growth, where customers vary their purchasing style over occasions, buy in bundles, and deal through buying groups.

Many a well-conceived hybrid idea fails because it is poorly implemented. Good implementation has four elements. First, the plan must be worked out in advance, in detail, and then communicated to all parties (including the direct sales force). Everyone needs to understand the rationale and the action plan. Doing so sends a signal that management believes in this strategy, and that it is not short term or expedient.

Second, accounts and prospects must be divided up fairly, for customer-based reasons. Here is a test: can you, the management of the manufacturer, visualize a strategy that offers all parties an opportunity to earn money without an untenable amount of infighting and politicking? If yes, the hybrid concept is implementable.

The third element of good implementation is to have top management's blessing and support for the move to a hybrid organization. Adding a vertically integrated group to outsourced selling, or adding third parties to a set of employees, is a major strategic decision. If it is left to the sales function alone, the decision will not hold up in the field. A hybrid structure inevitably generates high expectations, followed by a reality check. Without top management's support, the program will wither when the conflict, complexity, and overhead of a dual structure become apparent.

The fourth element of good implementation is to sort out the reporting structure. Making OSPs and employees report to the same manager puts that manager in a position of mixed motives, or conflict of interest. The success of one sales force can show up the other sales force and can be used by top management as a benchmark to criticize the manager. Further, many sales managers know little about Reps and will attempt to manage them in the same way as they manage employees. This is bound to fail. The best solution—have separate management, one for the Reps and one for the direct—removes the conflict of interest and allows the manufacturer to match the manager's skill sets to the task.

In a nutshell, the hybrid sales organization is an excellent idea in many circumstances. However, manufacturers should reason like botanists. When crossing two strains of roses, the idea is to create a new strain that has the best of both types. To get a superior hybrid, it is critical to keep crossing, ruthlessly throwing away the feeble Frankenstein roses that are bound to appear occasionally. Botanists keep crossbreeding until they get it right, and manufacturers need to approach hybrid sales forces in the same spirit. They must start with promising strains of roses (start with the right circumstances for using Reps and direct salespeople) and must keep adjusting until they find a superior rose (fine-tune the sales roles and get the implementation right). Remember that crossing just a handful of types gave rise to most of the roses being planted today and drove out the native roses of Europe and North America. When it works, it really works! Outsourcing the field sales force is not an all-or-nothing proposition.

CASE STUDY:
MATCHING THE ROLE TO THE PRODUCT AT
UPS MANUFACTURERS

An example of matching the role to the product is the manufacturing of uninterruptible power supplies, known as UPS systems. Originally UPS systems were meant to solve problems for large computers and other large systems that required a continuous and smooth flow of electricity to perform properly. The loss of electricity or violent spikes of power could do significant damage to the system. As time passed, newer applications for UPS evolved. Desktop computers, security systems, life support equipment (just to name a few) were natural users of UPS equipment. But these products were sold through different dealer and distribution networks. Hence, many suppliers of this equipment determined that they needed a different sales force or a different OSP network to penetrate these diverse markets. Since their existing sales structure was not always capable of providing the necessary coverage, multiple sales forces or OSPs were established. Either they adapted to needs of these emerging markets or lost enormous opportunities.

This need to adapt is obvious. So why doesn't every firm do it all the time? It's partly because sales structures have inertia: they are hard to change. But the more important reason is that managers don't want to subdivide sales roles because they don't want to create a sales infrastructure unless the role is a very big one. Managers want to preserve economies of scale. In the process, they lose sight of selling effectiveness. Managers imagine that salespeople and their managers can be chameleons, changing what they do each time they cross the boundaries of a sales role (which can happen several times a day with a varied product portfolio). But if salespeople are ineffective, what use is it to have economies of scale? Indeed, asking sales forces to be chameleons is a way to create *diseconomies* of scale: the operation is too big to do the job right.

ENDNOTES

1. Anderson, Erin, and Anne T. Coughlan (1987), "Distribution of Industrial Products Introduced to Foreign Markets: Integrated versus Independent Channels," *Journal of Marketing,* 51 (January), 71–82.
2. Scherer, F. M., and David Ross (1990), *Industrial Market Structure and Economic Performance.* Boston: Houghton Mifflin.
3. Fudge, William K., and Leonard M. Lodish (1977), "Evaluation of the Effectiveness of a Model Based Salesman's Planning System by Field Experience," *Interfaces,* 18 (November), 97–106.

   Lodish, Leonard M. (1974), "'Vaguely Right' Approach to Sales Force Allocations," *Harvard Business Review,* 52 (January/February), 119–124.

4. Lodish, Leonard (1980), "A User-Oriented Model for Sales Force Size, Product, and Market Allocation Decisions," *Journal of Marketing,* 44 (Summer), 70–78.
5. Zoltners, Andris A., and Prabhakant Sinha (1983), "Sales Territory Alignment: A Review and Model," *Management Science,* 29 (November), 1237–1256.

   Zoltners, Andris A., and Sally E. Lorimer (2000), "Sales Territory Alignment: An Overlooked Productivity Tool," *The Journal of Personal Selling and Sales Management,* 20 (3), 139–150.

6. Zoltners, Andris A., Parabhakant Sinha, and Greggor A. Zoltners (2001), *The Complete Guide to Accelerating Salesforce Performance.* New York: AMACOM.
7. Anderson, Rolph E., Rajiv Mehta, and Alan J. Dubinsky (2003), "Will the Real Channel Manager Please Stand Up?" *Business Horizons,* 20 (1), 61–68.
8. Kirmani, Amna, and Askhay R. Rao (2000), "No Pain, No Gain: A Critical Review of the Literature on Signaling Unobservable Product Quality," *Journal of Marketing,* 64 (April), 66–79.
9. Sa Vinhas, Alberto, and Erin Anderson (2003), "How Potential Conflict Drives Channel Structure: Concurrent Governance of Routes to Market," INSEAD working paper (November).
10. Rangan, V. Kasturi, and George T. Bowman (1992), "Beating the Commodity Magnet," *Industrial Marketing Management,* 21 (3), 215–224.
11. Kotler, Philip, Gary Armstrong, John Saunders, and Veronica Wong (2001), *Principles of Marketing* (3d European ed.). Englewood Cliffs, NJ: Prentice-Hall.
12. Mitchell, Vincent-Wayne, and Dominic F. Wilson (1998), "Balancing Theory and Practice: A Reappraisal of Business-to-Business Segmentation," *Industrial Marketing Management,* 27 (4), 429–445.
13. Dutta, Shantanu, Mark Bergen, Jan B. Heide, and George John (1995), "Understanding Dual Distribution: The Case of Reps and House Accounts," *Journal of Law, Economics, and Organization,* 11 (1), 189–204.
14. Ibid.
15. Torode, Christina (2003), "Partners: AT&T Lives by Channel Playbook," *CRN News,* 4 (September 2), 6–7.
16. Rodin, Robert, and Curtis Hartman (2000), *Free, Perfect, and Now: Connect-*

ing to the Three Insatiable Demands: A CEO's True Story. New York: Simon & Schuster.

17. Langerak, Fred (2003), "An Appraisal of Research on the Predictive Power of Market Orientation," *European Management Journal,* 21 (4), 447–464.

18. Rangan, V. Kasturi, Rowland T. Moriarty, and Gordon S. Swartz (1992), "Segmenting Customers in Mature Industrial Markets," *Journal of Marketing,* 56 (4), 72–82.

19. Kalwani, Manohar, and Narakesari Narayandas (1995), "Long-Term Manufacturer-Supplier Relationships: Do They Pay Off for Supplier Firms?" *Journal of Marketing,* 59 (January), 1–16.

20. Coughlan, Anne T., Erin Anderson, Louis W. Stern, and Adel I. El-Ansary (2001), *Marketing Channels* (6th ed.). Englewood Cliffs, NJ: Prentice-Hall.

21. Sa Vinhas, Alberto (2003), "Dual Distribution Channels in Business-to-Business Marketing: A Transaction Interdependencies View," Ph.D. dissertation, INSEAD.

22. Dirks, Kurt T., and Donald L. Ferrin (2002), "The Role of Trust in Organizational Settings," *Organization Science,* 12 (4), 450–467.

23. Williamson, Oliver E. (1993), "Calculativeness, Trust, and Economic Organization," *Journal of Law and Economics,* 36 (April), 453–486.

24. Dwyer, F. Robert, Paul H. Schurr, and Sejo Oh (1987), "Developing Buyer-Seller Relationships," *Journal of Marketing,* 51 (April), 11–27.

25. Mohr, Jakki, and Robert Spekman (1994), "Characteristics of Partnership Success: Partnership Attributes, Communication Behavior, and Conflict Resolution Techniques," *Strategic Management Journal,* 15 (1), 135–142.

26. Elliott, Heidi (2003), "Building a Big Rep with Reps," *Electronic Business,* 20 (April 15), 1–2.

27. Anderson, Rolph E., Rajiv Mehta, and Alan J. Dubinsky (2003), "Will the Real Channel Manager Please Stand Up?" *Business Horizons,* 20:1, 61–68.

5

Economic Arguments to Put to Reps—Or, Hitting the Optimal Window: The Role of Time and Commission Rate

The first thing a new professor in a business school learns to do is to lead a case discussion. A case is a description of the decision facing an executive, with some sketch of the situation. Business schools are notorious for relying on solving cases; the faculty want their students to soak up "process knowledge" (how to go about thinking about a problem). Process knowledge is tacit, so professors impart it by obliging their students to imagine playing a real role in business situations.

What do these cases impart? One of the most important points comes alive when 90 intelligent, educated, prepared, passionate young people spend an hour arguing a case, only to see a single student settle the argument in minutes. How? *By calculating out the costs and benefits to all the players.* Eventually, students come to realize that in business a well-crafted economic argument carries the day. Economic arguments transcend viewpoints and values. Cost/benefit analysis has a way of bringing decision-makers to agreement.

But it's not just the accounting costs and benefits (the ones you can specify). Case analysis convinces students that the most important costs must be framed as opportunity costs—what you forego by doing something other than your best course of action. In short, case analysis serves to teach young people one of the most fundamental things that managers learn by experience—always do a cost/benefit analysis, focusing on the best use of the resources a firm has. Don't rely solely on lists of pros and cons. Calculate. Do the economics. Accept that you can only approximate, but do not fail to quantify.

It should be no surprise that this way of approaching a problem is extremely effective in dealing with the OSP. The OSP is a business, and so is a manufacturer. To persuade and inspire the Rep, work out the economic arguments, and rely heavily on them.

This is easier said than done, because the economics of the Rep are quite different from the economics of the manufacturer. While most manufacturers focus on two things: time (how much are they getting from the Rep) and commission (how high or low to set it), Reps evaluate a deal on a much more complex set of issues.

This chapter attempts to debunk the myth that getting the most time ("mind share") out of a Rep at the least possible commission is the ideal scenario. In fact, you will discover that time and commission are often moving targets, and hitting that small window of optimality is how to create an effective partnership with an OSP—*effective in getting sales, profit, and market share results.*

When we present this argument to managers, we immediately get resistance. Reps are profit-seeking organizations, but they are run by people. Don't the personal, emotional, noncalculative elements play a role? Isn't it possible for a principal to become the Rep's emotional favorite? And doesn't that get results, too?

Yes, yes, and yes. This chapter is based on a major study of how OSPs divide their resources, financial and human.[1] This study documents what experienced managers know: the human element is terribly important. This said, the economic element is even more important. No business can meet a payroll on positive feelings alone. The money has to be there, now and in the future. This chapter is about financial arguments only. Chapter 6 rounds out the picture by adding in the human element, which is very substantial. Together, Chapters 6 and 7 tell you how to motivate your Rep to achieve tangible results, quickly, on your behalf.

WHAT ARE YOU WORTH? CALCULATING THE OPTIMAL ALLOCATION

A lot of manufacturers worry about getting "mind share" from their Rep firms. As we have already said, and will continue to say, what matters most is *market* share, not *mind* share. Anticipating that you may not agree with this statement, we've put together a little brainteaser that speaks directly to this issue. We assure you that you will be floored by what it illustrates.

Table 5-1. Brain Teaser: How Calls Produce Sales Results

ACCOUNTS	0	1	2	3	4	5	6
Alpha	20	200	205	208	213	217	220
Bravo	10	30	50	68	80	90	95
Charlie	0	5	40	45	50	55	55
Delta	0	100	250	300	340	375	400
Echo	0	5	10	15	20	25	25
Foxtrot	200	220	230	240	245	250	260
Golf	0	10	20	30	30	40	45
Hotel	0	50	110	150	180	100	215

Present hours allocated:
Total hours allocated: $5 + 1 + 2 + 3 + 1 + 5 + 2 + 1 = 20$
Sales with present allocation: $217 + 30 + 40 + 300 + 5 + 250 + 20 + 50 = 912$

Source: Based on research reported in Lodish, Leonard (1980), "A User-Oriented Model for Sales Force Size, Product, and Market Allocation Decisions," *Journal of Marketing*, 44 (Summer), 70–78. Used with permission.

The brainteaser starts with a saleswoman (let's call her Jill) who has 8 accounts. Jill has enough time that she can make 20 calls a month on them. The accounts "respond" to her call efforts by giving her some level of sales. As a practical matter, no account will accept more than 6 calls in a month. Jill controls her time: she can make no calls on an account if she chooses. Management holds her accountable only for her sales results. Table 5-1 shows us what would happen in each account at each level of sales call. The shaded cells in this matrix show what Jill is actually doing now and the results she is getting. For example, Jill makes one call on Bravo, which generates sales of 30. Jill would get sales of 10 even without making any calls, and sales of 95 by making 6 calls. Jill is working to the limit: 20 calls. Her call pattern is indicated by the shaded cells, which add up to sales of 912 from the 8 accounts together. Here is the challenge: find the best way to reallocate Jill's time over the same accounts so as to increase sales without making Jill work any harder. In other words, maximize Jill's sales at the same level of effort (20 calls).

The Optimal Allocation of Time

The brainteaser in Table 5-1 is often given to managers and sales-people in meeting rooms. People hold up their hand when they think they've got the best possible way to invest Jill's time. Some people figure it out in less than 2½ minutes. Within 3½ minutes, most businesspeople get close to the optimal allocation of Jill's time. But in under 4 minutes, few people actually do find the one best (i.e., optimal) allocation, the one that gives the highest sales results without going over Jill's available time. Eking out the last few dollars is a tedious exercise.[2]

Who does this task fast? It's a matter of practice. People who are used to managing limited resources and can see some sort of results tend to be good at it. For example, logistics managers juggle warehouse space (limited shelf space) and are judged on inventory holding costs and delivery times (results). They find this brainteaser relatively easy. Another group that does this task well is experienced salespeople. Indeed, the under-2½-minutes crowd usually turns out to be top salespeople—in companies that pay sizeable commissions and bonuses—who are motivated to practice this kind of thinking.

The key here is to think in terms of *trade-offs* across the *whole set of possibilities.* People who do this task slowly start by thinking in 1-hour increments (call) at a time and looking at one account (one row of the matrix), moving from one account to another. Fast problem solvers look at blocks of time (3 or 4 hours) first, glancing over the accounts (rows). They're looking for big swaps with big payoffs (for example, moving 3 hours from Alpha to Hotel). Fast problem solvers are willing to shift the call pattern dramatically over accounts. They know that making real sales gains requires making sacrifices in order to find the resources to bet on the most promising prospects. In contrast, slow problem solvers hesitate to cut way back on some accounts. Thus, they can't make big shifts to other accounts and burden themselves with the idea that they have to make minimum calls on everyone. (Some people even insist that was in the instructions and won't drop their claim until they hear audience members laughing.)

This way of thinking is one of making trade-offs to maximize results. The thought process is something like this: if I take off 3 hours over here, I lose 12, but if I put it over there, I gain 130, so I'm net 118, and now can I find cuts and gains that are better than 118? The *opportunity cost* of not changing is 118. Fast problem solvers are sensitive to low losses (an hour or so less doesn't make much difference, as in Alpha or Foxtrot) and to high gains (more time means a lot more sales, as in Hotel or Delta). Economists have a term for this. Low losses mean sales are *inelastic* with respect to effort. High gains mean sales are highly *elastic* with respect to effort. Fast problem solvers take effort from the inelastic accounts and give it to the elastic accounts.

When the session moderator asks the fast people to describe how they reason through it, most of them use pictorial language. They're looking for "jumps," "spikes," "leaps," "heartbeats," and "peaks." They put time there. To find time, they look for "the flats," "the plains," "the prairies," "the dead pulses," the "flatlines." That's how they quickly find the opportunity cost of suboptimal time allocation.

These fast problem solvers are visualizing the sales response functions. Figure 5-1 shows us what they see: numbers transformed into graphics. (Some people actually do this with the raw numbers and skip the visual stage. They sense big or small numbers without needing to "see" them.)

But it's not enough to understand how sales respond to effort. Fast problem solvers are always looking for opportunity costs, gains from doing better. They are ready to reshuffle, dramatically if need be, to bring the opportunity cost down to zero. They accept, with little emotion, that if you're working at the limit of your resources, *you can't invest in one place unless you take it from somewhere else.* They are not wishful thinkers. They accept the inevitability of trade-offs.

The Optimal Allocation of Time and Commission Rates

Now, let's try the same exercise, this time for a Rep. The management of a good OSP wants to maximize its total profit. The Rep's revenue is its sales times its commission rate. Since most of the Rep's resources are its salespeople, most of the Rep's expenses follow how those people invest their time. If we focus on the function that expresses how the Rep's commissions respond to the salespeople's time, we've got the essential elements of the Rep's profit function. That means that if we maximize the OSP's revenue (commissions) in function of how the salespeople, taken together, invest their total time, we maximize the Rep's profit.

Figure 5-2 shows several functions relating the Rep commission to how its salespeople invest their time. Remember, the Rep is a company, so this is the total sales time of multiple salespeople related to total commissions. Each function applies to a principal, that is, a manufacturer of a product. The horizontal axis shows what fraction of the company's total pool of sales time could go to selling on behalf of that principal. The vertical axis shows the commission to the Rep company that would result from that fraction, that is, the OSP's revenue. The response function covers the range of theoretical possibilities, from giving the principal zero time

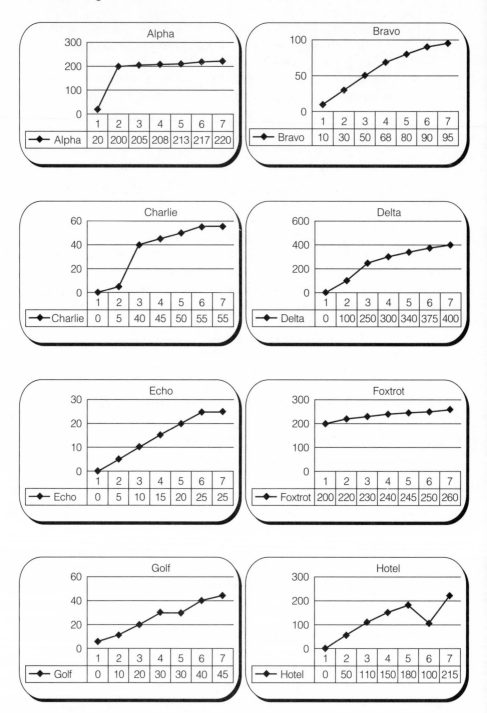

Figure 5-1. Brain Teaser as Images

Line Sales ($)

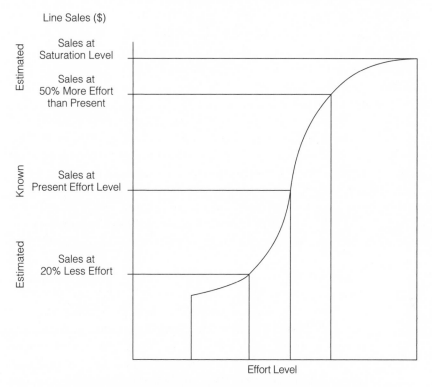

Figure 5-2. How the Rep's Sales Respond to Its Efforts
Adapted from Anderson, Erin, Leonard M. Lodish, and Barton Weitz (1987),
"Resource Allocation Behavior in Conventional Channels," *Journal of Marketing
Research,* 24 (February), 85–97.

to giving the principal all the Rep's time. In practice, Reps usually
operate in the zone of 1 to 33 percent of their time for any one
principal. This estimate can, and usually does, vary between salespeople within the firm since their individual customer assign-
ments may have different needs.

When framed like this, it's easy to see that this problem is no
different from the brainteaser in Table 5-1. Given a portfolio of
principals and a finite pool of selling time, there is an optimal allocation, that is, a division of selling time that maximizes the Rep's
revenue. What maximizes the Rep's revenue also maximizes its
profit (since expenses follow time).

Good salespeople have a feel for the best use of their time
given their customers. In the same way, good Rep management
has a feel for the best use of its salespeople's pool of time, given
the OSP's principals.

There is one nuance that complicates the picture. Good Rep management senses the minimum time allocation each principal will accept. For example, if a principal will terminate a Rep that devotes less than 6 percent of its time to their line, there is no point in giving that principal 5 percent of time, even if 5 percent is what maximizes the Rep's revenue. Allocating the principal 5 percent of the pool of selling time is a false maximization, because the Rep is investing in a soon-to-disappear relationship. Instead, the Rep's true maximization comes from replacing the principal. Why? That the optimal allocation (from the Rep's standpoint) is less time than the principal will accept can only mean one thing: the Rep has other principals that offer a better return on the Rep's time. To meet the principal's minimum-time requirement, therefore, profit must be sacrificed. This is an opportunity cost.

Top Reps are highly sensitive to the optimal allocation of their pool of selling time across their set of principals. Like top salespeople who are paid for results, managers of well-run OSPs are keenly aware of the opportunity costs of their company's sales time. And like top salespeople, management doesn't just stockpile that knowledge— they put it to use. Just as top salespeople alter their call patterns across customers to maximize their individual revenue, so Reps alter their time allocation across principals to maximize their company's profit. This means the OSP's management actually tracks, directs, and redirects how salespeople invest their time. OSP managers don't let their salespeople follow their private ideas about which lines deserve more effort.

Optimality, Not Time, Is the Ultimate Argument

Seen from the Rep's viewpoint, each line gets the time it "deserves," according to what is in the Rep's economic best interest. This is the single biggest driver of how much time the OSP's salespeople will devote to a line. If you try to fight that, you are trying to make water flow uphill. This doesn't mean that raw economics (current profit) is the only factor that matters, but it is the biggest single factor. (In the next chapter we will look at the benefits of becoming the Rep's "emotional favorite.") Reps learn the hard way that if they don't maximize their income, they won't survive. They won't be able to weather the bad times as well as prosper in the good times. It's Darwinian economics: those who pay attention to their opportunity costs are selected out to survive. Sooner or later, the rest fail. Because Reps have no corporate parent to bail them out, they simply go under—unless they ruthlessly pursue their economic self-interest.

That means the *single most effective way to induce a Rep to devote more time to a line is to be worth more time* from the Rep's perspective. This may sound confusing since we have just insisted that market share (that is, your results with customers) *not* mind share (share of the Rep's time) is the real indicator of your success. Yet, that said, there is an *optimal* amount of time you want a Rep to devote to your product, and you need to be worth that time.

Being Worth More Time: Three Possible Routes

There are three ways to be worth more time: (1) have a better (higher, steeper) sales response curve, (2) be sure to sign up with a Rep whose other lines are not very saleable, so that you are the Rep's best option, and (3) raise the Rep's commission.

Although option 2 is obviously silly, many manufacturers do this. Of course, they don't explain it as, "We're going to line up a mediocre Rep that we can dominate." They have a better-sounding way of putting it: "We want to have some influence over our Rep, so we make sure to deal with them only if we can be an important principal."

If your products appeal to the Rep's portfolio of customers, you *are* an important principal. And if your products don't appeal, a good OSP won't carry them anyway. A manufacturer should not hesitate to work with a Rep whose other lines merit a good deal of sales attention. These are good lines, and a manufacturer should want to be in their company.

Nonetheless, some manufacturers insist on "being the important principal" and think this means commanding a large part of the Rep's attention. In fact, one of the most common questions asked during a Rep interview is that of mind share: "How much of your mind share will we get? The only way that we can obtain the desired results that we seek is if we are at the top of your line card. We need to get a disproportionate share of your organization's time."

But does it really matter how long someone takes to get the job done or how much they think about the job? Has any company ever published a stockholder's report that showed "efforts per share" versus "earnings per share"? In many ways, the Nike slogan applies here perfectly: *Just do it!* Because the objective is not to have a high "share of mind" or even a high "share of time."

WHEN MIND SHARE MATTERS

Capturing of mind share does have its application in some instances. Let's look at a distributor's or a dealer's sales organization. They have multiple suppliers for each category of products. How does a manufacturer (and/or their Rep salesperson) capture the attention of those salespeople and get them to focus on and sell their product versus the other three of four competitors they are selling? The question here is, "What can we do to keep our products foremost in their minds?" The distributor/dealer salesperson most often has options that she or he can exercise if so motivated.

Normally, manufacturers attempt to gain a distributor/dealer salesperson's mind share through a series of activities including market-oriented sales meetings, sales promotions, and "spiffs of all sorts" (monetary rewards, trips, gifts, etc.). More thought given to staying "in their mind" will probably accomplish results. Most often, however, the extra effort obtained as the result of a promotion is short-lived, and so the process begins again. Of course, because all of the competing manufacturers are attempting to accomplish the same thing, the "mind share" competition is very real and requires consistent resuscitation and innovation. Who has the better promotion this week or month?

Unfortunately, many people in sales management believe that the same issues and methods that apply to working with distributors and dealers should apply equally to Reps. Not so! Let's look at a few reasons why this approach does not apply to Reps and indeed may even be counterproductive.

1. Reps do not carry competing products. They either sell your product or they make no sale at all. They have no options. They are principal loyal.
2. Other principals are not competitors; they're complementary products that add synergy and leverage to their selling efforts. Selling one product often leads to the sale of other products, a major advantage of the Representative function. This has been well covered in previous chapters.
3. Their portfolio of products takes a long time to develop. Getting the right mix of principals that don't compete yet complement one another lends strength to their position with customers in their market. Some principal product or name recognition assist in "pulling through" the sale of other principal's products, which is where the application of economies of scale and scope come into play, as discussed earlier and throughout this book.
4. If they expend a disproportionate amount of time on a given principal, the Rep firm may jeopardize their relationship/performance with other principals and risk termination. This weakens their portfolio and may have financial consequences to the Rep firm that even you won't like, such as staff reduction (popularly referred to as "right sizing").

Good Rep managers determine how much time it takes to develop a principal's potential. The potential does not have to generate immediate sales dollars to the Rep firm in order to capture and hold their attention. Often it requires considerable time and resources to accomplish sales goals. In the electronic component industry, for example, some efforts require years of work. The process of working with people in various levels of project management, engineering and design development, multiple sampling efforts, vendor approvals process, manufacturing department approval, purchasing negotiations, and so forth can represent a substantial investment in resources. Even after that effort is expended, the project may be dropped and no purchases are ever offered to anyone. That's all part of the risk/reward formula.

The objective is to have high sales, high market share, and high sales growth. The objective is expressed in absolute results. *It is not a matter of share of the Rep's mind, or anything else about the Rep.* A small share of a great Rep's time (or mind) will get far better results than a large share of a mediocre Rep's time (or mind).

Actually the best way to be worth more time is to have a better curve (option 1). Curvy is better, especially if the curve is up high. We mean that literally. The higher the curve (on the vertical axis), the bigger the commission at any level of sales effort. And to be curvy means that sales turn up. It means that sales effort creates sharply increasing returns. This is an elastic response function; it trumps inelastic response functions and therefore pulls the optimal allocation.

In turn, how do you develop a high, curved response function? Serve the market well. *Good marketing is the key to a sales response function that attracts the Rep's time.* It means the product is appealing, saleable, to at least one sizable segment of buyers. A number of factors make this happen, such as reputable brand name, superior product performance and reliability, good design, appealing points of uniqueness, satisfactory lead times for delivery, and pricing that fits the value the customer perceives in the product (not out of line with what the customer perceives to be the competition). In short, if a brand does a good job of meeting market needs, it has the sales response curve that draws time. Giving time to the brand fits the Rep's economic self-interest.

Having a high, elastic sales response function is critical because the Rep's revenue is sales driven. But the OSP isn't maximizing your revenue—it's maximizing its own revenue. That's your revenue times the Rep's commission. The pie here is total revenue from selling your product. Raising the commission rate gives the Rep a larger piece of the pie, which raises the curve the Rep relies upon to determine optimal time allocation. So wouldn't it make sense to raise the commission rate?

Table 5-2. Diminishing Returns to Higher Commissions

GAIN IN COMMISSION RATE	GAIN IN TIME
First ¼ percent	10 percent more than you were getting
Second ¼ percent	8 percent more
Third ¼ percent	6.4 percent more
Fourth ¼ percent	5.12 percent
Continuing increases	Eventually approaches no gain

Yes and no. Option 3, raising commission rates, is a very sticky issue, precisely because much like time, commission rates hit a point of diminishing returns at some point along the sales curve. Obviously, a higher commission rate is more appealing to the Rep, if all else is constant. But let's take a look at what happens when the manufacturer relies exclusively on this strategy to motivate the OSP. Table 5-2 shows a typical result. In step 1, the principal is paying a 5 percent commission. To become more economically interesting to the Rep, the principal raises the rate by one-fourth of a percentage point, to 5.25 percent. The result is gratifying: the Rep increases its time allocation by 10 percent. Thus, if the Rep were giving the principal 8 percent of its time at 5 percent commission, the Rep goes to 8.8 percent of its time (that is, another 10 percent of the base share) at 5.25 percent commission. So far, so good.

Since that worked, the manufacturer does it again: another one-fourth of a percent raise in commission rate, in expectation of another 10 percent gain in time share. That works, but not as well as expected. The Rep adds 8 percent time share, not 10 percent. Now the Rep has added 18.8 percent to its original time share (1.1 × 1.08), and the commission is at 5.5 percent.[3] Still, a time gain is a time gain, so the manufacturer raises another one-fourth of a percentage point, expecting another 8 percent time gain. On this round, the gain is only 6.4 percent—but that's not bad.

This is a scenario of diminishing returns to the manufacturer's incentive. For every (constant) percentage increase in commission rate, the Rep adds a time share that is not constant. It is 80 percent of the gain on the last round. The return to more incentive declines slowly but steadily, eventually coming close to zero return.

The precise rate of decline varies from case to case. The principle, though, is general: raising commission rates is a strategy that works but not indefinitely. It is a strategy of diminishing returns.

Why does this happen? One reason is that all manufacturers have an upper limit to their sales potential. More effort (in response to higher rates) eventually drives the Rep into the zone of diminishing returns to effort. The OSP enters the inelastic zone of the manufacturer's sales response function. Thus, the improvement in the Rep's share of the pie is offset by the saturation effect: the pie can only grow so much.

But there is a more subtle reason. A commission rate is a *credible signal*: by its very existence, it says something powerful about what the manufacturer believes and intends. There is a proper level of commission rate. It rests on a fair rate of return for efforts exerted and risks undertaken. If the Rep must devote high efforts and take high risks, a very high rate is justified. But raising commission rates eventually takes the principal to a level that is unreasonably high. The Rep knows this and assumes the manufacturer knows it too (or will figure it out quickly).

So, what signal does an unreasonably high commission rate send about the manufacturer's beliefs and intentions? The signal is that something is wrong somewhere. Now comes speculation time: what could that be? Here are some possibilities that could occur to any manager of the OSP.

- There's something wrong with this product. They want us to drop everything and sell it fast, so they make their numbers before the market finds out what the problem is.
- They want to see, and quickly, what is the potential out there, without investing much. If we do well at high sales effort, they know the potential is high. If we do badly at high sales effort, they know it's low.
- If they learn that potential is low, they'll cut back—and we'll be left having overinvested.
- If they learn that potential is high, they'll invest more. Maybe they'll invest in us—or maybe they'll go direct, or switch to another Rep who will work for less. They can do that, if we open the market first.
- Or maybe the management of this manufacturer really doesn't know what a fair commission is. That means they won't last long.

There is no attribution on this list that is encouraging. Either manufacturer management is incompetent, or it is hiding discouraging beliefs (something's wrong with the product) or damaging intentions ("They want us to overinvest so they can see whether the demand is there, and then . . ."). A sky-high commission rate is too good to be true, too good to last. Management of a good OSP will not count on luck. They will hold back on efforts.

When you think about it, this makes complete sense. Indeed, you probably think the same way about your own business: if something is too good to be true, you proceed on the assumption that it's false. Nonetheless, we have seen a number of manufacturers that blindly persisted in raising commission rates to the sky. They explain it this way: "You have to show the Rep the money, or they won't sell for you." True—but an unreasonably high commission rate does not show the Rep the money. It shows the Rep a reason to be worried.

The real reason managers keep raising commission rates is that they lack the knowledge, imagination, or power to manage their Rep relationship any better. The rest of this book will fix the knowledge gap and fire up the imagination. But the power is another matter. In many cases, the product itself has serious marketing deficiencies—and the manager doesn't have the vision or the organizational influence to fix *that*. So, rather than make a better product and market it better, managers try to bribe their Reps to push it harder. Is it any wonder that this strategy runs into diminishing returns? The Rep that pushes an inferior product endangers its business.

By the way, another solution to this problem is to hire a direct sales force, then pressure employees to sell the product, marketing problems and all. But employee salespeople will also have trouble selling it. The result? The better salespeople leave, especially if their pay includes an important variable component.[4] The rest resist passively and thereby fail to generate results.[5]

This chapter is about using economic arguments to motivate the OSP to give you attention and its attendant results. We've covered optimality and commission rate, one principal at a time, in the context of the OSP's portfolio of principals. Now we turn to four other factors that influence the financial rewards the Rep gains from each principal. These are (1) synergy and leverage, (2) ease of sale, (3) growth potential, and (4) forecastability.

SYNERGY AND LEVERAGE WITH THE OSP'S PRODUCT PORTFOLIO

The heart of the OSP's value proposition is a portfolio of products. A portfolio is not a collection or an assembly of diverse things. A portfolio is a carefully designed set of products, designed to work together to solve customers' problems. Thinking about the products line by line, response function by response function, overlooks the essential idea that the Rep is playing on the synergy among the lines.

Reps don't overlook synergy. They give more effort to product lines that fit nicely in the portfolio, products that help to sell (leverage) all the other lines. By itself, a synergistic line may not merit much effort. But the Rep will devote selling time to it anyway, knowing that the economic value of the line shows up in the sales of the other lines and in the satisfaction of the customer base.

This effect is symmetric, meaning that it cuts both ways. A line that has negative synergy that detracts from the sales of the rest of the lines will receive less time than it merits all by itself.

An example comes from the 1980s, the era of the discotheque. Discos are heavy users of all sorts of electronic and electrical paraphernalia. We know an electronic components Rep who did a good business serving discos. The owner had a friend who had a side business making the mirrored globes that hang from the ceiling and turn, sending reflected light all over the dance floor. Seeing that the Rep had the attention of disco managers, the manufacturer asked his friend to take on the mirrored globes. In a moment of weakness, the owner agreed. A few months later, it was clear that the Rep's salespeople were losing their technical credibility and hastening the end of the call every time they brought up the globes. The globes were hurting sales of the other lines. Seeing this, the salespeople were leaving their sample globes in the trunks of their cars. (The owner then did the right thing by resigning the line.)

In short, adding synergy to the Rep's portfolio has a payoff: the OSP will give the line its proper time. This means that manufacturers should make it a point to select Reps whose portfolios fit what the manufacturer makes. Of course, the customers, not necessarily technical considerations, determine fit. If customers want to see the line when they consider how to solve a problem, the line adds synergy to the Rep's portfolio. (In contrast, the technicians who set up and maintained the discos did not want to see mirrored globes when they bought electronic components—globes are décor, to be settled on a different occasion, perhaps by different decision makers, in conjunction with a different set of related purchases.) And if a line gives the salesperson the ability to probe, or the ability to get an appointment, or the ability to get to the first yes, it is particularly synergistic. OSPs put their efforts behind such a line.

It behooves a manufacturer to keep pointing out to the Rep the synergy that its line offers. This is communication, a powerful tool (which we cover in detail in Chapter 6).

ARE YOUR PRODUCTS EASY TO SELL?
THE HIDDEN BONUS

Up to this point, we have focused on return per unit of time (commission as a return to collective sales effort). Implicitly, this assumes that one hour is just like another hour. But that's too simple.

Everyone has his or her best time of the day, usually no more than 2 to 4 hours long. Morning people are in top form early, sometimes in the wee hours. Afternoon people feel a surge as the day goes on, sometimes going into overdrive in the last couple of hours of the workday. Evening people come alive after dinner and like to stay up late. Whatever your type, it pays to identify your best 2 to 4 hours and accept that you can't extend them (to, say, 6 hours) or displace them (move them to another part of the day). Then it pays to plan your work to match the most challenging tasks to your best time. Easier tasks should be deferred and performed only when your best hours are over. This is one reason why people who have control over their time should be expected to be more productive. They can match their hardest jobs to their best hours.

Not all time is of equal value, not all work is of equal difficulty, and after some point, putting in more hours will not get more work done—unless some of the work is easier. This is true for businesses, just as it is true for individuals.

In any sales organization, some lines are harder to sell than are others. These lines demand not just more time but the *best* time. They demand the salesperson's *better* efforts. This puts a strain on the sales force. Naturally, therefore, easier-to-sell lines receive a bonus. All other constant, easier-to-sell lines will get more time than the harder-to-sell ones. It's because the harder lines drain the best time, which is in limited supply. The easier lines get more time because that time can come from the larger pool of sales time that is good but not prime. It's analogous to buying airtime on TV or radio. Drive time (radio) or evenings (TV) is limited. A given advertising budget will buy much more time if the message can be effectively delivered outside of these prime hours.

In short, if your line is hard to sell, you will draw less selling time than if it is easy to sell. Easier-to-sell items get a hidden bonus: they are pulled out of the salesperson's bag more often and presented at greater length.

This means it pays to make your line easier to sell, and one of the best ways to do this is to offer technical support to the Rep's salespeople. Outsourced sales professionals do have their own technical support and will "cover" for you if you don't provide any. However, if you assume part of the technical support task yourself, you make it easier for the OSP to sell your product, which will gain you more selling time. As an added benefit, your technical support people open up a new line of communication to your OSP and help to deepen trust between your organization and theirs. Chapter 6 underscores the value of these ties, even though they don't translate directly into financial terms.

DOES YOUR PRODUCT CATEGORY HAVE POTENTIAL TO GROW?

So far, we have focused on a brand, that is, one line of one principal. But those brands belong to product categories. For example, brands fit into types of resistors, or types of semiconductors. A brand fits into categories of greeting cards (congratulations, birthday, friendship). The idea is that the brand's potential is linked to the category's potential, and the OSP invests more time in a brand if it belongs to a *product category* that has the potential to grow.

For example, in the appliances industry, the category of standard clothes washing machine has little growth potential. Most people who want such a machine have one, so the market is largely replacement. However, there is a new category of extremely high-end washing machines with prices that start at least three times higher. These machines fit a new lifestyle trend, which is to create a family room around the laundry room. High-end machines are fast (short cycle), efficient (little water or power), versatile (they can do hand laundry, curtains, or upholstery), effective (they remove special stains), silent, and reliable. That's the performance side. On the aesthetic side, premium machines don't look like washing machines. They feature colors and European design and are almost attractive (almost, because these are, after all, clothes washers).

The superpremium designer washing machine does not face a large market now, but that market is growing extremely fast. A Rep would give a brand in this category more time than it deserves based on current profitability alone. The Rep is betting on the future, building the base of its business, and positioning itself as well placed to meet a latent but emerging need of its customer base.

In other words, if your product category is declining, your line will lose time. If it is the 1930s and you make buggy whips, you cannot induce your Rep to give you a great deal of time. The Rep senses the decline. Current profitability is still there, and the Rep will respond to that. But the OSP will subtract some time and will put those resources elsewhere to build the future. In contrast, if your category has growth potential, the Rep will anticipate future returns and give your brand more time than its current economics are worth.

Of course, this works only if the Rep *perceives* that the category has growth potential. All too often, manufacturers think the category will grow and assume their Rep shares that opinion, but often the Rep does not. In general, manufacturers (upstream in the value chain) and downstream members of the channel of distribution tend to be far apart in their perceptions and forecasts.[6] It's because they live in different worlds and see different pieces of the total picture.

Therefore, it is important that the manufacturer communicate what it expects from the market and why. Communication is two-way. By sharing its expectations and information, the manufacturer spurs dialogue with its Rep. The Rep, in turn, has valuable market insight to share. When the manufacturer and the Rep pool their information and conclude together that the product category will grow, the manufacturer collects a bonus: greater sales effort.

ARE YOUR SALES FORECASTABLE?

You compose your personal investment portfolio by the principle that greater risk demands the prospect of greater return. Conversely, lower expected returns are attractive only when accompanied by lower risk. You allocate your resources (i.e., your money) to different investment choices by this principle. You seek not mere return, but risk-adjusted return.

Management of OSPs will follow the same principle in allocating their company's resources (i.e., total selling time) to different principals. They seek to diversify their risks. Given two lines that offer the same expected return (commissions), the Rep allocates more selling time to the lower-risk line. Risk means forecastability. Reps always forecast returns to selling time. When a line is forecastable, Reps have confidence in their estimate. This is a lower-risk line. But when a line is hard to forecast, Reps have little faith in their own estimate. This is a higher-risk line. To induce the Rep to give it more time, the line needs to offer a higher return.

It pays for a manufacturer to help the Rep forecast. Sharing information can do this, including sharing the manufacturer's own forecasts and information sources. In particular, the manufacturer should have information about demand for its product over multiple markets. The Rep knows its own market but lacks the reference to other markets. Manufacturers, by sharing information, provide a market benchmark to their Reps. This improves the Rep's confidence by imparting the sense that sales are forecastable, that the forecast is not arbitrary or imaginary. The Rep's perception of risk comes down. The manufacturer benefits by winning more of the Rep's time.

SUMMARY

You want to motivate an OSP to generate hard results for you, results your accountant can tally up: sales, profits, market share, and growth. The best, most effective arguments you can make are economic. While this is true in most competitive business situations, it is particularly true when motivating OSPs. Their management has learned the hard way that survival and prosperity depend on managing their businesses tightly, focusing on generating current profits and cash flow. Therefore, OSPs have honed a keen appreciation of profit-maximization principles. The most important principle is to take resources from lines whose returns to the Rep are inelastic (relatively flat, or insensitive to effort) and redeploy those resources to lines whose returns to the Rep are elastic (sharp returns to more effort). The resources are, of course, aggregate selling time (all salespeople pooled).

The management of a well-functioning OSP will not leave the deployment decision to each salesperson. Instead, management will determine the allocation of time across principals (lines) that maximize the organization's revenue (that is, total commissions) and will oblige its salespeople to follow this optimal allocation. In so doing, Rep management is hard nosed, meaning calculating and firm. Managers sense what is the minimum attention a principal will accept. If the Rep's economic self-interest dictates the principal merits less time, the Rep won't bow to the principal and incur an opportunity cost by allocating the principal's minimum demanded time. Instead, the Rep acts proactively. Rather than invest the (unacceptably low) time to the line that maximizes immediate profit and risk being terminated, management of the OSP replaces the line. OSPs don't invest in lines that are bound to disappear from their portfolio.

There are three ways to gain the Rep's time. The worst way is to sign on with a Rep whose other lines don't merit much attention. Your line then becomes the most appealing in the set and will win a high share of time, but this means being the best of a bad lot. It's great for your ego to be powerful, but it's not profitable. Being sold alongside second-tier brands does no good for the manufacturer's results or for its brand equity. The objective is financial results.

The best way to gain the time of any Rep is to offer a brand that has genuine market potential. Such a brand offers the OSP an appealing response function, high and curvy. Such a curve offers returns even at low levels of sales effort, and those returns increase sharply with more effort (returns are elastic). In contrast, a flat response function (inelastic) invites the OSP to take selling resources away, since the cost of so doing is small. In turn, an elastic response function is the result of good marketing.

Another way to gain the time of any Rep is to increase the rate of commission. At every level of sales, the Rep's return goes up, making the line worth more sales effort. However, it is dangerous to rely exclusively on commission rates to motivate the OSP. Eventually, the strategy of raising rates to gain time runs deeply into the zone of diminishing returns: the Rep ceases to reciprocate commission increases with time increases. This is partly because as the OSP adds effort, its salespeople enter into saturation zone: more effort doesn't increase the principal's sales much. More commission is useless if there are no more sales to be had. But commission increases also enter the zone of diminishing returns (less effort gained with each increase) because the OSP will question a commission rate that is significantly out of line with what is equitable for that brand. If the rate is too good to be true, the OSP is likely to suspect it is not true, that indeed something is wrong. Thus, the OSP will hold back additional effort.

In short, how much commission the line generates vis-à-vis the Rep's other lines is the single biggest influence on the Rep's time allocation. The best way to gain more time is to be worth more time from the standpoint of maximizing the Rep's current income. But this is not the whole story. Reps devote effort to lines that help sell the rest of the portfolio. That's leveraging one line to help sell other lines. Synergistic lines gain time. Lines that pull the rest of the portfolio down (negative synergy) lose time. Manufacturers gain the Rep's sales efforts by selecting Reps whose portfolio fits with its products and then communicating the message that synergy is there.

The OSP is an ongoing private business, intended to survive. Rep management will lay the foundation for future growth, although it will not wait indefinitely for the payoff. If your brand does not have high sales potential in the short term, it will still get current sales attention—if it is part of a product category that has potential to grow. It is important to share information with the OSP to gain its agreement that the category indeed does have potential. Why? *Because it is always dangerous to assume that another organization shares your perceptions and expectations.* This is particularly true when the two organizations operate in different environments. The manufacturer and the OSP have very different spheres of operation. Supplier management and Rep management are unlikely to agree about the product category's growth potential unless they communicate actively.

Another boost to sales effort comes when your brand is relatively easier to sell. Such brands get more time because they can be presented all day, every day, to anyone in the customer portfolio, by anyone in the Rep organization. In contrast, hard-to-sell brands demand not only hours of effort, but also the prime hours—and these are in limited supply. Making it easier for the Rep to sell your brand pays off in increased sales effort.

ENDNOTES

1. Anderson, Erin, Leonard M. Lodish, and Barton Weitz (1987), "Resource Allocation Behavior in Conventional Channels," *Journal of Marketing Research*, 24 (February), 85–97. This chapter is based on the findings of this original, large-scale field research.

2. The optimal allocation is Alpha = 1 call, Bravo = 4 calls, Charlie = 2 calls, Delta = 6 calls, Echo = no calls, Foxtrot = 1 call, Golf = no calls, Hotel = 6 calls, which totals 20 calls and sales of 1,155.

   This can be found by fitting the numbers in each row (account) to an equation. This equation is the sales response function, which summarizes how sales respond to effort. One can then solve for the optimal effort level in the set of eight equations, that is, maximizing total sales subject to a constraint of 20 calls.

3. For example, suppose the Rep had been giving the principal 7 percent of its pool of selling time. The first raise brings the time to 7.7 percent ($.07 \times 1.1$). The next raise brings the time to 8.32 percent ($.077 \times 1.08$).

4. Cappelli, Peter (1999), *The New Deal at Work*. Boston: HBS Press.

   ———. (2000), "A Market-Driven Approach to Retaining Talent," *Harvard Business Review*, 46 (1), 45–55.

5. Anderson, Erin, and Thomas S. Robertson (1995), "Inducing Multi-Line Salespeople to Adopt House Brands," *Journal of Marketing*, 59 (April), 16–31.

6. John, George, and Torger Reve (1982), "The Reliability and Validity of Key Informant Data from Dyadic Relationships in Marketing Channels," *Journal of Marketing Research*, 19 (November), 517–524.

6

Enhancing Relationships with Your Reps: Become the "Emotional Favorite"

Chapter 5 covered ways to motivate the OSP that are directly connected to financial returns. This chapter covers the socio-psychological side of the picture, which is of tremendous importance. We explain how to enhance a relationship with the OSP, and, in particular, how to create a stellar asset: status as the Rep's emotional favorite. To begin, let's consider what it means to be an "independent" sales agent.

Are Reps Independent or Interdependent?

Speakers, textbooks, white papers, trade magazines, and everything else that has ever been written or spoken about Reps refer to them as "independent" Reps or "independent" agents. The term "independent" has become so well utilized that it is automatically injected in order to establish a distinguishing and limiting classification of the Rep function. As far as we can tell, every trade association of manufacturers' representatives/agents refers to their members as being "independent." Legally speaking, a Rep firm is "independent" insofar as it is a privately owned business responsible for its own actions and finances. Attorneys who write Rep agreements stress the independence of their Reps in order to make it clear that the Rep firm is a totally separate, legal entity from the principal. Such language portends to make it very clear that the manufacturer is not responsible for any action (or nonaction) taken by its Representative unless specifically approved in advance by the manufacturer. Some contracts go to extraordinary lengths (and chilling detail) to emphasize the point and to illustrate the ramifications of such behavior. And yes, the Internal Revenue Service also considers a

Rep firm an "independent" entity. But that's where the term's usage should end.

Although they are legally independent, Reps and principals are quite *interdependent*. In the real world, most principals treat their Reps as pseudo-employees and hope that the Reps will act and feel the same way. The term "independent Rep" is almost an oxymoron.

The success of the Rep firm is inextricably tied to its principals' success and vice versa. The interdependent relationships that should exist between Reps and their principals are similar to the good and valued relationships that exist in good partnerships, good marriages, and good friendships. Interdependence generates the synergy that everyone seeks in a relationship. This is how win/win relationships develop and grow between Reps and principals, in spite of the legalese contained in the contract.

Getting the Extra Effort Out of Salespeople

Maximizing the relationship with Reps is the goal of every manufacturer that utilizes a network of Reps. Some manufacturers, however, believe that the way to achieve that goal is by getting greater mind share of their Reps. *More mind share should equal better sales performance,* they theorize. Sounds logical. But as we already discussed in the previous chapter, mind share does not automatically translate to market share.

Even worse, if a principal succeeds in coercing a disproportionate amount of the Rep firm's time and resources, other principals will more than likely suffer and perhaps even terminate the Rep. If dropped by other principals, the Rep will actually be less appealing to potential customers because of a reduced portfolio, making it harder for the Rep to sell your product. Ironically, the principal would have gotten what he wanted, but to his own detriment. Be careful what you wish for!

Other principals exert pressure on their Reps in the form of constant threats. They often overload their Reps with requests for unnecessary and burdensome chores, thinking that these actions get and keep their attention, as well as keep them from spending time with other principals, whom they view as competition. But in most cases this approach backfires. Persistent threats generate a concern of imminent termination, so the Rep begins to keep an

LOTS OF SMOKE, NO FIRE

In a paper titled "The Input Bias," professors K. E. Chinander, Ph.D. (University of Miami), and M. E. Schweitzer, Ph.D. (Wharton School of the University of Pennsylvania),[1] reveal that people tend to be more influenced by the apparent *quantity* of an output instead of the *quality* of the output. In other words, when managers see employees running around appearing to be very busy, they believe that person is doing a good job.

The idea behind their research was comically illustrated in an episode of the popular television program, *Seinfeld.* In the episode, Jerry Seinfeld's friend George leaves his car parked in the company's parking lot in order to create the impression that he is working long hours, even though he is not. He believes that by doing so, his boss will give him more favorable reviews and hopefully a bigger pay raise. Professors Chinander and Schweitzer call this behavior "an attempt to invoke the input bias . . . the use of input information (in this case the false impression of long hours) to judge outcomes." They contend that "many business decisions are made based on input information that is either biased or manipulated." They define input bias as "the systematic misuse of input information in judgments of outcome quality."

While Chinander and Schweitzer relate that the quality of the decisions is often based on the quantity of information (suggesting a positive result), the quantity of input is not always related to a quality output. They conclude that, "In many cases inputs are misused, misinterpreted, or even negatively related to outcome quality" by managers. They contend that some people are impressed with the volume of information or have a preconceived bias toward the information even if it is not at all relevant to the matter being considered. In other words, lots of smoke, but no fire; lots of action, but not results; lots of mind share, but no market share. That's majoring in minors!

---

eye out for their next opportunity, effectively "checking out" from the current relationship.

Again, seeking to manage mind share instead of obtaining the right amount of market share (outcome) is focusing on the wrong issue. Indeed, as we pointed out in the previous chapter, how many annual reports show "Efforts per Share" instead of "Earnings per Share"? Interestingly, recent research shows that many of us fall for the old, "Hey, look at me! I'm doing lots of work!" charade, when in the end, getting the job done is the only thing that really matters and is what good Rep firms are geared to do.

An autocratic and confrontational style is clearly not very effective in managing, directing, or motivating any type of salesperson today, particularly Reps, who have different needs and should be worked with quite differently from an in-house sales force.

NOT ALL SALES PROBLEMS CAN BE BLAMED
ON THE SALES FORCE

There is an old sales meeting story about a dog food manufacturer and their annual meeting with their nationwide network of Reps. The sales manager was doing his best to light a fire under his team of Reps because the sales of their new dog food product was far below their budget commitment and corporate expectation. The company president, who by nature is an impatient and intense man, was squirming uncontrollably at the prolonged proceedings, which seemed to be going nowhere and not getting to the crux of the matter.

He couldn't stand it any longer. Without warning, he jumped out of his chair and grabbed the microphone from the startled and embarrassed sales manager. With a loud and emotional tone to his voice, he questioned his Rep audience, "Whose dog food offers the most nutritional value in the business?" The Rep crowd, recognizing his demeanor, loudly responded, *"We do!"* The President then asked, "Who has the best advertising and best distribution network in the dog food business?" The audience again loudly proclaimed, *"We do!"* And with growing confidence the President then asked, "Who has the lowest prices in the dog food industry?" And with much gusto, the Reps loudly and enthusiastically yelled, *"We do!"* Feeling very confident that he had the audience exactly where he wanted them at that moment, the head man leaned forward and then fired off his closing question with startling directness induced by intense displeasure: "Okay, if we're so damned good at everything, how come you guys aren't selling more of our dog food?" It was as though someone had suddenly sucked the oxygen out of the room. The silence was deafening. Nobody blinked.

Finally, someone from the back of the room summoned up some courage and responded: "Because the dogs hate it!"

It's management (principal) to management (Rep), just as with any other outsource partner, not boss to employee. A major reason for utilizing OSPs in the first place is that they manage themselves.

Indeed, as Michael Useem, professor of marketing and director of the Center for Leadership and Change Management at the Wharton School, has found: "Firms involved in outsourcing need managers with capabilities for lateral leadership—the ability to negotiate results outward across boundaries rather than issue orders downward through a hierarchy."

UNDERSTANDING THE REP PERSPECTIVE

A first step to "managing outward across boundaries" begins with understanding what motivates the Rep. In fact, the best Reps have a very clear litmus test for determining whether to take on a new principal. We highlight seven factors.

1. Their Marketplace and Customer Potential

Well-established Reps ultimately obtain from a variety of sources the potential purchase volume of major customers, distributors, dealers, and so on, and develop estimates of total available market (TAM) and served available market (SAM) for each product line. Some firms regularly track the sales numbers of their competitive suppliers and develop estimates of market share and their trends. The information is constantly updated. Many Reps accumulate this information for products that they don't even sell, just to have it handy should the opportunity to represent a company that manufactures such products is ever offered to them.

2. The Principal's Potential in Serving That Marketplace and Customer Base

Principals may vary in their ability to meet certain customer's requirements. For example, certain products may have huge potential if you have computer manufacturers in your territory yet be of little value to a Rep territory that has none.

3. The Strength of Competition

It may take time to dislodge a competitor or at least become a qualified vendor. Reps will weigh whether the principal's returns are worth the risk that the payoff will be too long or too difficult to achieve in light of the competition in the market.

4. The Potential Earnings for the Rep Firm

Reps are not charitable institutions; they're businesspeople looking to make a profit. They live or die based on the intelligent utilization of their resources and the return that they make on that investment. If the potential financial return does not equal the expenditure of resources, that differential represents a problem that both parties need to address. Realistic goals and the commitment by both parties to achieve those goals are essential to the longevity of the relationship and the strength of the commitment.

5. How Each Principal's Product Offering (Synergy) Fits in Their Portfolio

The Rep's focus is on creating a portfolio of products or services that makes sense to their customer base. Thus, the Rep will look closely at new principals in order to determine if their product will help create an ideal product portfolio. Synergy really works in both directions, for the principal and for the Rep firm. If there appear to be slight overlaps of products or technologies, the Rep will need to have open dialogue with both principals to determine if the problem is livable for everyone. Top-notch Rep management can and will work on this puzzle quickly. When products fit together, that's when the bells and whistles sound. That's classic multiple-line selling strategy.

6. The "Pain Level" versus Income Potential of Each Principal

Pain level is a term that Reps use when certain elements get out of proportion or out of control. Some of these factors are (a) the principal's attempt to micromanage the Rep firm, (b) interference in Rep firm personnel issues, (c) unreasonable demands, (d) the constant changing of contract or compensation terms and conditions in a negative direction, (e) frequent nonpayment or nontimely payment of commission, (f) having to work with unprofessional or unethical local management, and (g) principals that are very difficult to do business with.

7. The People Factor (the Emotional Favorite)

Perhaps this is the least understood—yet one of the most important—considerations for most Rep firms. An emotional favorite can be a large principal or a small principal in terms of income. It is a chemistry that emerges among the parties involved, a simpatico blend of philosophies and likenesses of business styles.

A Rep's portfolio (line card) of principals is their lifeline and their image. It takes years to develop the right combination of principals that complement one another, fit the Rep's skill level, don't compete with one another, and fit to their market and customer base. Making all of these ingredients fit together is a major concern for Reps and explains their willingness or reluctance to take on new principals.

WHY INCENTIVES DON'T WORK

Offering trips, steaks, prizes, and so forth often works well for employee sales-people, but it is not always warmly received by Reps. Reps are companies. They cannot divide up a trip. The Rep's results are produced by groups, not by individuals.

Some manufacturers (principals) go around this issue by offering incentives directly to the Rep's employees, but this creates chaos. Effectively, the principal is trying to buy the employee's time. But the Rep is charged with managing a pool of employees to leverage the synergy of the entire product portfolio to meet the customers' needs. Incentives can skew the salesperson's attention, to the detriment of a customer orientation and the exploitation of sales synergy in the product portfolio. What works is to provide economic rewards, direct and indirect, to the Rep, and then let the Rep motivate and manage its own staff and hold them accountable for results.

Why, then, is it more common to offer incentives directly to a distributor's salespeople? The reason is the fundamental difference in what Reps and distributors do. Reps generate demand and fill factory orders (delayed delivery) *for only one manufacturer in each product category*. Reps solve customer problems by leveraging the synergy of complementary product categories. To do this, they must focus on the family of needs (implicit or explicit) that a customer addresses in a sales call. Exploring latent needs must be uppermost in the salesperson's mind. In contrast, distributor salespeople tend to focus on fulfilling needs, often well-identified needs. Distributors typically offer tremendous depth of assortment (multiple brands in each product category) as well as immediate delivery. Offering an incentive to a distributor salesperson does skew his or her attention from one brand to another, but this is frequently *within one product category*. The competition is between brands in a category, and many customers have already identified what category they want to purchase for immediate delivery. Therefore, less damage is done by offering incentives to distributor salespeople than to Rep salespeople.

This said, even going directly to distributor salespeople is a flawed idea. Offering "spiffs" to distributor employees should be a short-term way to get attention for something new. Instead, it all too often degenerates into a semipermanent reward that is much less effective than other ways to motivate distributors. These other ways focus on the fact that the distributor is also a company. What works best is to play to company-level interests. The company wants to be profitable, stable, and differentiated. Good marketing, equitable financial returns, and supporting the distributor in such a way as to enhance its capabilities—these are the levels that work with distributors.[2]

THE EMOTIONAL FAVORITE

Of the seven items listed previously, being the "emotional favorite" is perhaps the most important. It is the most difficult to define, although we have all experienced it. For example, we prefer going to a particular tailor or a specific accountant because we like and trust that person. All things being relatively equal—quality of the work, price, location, ease of interaction—we will do business with the provider who is our "emotional favorite." This phenomenon holds true for Reps, who will go the extra mile for principals that they consider their emotional favorite. This extra mile can turn into significant benefits for the principal.

For example, the biggest asset an OSP possesses is in-depth customer knowledge and long-term relationships throughout their entire territory. This is an asset you can use. The Rep sees the larger need that your products help to fill. You are a piece in a jig-saw puzzle, and the Rep has put it all together. This means that you can use the Rep as an independent counsel, a second opinion, a sounding board, and a market research house—all wrapped up in one package. Indeed, producers who *do* use their Reps this way not only improve their own marketing—they also enjoy a better, more productive relationship with them![3]

Genuinely liking and trusting the principal evokes immense loyalty and dedication from the Rep. After all, Reps are un-abashedly people-oriented—you have to be if you're going to be successful in the business of professional selling. Developing a relationship with people is their stock-in-trade. Reps develop an immense and enduring loyalty toward those principals who treat them fairly and who communicate openly and honestly with them. This feeling grows and deepens with time. It is not too difficult to understand why: everybody would rather work with, or for, a boss whom they like and respect.

Those principals who understand this normal tendency of the Rep to become emotionally attached to their principals seem to unconsciously do certain things that promote this relationship with their Reps. It's like walking and breathing to them: they don't have to think about it, they just do it.

So what is it that they do? Not surprisingly, they treat Reps the same way they themselves would like to be treated (a bit of the Golden Rule effect). Based on our research, we have identified several major components of this special relationship: fairness and trust, openness and candor in communications, ability to commu-nicate with top management, quality of staff, openly committed to the Rep function, and being treated like part of the family. We'll talk about each of these in turn.

Reputation for Fairness and Trust

The way to gain a good reputation is to endeavor to be what you desire to appear.

—*Socrates*

A company's reputation for fairness is an essential ingredient. This applies to Reps as well as manufacturers. Nothing can make up for a lack of fairness. Good Reps have a *sixth sense* in detecting people and companies that are fair. They feel it as much as see it. They respond in a very extraordinary way to the folks who treat them fairly!

Interestingly, economists have been trying to figure out for years how business relationships really get done. To their great frustration, their models cannot clearly explain the phenomenon. Many business relationships perform far better than economic models say they should, leading many economists to consider that the elements their models are missing are, in fact, trust and reputation. This issue tends to agitate economists because it doesn't fit nicely into the hard, rational, and observable nature of most economic arguments. But other academicians are taking note; one journal recently called for economists to "face the music" and to begin studying trust and reputation. The article argues that 200 years of economic research have shown that these factors are hugely important and that the fact that they are difficult to model should not be an excuse to ignore them.[4]

Reps give a lot of weight to the decision to represent a company based on that company's reputation for fairness. Treating people fairly is a traceable trait of any company. Throughout this book, many references are made to how well good Rep firms network with others. Any Rep firm worth their salt will burn up the phone lines with calls to other Reps (past and present) throughout the country to collect information about a prospective principal's reputation concerning fairness. Getting positive feedback from other Reps carries a huge qualitative value in the selection criteria from the Rep's point of view as it should from the principal's perspective, too.

Trust and fairness establish the cornerstone of the emotional favorite relationship. Earlier in the book we introduced Dr. Stephen Covey's idea of an "emotional bank account." Covey identifies six major deposits (for the metaphorical emotional bank account) that build a sense of fairness and trust: (1) understanding the individual, (2) attending to the little things, (3) keeping commitments, (4) clarifying expectations, (5) showing personal integrity, and (6) apologizing when you make a withdrawal. Any company who adopts this kind of philosophy and puts it into practice reaps big rewards from their Reps (as well as everyone else). Reps relate to this kind of company with an almost religious fervor. The company's reputation establishes itself as a blue chip organization and one that any Rep firm would be proud to represent. Every Rep in every industry knows which companies are—and which are not—in this category.

Openness and Candor in Communications

Everybody prefers to deal with a "straight shooter." Knowing that you're getting honest opinion, even when it's criticism, is preferable than dealing with someone who holds back on the facts, skirts the issues, or worse yet, leads you astray with a hidden agenda. When the senior management of a principal are a core of "straight shooters," their example becomes the way that their subordinate managers deal with others under their charge. Indeed, they insist on it. As it has been said many times, like attracts like!

In turn, these principals want their Reps to respond in kind. They want honest and open feedback from the field. It's a two-way street. Reps generally respond favorably to this open communication style, provided they are not subjected to the "shoot-the-messenger" syndrome. Reps tend to be more open than their factory direct employee counterparts, since they are less concerned with company politics. Obviously, diplomacy needs to be exercised by all parties, as opposed to the sharp-stick-in-the-eye style of some folks.

Even though there are no statistics to back this up, we believe that more Rep firms are terminated for poor communications than for poor sales performance. This complaint from manufacturers has been around for years. While most quality Rep firms have corrected this deficiency, still some have not gotten the message. All Rep firms need to underscore to their entire staff the importance of communications with their principals. A lack of quality communication is absolutely inexcusable when all sorts of tools are available. There's a saying, "Silence is golden." From a principal's perspective regarding its Reps, silence is commercial suicide. If they don't hear from their Reps, regardless of their sales stats, the principal believes that they aren't really working for them. Representing themselves back to the principal should be standard procedure; a flow of good communications is part of that essential process.

Successful Reps are good communicators! Communicating in the sales business is as important as hand-eye coordination to the athlete. This is not considered a "big plus"; it's unquestionably a prerequisite. Extraordinary communicators have the potential to become great leaders of business and countries. For example, most historians believe that Winston Churchill's communication skills made him the single most significant communicator in the free world; this had an immeasurable impact on the outcome of World War II.

One of the most utilized forms of communications between a network of Reps and principals is the Rep council. (We will go into this in greater detail later in the chapter.) Utilizing a Rep council provides a vehicle to give and receive candid comments about the Rep relationship and demonstrates the company's appreciation of the Rep's managerial skills, ideas, and experiences.

Opportunity to Communicate with Top Management

Communicating from the "top down" on a regular basis promotes a strong feeling of family among all salespeople, especially among Reps. As Tom Dalton, vice president of worldwide sales for Honeywell Sensing and Control, noted, "An excellent Rep network without the proper interface between the network and the principal in essence dilutes the effectiveness of the sales channel. Our efforts now are to build the right supporting infrastructure to support the Rep organization and make it a success."

Indeed, the best company leaders, regardless of their titles, like to mix it up with their *sales types,* and that speaks volumes about the company's willingness to listen. Good companies manage to let the voice of the field be heard and understood.

In years past, company presidents were often active participants in all sales functions. In some cases, they dominated the meetings, much to the chagrin of the sales manager. But their presence was an important ingredient in the bonding of the sales organization with top management. It added a sense of openness and inclusion and further served as an opportunity for the field to communicate with the top officials of the company.

Unfortunately, this has changed in recent years. Few top executives or company presidents spend much time around the sales organization. They relegate that responsibility to lower level managers who have limited decision-making authority. On occasion they might drop in on a meeting and give a brief address, much in the way they would at a stockholder's meeting. Yet, those top officials who insulate themselves from the field organization are doing themselves a great disservice by missing out on the benefits that come from being the emotional favorite.

Quality of Staff

Dealing with well-trained staff and customer service personnel isn't just a pleasure for customers; it a real pleasure for the Rep firms as well. The emotional favorite employs competent people who have good values and who have been trained in working with field sales issues and manufacturers' representatives. Many companies select one of their Rep principals or a paid consultant to help educate and train company employees, particularly those who will interface with the field sales organization, on the Representative function. Promoting staff people who have not been properly trained in this area (or in sales in general) can do substantial harm to the process. For example, a good field application engineer does not automatically qualify as a district manager or a regional manager.

Open Commitment to the Rep Function

Companies that change from a direct sales force to a network of Representative firms often overlook the importance of educating their staff about Reps. In some cases, the Rep firms are treated as outsiders. Sometimes the change to Reps is viewed by the uninformed as a temporary measure "until business picks up again." In most cases, this is not an overt act on the part of the principal's management but a lack of understanding of how the new Rep organization(s) fits into the scheme of things and how the strategic decision to outsource field sales was made.

An open commitment to the Rep function and an open demonstration of that fact in both word and deed is an important indicator of the commitment to this new or existing field sales force. Unskilled managers who continually threaten their Reps with going direct again lose what they hope to gain. Good Reps know that they're in the performance business and don't need to be reminded of the consequences of nonperformance. Productive, individualized critiques work best, as opposed to a broad-brush castigation or threat.

THE REP COUNCIL

A Rep council is a powerful way to build a strong relationship between the outsourced field sales Rep and the manufacturer. It is an open forum that allows for candid discussion of problems and opportunities in the marketplace. It can provide a manufacturer with the opportunity to learn from the successes and failures of programs and policies of other manufacturers without paying the high price of learning by experience. In other words, it's learning from other people's experiences. The Reps' experiences and insights from different manufacturers make this possible.

Any subject that influences the Representative and manufacturer relationship can be addressed at a Rep council. These formalized meetings provide a vehicle to discuss, analyze, review, suggest, and implement new policies, procedures, and strategies that can have a positive impact on the sales and marketing of a manufacturer's products. Interestingly, it seems that most companies that do a good job of running Rep councils become an *emotional favorite* of their Reps, regardless of company size.

What Is a Rep Council?

A Rep council is an advisory group comprised of top principal management and individuals selected from the manufacturer's Representative organizations. The principal can invite any individual from any organization it believes can make a significant contribution to the discussion. However, the Rep council meeting is a business planning meeting, not a sales meeting. Nor is it a bitch session! (Nit-picking is a killer to any Rep council!) Kept to its original purpose, a Rep council can provide an excellent sounding board for new ideas. It must operate in an open, positive, and free manner. An atmosphere must be created and maintained that allows the discussion of controversial subject matter without recrimination.

The Rep Council Agenda

A wide variety of subjects is appropriate for discussion, among them:

- The principal's policies and procedures, including
  - Representative contracts and agreements
  - Termination policies

- Split commission and point of sales policies
- Guidelines for sales Rep performance and evaluation
- Sales meetings and product training
- Customer/principal policies and procedures
  - Pricing strategies
  - Competitive promotions
- Marketing strategies
  - Increasing performance in specific or new markets
  - Utilizing other Rep firms to penetrate markets not presently covered
  - Determining TAM and SAM for major customers and distributors
  - Evaluating the strengths and weaknesses of the principal's competitors
- New product possibilities and possible acquisitions
  - Significant product opportunities (that competitors have)
  - Packaging issues and suggestions
  - Shipping methods
- Catalogs and literature
  - Quality of literature
  - Need for and suggestions for promotional material
  - Advertising
  - Opinion of current advertising
  - Trade magazines to be utilized
- Trade show participation
  - Which shows are hot and which are dying
  - How to maximize the expense of participating in trade shows

Generally, the Representative members of the council are responsible for soliciting input from or conducting surveys of their fellow Representatives on a variety of subjects. This input may take the form of a formal evaluation process, as requested by the principal. Typical areas that are commonly evaluated by Rep councils are customer service, customer acceptance, product capability, delivery and quality, competitiveness, advertising, and literature.

It is very important that the anonymity of any individual Representative responding to a questionnaire be maintained when the answers are compiled and submitted to the principal. Without this protection, it is hard to ensure honest appraisals by the Representatives. Similarly, it is incumbent upon all participants to present their opinions in a positive and productive manner. Additionally, it is extremely important that a report, which should clearly outline agreed upon action items, be distributed to all of the company's Representatives following a Rep council meeting.

Participants

The principal's sales and marketing executives should be the key participants. Depending on need and/or direct involvement, key "decision makers" such as the CEO may be included on the council for all or parts of the meeting. Managers from disciplines such as manufacturing and advertising can also participate for special meetings (or portions of the meeting) of the council. It is important that the principal's participants have the authority to effect most changes that are recommended by the council.

Generally the owner, CEO, or general manager of selected Rep firms participates, especially at the first meeting. The principal should look for members who will bring a variety of viewpoints to the council. Members should be well versed in areas of marketing, product, and the competition. Normally, it is best for Representatives from some of the principal's major territories to be involved in the council. Furthermore, it is beneficial for some of the Representatives on the council to have length of service with the principal so that they are familiar with the principal's policies and general operating philosophy. Normally, one of the Representatives is elected or appointed council chair (by the principal). He or she chairs the meetings and is responsible for coordinating the preparation and follow-up activities of the other Representative members.

There is no hard-and-fast rule as to how many participants should be on the council. Most councils consist of two to four members from the principal and four to six members from the Rep force. Some companies establish a length of term for the Rep participants, usually for one year, with some type of staggered rotation so that the entire council does not change all at once. Typically, the most qualified Reps tend to stay on for longer periods of time, although principals should make periodic changes to ensure fresh input and different points of view. The principal's participants will generally remain constant from year to year.

Meeting Schedule

Normally, Rep councils meet once a year. However, special meetings or conference calls can be scheduled if a situation warrants.

In some cases, meetings become less frequent as problems are solved and the apparent need for meetings diminishes. However, beware of the trap we describe in Chapter 7: firms often take their older, established relationships for granted and let communication wither. Insidiously, the players' trust withers as well. One day there will be a crisis that shows that things are not as good as they seem. By that time, the relationship may be seriously damaged. Therefore, it is a bad idea to skip Rep council meetings twice in a row.

Meeting Preparation

The meeting chair should circulate a preliminary agenda to the Representative members at least 60 days before the meeting date. The Representatives should be encouraged to suggest additions and/or changes before the meeting's chair and the principal finalize and distribute the agenda. On the Rep side, those attending the meeting should solicit ideas for discussion from their fellow Representatives, thus ensuring that a range of issues is addressed. Both the Representatives and the principal participants should come to the meeting well prepared.

Meeting Location

Meetings should be held off site so that interruptions can be kept to a minimum. It is recommended that the meetings be held near a principal facility *if* the participation of noncouncil personnel is required for a portion of the meeting. Today, because everyone is conscious of costs and time, many companies have begun using teleconferencing and videoconferencing (at a commercial host site, such as Kinko's) in lieu of interim meetings in order to reduce expense and keep travel time to a minimum. A principal's upcoming sales meeting would be an ideal time to kick off its first Rep council meeting.

Although length will vary, depending on the complexity of the agenda, location, availability of personnel, and so on, the maximum duration for a Rep council meeting is one and a half days. Meetings should be planned for early or late in the week to allow the participants a minimum amount of time away from the office or out of the field. However, some companies plan meetings at resort locations, allowing individuals to come a day early or stay a day extra (or both) for a little socializing and golf.

Rep Council Summary

A Rep council involving responsible, knowledgeable, and successful Representative participants can provide an outstanding vehicle
for a manufacturer to obtain meaningful field feedback in an
efficient, cost-effective manner. All participants should approach
the council meeting as though it were a "staff meeting" designed
to deal with planning and strategies around issues that affect
the overall health and success of the principal. At the same time,
the benefits to both the principal and its Representatives are
obvious. With a sincere effort and a willingness to consider change
on the part of all participants, a Rep council can make a substantial contribution to the overall success of the principal and its
Representatives.

SUMMARY

While Reps are legally independent from their principals, the two
entities are in fact quite interdependent. The success of the Rep
firm is inextricably linked to its principal's success and vice versa.
In their effort to get more "mind share" from their Reps (thinking
that it will translate to more market share), many principals use
threats or coercion. In fact, getting more "mind share" is not a
recipe for success.

The best Rep/principal relationships are like the best friendships or marriages; they are based on trust and respect. A first step
in the manufacturer's process of building a relationship is understanding what motivates a Rep organization. The best Rep firms
have high standards and consider a variety of issues before agree-
ing to take on a new principal. They include

1. Their marketplace and customer potential
2. The principal's potential in serving that marketplace and
   customer base
3. The strength of competition
4. The potential earnings for the Rep firm
5. How each principal's product offering (synergy) fits in their
   portfolio, which assists in leveraging the Rep's position
6. The "pain level" versus income potential of each principal
7. The people factor (the emotional favorite)

Becoming the "emotional favorite" can provide significant
benefits to the principal. Reps will "go the extra mile" for their

emotional favorites, often serving a critical role as "eyes and ears" of the market and competition. How does a principal go about being the emotional favorite? They follow the Golden Rule—they treat their Reps with the respect and care they would want to be treated with, specifically fairness and trust, openness and candor in communications, opportunity to communicate with top management, quality of staff, and an open commitment to the Rep function.

One of the most effective ways of enhancing the Rep/principal relationship is creating a Rep council. The concept allows for a venue where selected Reps and employees of the principal come together to discuss a variety of issues affecting the relationship. The chapter concludes with the case study of an electronics company, Zero Zone, whose president recounts the company's success with Rep councils.

In the next chapter, we will look at how to take the Rep/ principal relationship to an even higher level.

CASE STUDY:
BENEFITS OF A REP COUNCIL AT ZERO ZONE

A Rep council was established, outlining very specific goals and objectives. Four representative principals and two company employees, the president and the vice president of sales and marketing, meet two times per year. The meeting chair is one of the Rep principals and the secretary is the Zero Zone president. Topics of the meeting are wide open but must be issues that are important to all representatives and are not supposed to be specific to one representative's issues. Each Council member has anywhere from four to six other agencies that supply them with topics. An agenda is prepared and agreed upon in advance and minutes are published and circulated to all agencies of the company. Comments are solicited. Task lists are then circulated to the Rep agencies for them to act upon and to company management to provide action or comment.

All of the items are reported back to all agencies as they are completed. Both sides are held accountable for their actions and reactions.

The question always come up, "How come your Rep council works?" I personally credit a few of our very professional representatives that agreed with me to make it work. They were involved in councils with other companies, both successful and unsuccessful, and showed me the way from their own experience. I capitalized on what they conveyed to me, added what I knew about treating employees properly, and threw in a few oddball items as incentives and arrived at a Rep organization that would rival anyone else.

I believe we can credit our council today with good and accurate feedback on new products, revisions to existing products, contributions to processes, solving of Rep/company issues and concerns, increased sales, and better communication between our sales force and the company. Have we resolved everything? Absolutely not, but quite frankly neither has my staff. Do we ever have to replace Reps? Those who do not follow closely what the Council is doing and thereby increase their cooperation and communication have no place at Zero Zone, so yes, we still have to replace Representatives, or salespeople. Given all of the circumstances, has an effective Representative council improved our business? You bet. I wouldn't have it any other way. They may be independent ornery entrepreneurs, but since I am one, why would I want it any other way?

Jack Van Der Ploeg, President, Zero Zone, Inc., North Prairie, Wisconsin

ENDNOTES

1. Chinander, K. E., and M. E. Schweitzer, "The Input Bias: The Misuse of Input Information in Judgments of Outcomes," (2003), *Organizational Behavior and Human Decision Processes.*
2. Narus, James A., and James C. Anderson (1988), "Strengthen Distributor Performance through Channel Positioning," *Sloan Management Review,* 29 (4), 31–40.
3. Anderson, Erin, Leonard M. Lodish, and Barton Weitz (1987), "Resource Allocation Behavior in Conventional Channels," *Journal of Marketing Research,* 24 (February), 85–97.
4. James, Harvey S. (2002), "The Trust Paradox: A Survey of Economic Inquiries in the Nature of Trust and Trustworthiness," *The Journal of Economic Behavior and Organization,* 42 (2), 291–307.

7

Building a Long-Term Strategic Alliance with Your Rep

Strategic business decisions have three features: they require committing substantial resources, they are hard to get into (barriers to entry), and they are hard to get out of (barriers to exit). Consequently, strategic moves should be made only when they are likely to generate enduring returns that are much better than the returns from decisions that are easier to reverse.

It is one thing to have a good relationship with your Rep, or OSP. This is the normal state of affairs and generates excellent returns when done right. But it is quite another thing to have a long-term strategic alliance with your OSP. This is a relationship so close that it approximates vertical integration. A true strategic alliance between a Rep and a manufacturer (the "principal") is capable of delivering extraordinary returns. Most manufacturers would benefit from bonding like this with at least some Reps, but the costs of an alliance can overwhelm the benefits. Consequently, not every OSP/principal relationship results in—or even *should* result in—a long-term strategic alliance.

In this chapter, we draw on a large body of research on what works and what doesn't in forging an enduring relationship between two organizations, with emphasis on upstream-downstream marketing alliances. The focus of this chapter is on how to build ties so tight that the Rep and the principal could almost be the same company. Alliance building is a competence, an organizational skill, and some companies are better at it than others. Nonetheless, alliances *can* be manufactured, and most Reps and manufacturers are capable of creating a tight coalition.

In the previous chapter we reviewed how a manufacturer can become the Rep's "emotional favorite," which involves building a relationship based on trust, fairness, and respect. Here, we will look at taking the relationship to the next level. This high level of alliance involves a leap in capabilities—*and* a leap in investments. Jumping from medium to high strength of ties demands that each party (manufacturer and OSP, or principal and agent in legal terms) *perceive* the other is committed to the relationship.

RETURNS FROM A STRATEGIC ALLIANCE

Why go to such lengths to enhance the manufacturer/Rep relationship? When an upstream company and a downstream company manage to create a powerful and enduring collaboration, they generate a long, long list of benefits, which have been documented in extensive field research.[1] From the manufacturer's standpoint, the benefits fall into three categories: joint action, current operating results, and long-term capacity.

Joint Action

Alliance partners support each other by coordinating their efforts. For the manufacturer, this means that its marketing strategy is better executed: the downstream partner is more cooperative, works harder and smarter, and shows less passive resistance and more enthusiastic effort. Economists describe these relationships as having lower levels of "haggling" or "friction." It's simply easier to get things done. Manufacturer and Rep come to a meeting of the minds faster and more easily. They share information more openly, more completely. Together, they are faster at spotting a better way to do things and then carrying it out. They seize more opportunities, and they offer each other a helping hand, going beyond the normal limits of their role. For example, a committed Rep will help a principal find Reps in other territories. It's hard to put a dollar figure on the value of smooth joint action. But the value is there and helps the manufacturer/OSP pair to achieve lasting competitive advantage.

Current Operating Results

Joint action ought to produce better current operating results, and indeed it does—usually for *both* parties. Committed partners tend to "grow the pie": they create a much bigger pool of rewards. For example, they don't just gain market share from another player (a secondary demand effect). They actually make the market bigger (a primary demand effect) by bringing new customers into the market and by inducing current customers to devote more money to the product category.

Sales and growth are welcome results, but that's not all. Because alliance partners work hard to collaborate and coordinate, the manufacturer actually enjoys a better quality of business. For example, the insurance industry in North America is not known for close upstream-downstream ties. Few independent insurance agents forge a long-term strategic alliance with any company that writes insurance, and, like distributors, they usually carry competing brands. Arm's-length relationships are the norm, and semi-adversarial relationships are, unfortunately, fairly common. But some insurer underwriters buck their industry's trend, forging strong links with a handful of selected agents. Their payoff comes not only in the *quantity* of the business independent agents write for them (total insurance premiums) but in the *quality* of the business.[2] The less committed an agent the more he or she knowingly underprices, then passes on some bad risks, which the insurer will discover too late. Committed agents do a better job of screening risks: they match the premiums to the customer's actual risk more accurately. The result for the underwriter (manufacturer) is a lower ratio of claims to premiums, a crucial operating result in the insurance industry.

In short, better quality business means more profitable business, not just more revenue. A committed field sales force tries harder to bring in the type of business the principal wants, whatever that is, and those efforts pay off.

Long-Term Capacity

The benefits of a long-term strategic alliance start with the here-and-now (joint action) and extend to this quarter, or this year (current operating results), but they don't stop there. Because alliance partners support each other, they enhance each other's capacities. The result: the manufacturer gains abilities that pay off in the future. The best place to see this is in new product development. Downstream members of the value chain (such as Reps) possess very different information than do upstream members (such as manufacturers). Alliances put these information sets together quite well, which results in new products that are better suited to the market. When Reps and manufacturers bond, new products stay out of the R&D trap, wherein technically impressive products fail to connect with the market because they don't meet a need that customers have—or can be persuaded that they have. In a Rep/principal alliance, the two work together to shape the product to fit market segments. Reps excel at this because they see their customer's family of needs, not just the need connected to what the principal currently makes.

An alliance has "social capital," meaning a dense set of ties and obligations that allow a firm to ask a great deal of another firm—and get it. Alliances repeatedly go beyond what is normal for a Rep/principal relationship.

THE COSTS OF A LONG-TERM STRATEGIC ALLIANCE

It sounds good, doesn't it? And it is, if one considers only the benefits. The other side of the coin is that alliances are quite costly. Building them is an arduous affair, requiring time, effort, and money. Because the firm cannot build one every time it outsources, it's critical to target the right organization, which is more easily said than done. A firm can bond to an inferior partner, then find it difficult to exit—and difficult to attract a superior replacement. Or a firm can bond to the right partner today, only to need a different partner as circumstances change.[3]

It is hard for either party to exit a long-term strategic alliance. Perversely, this dampens the parties' incentives to continue to perform, to make their best efforts, and to share information. Why? Because it is all too tempting for either alliance partner to become complacent and to fail to execute its obligations, knowing the arrangement is costly for the other party to terminate. Within limits, the other party will complain but will tolerate reduced quality and quantity of effort from its partner. Tolerance is cheaper than switching.

However, if the other party comes to believe its counterpart is reneging on their business understanding (a situation economists call "opportunism"), the relationship will become strained.[4] Even the mere *suspicion* of opportunism weakens an alliance. It is difficult to prove one's innocence (how do you convince a wary manager that you really are making your best efforts and being completely candid?). And suspected opportunism erodes trust and invites reciprocity. The accused may decide to start exercising some real opportunism, which invites retaliation in kind. As a result, once-close relationships can degenerate into accusation, deception, disillusionment, and disappointment.

In short, long-term strategic alliances are difficult to manage. They have been compared to a marriage: How do you know you married the right person? How do you know your spouse is still the right person? How do you keep your marriage vibrant? How do you keep your partner motivated to live up to his or her promise to be a good spouse? How do you adapt your marriage to new demands (children, illness, finances, career)? And how do you make sure that all these worries and doubts, *by themselves,* don't undermine even a good relationship? There are plenty of great marriages out there, generating psychic payoffs to the partners—but there are plenty of failures, too.

The marriage metaphor isn't perfect. Business alliances aren't intensely personal—they are based on economic calculation, and you *can* have more than one of them at a time—but there's some truth to the marriage analogy. We're not advocating that every Rep/principal relationship be a long-term strategic alliance. It doesn't always fit the costs and benefits of bonding. Following the guidelines of Chapter 6 and "becoming the Rep's emotional favorite," will create a good business relationship. It will be less than a long-term strategic alliance, but it will work very well—and will be good enough for most situations.

However, every manufacturer can use at least some favored relationships in its portfolio of outsourced field sales forces.

Should I Invest in This Rep?

Alliances work well in growing markets full of opportunity. They help to exploit that opportunity to the fullest. In such a situation, it pays to ally—if you find the right Rep. The right Rep has three characteristics.

First, the company enjoys a strong reputation in the target customer base.[5] This kind of OSP is doing many things right. Reputations are images, which are slow and painful to build. An OSP that customers know and hold in high esteem is a well-managed organization. Such a Rep is a particularly appealing partner.

Table 7-1 develops the facets of reputation, scoring them from 1 to 7. (Note this is a generalized reputation, not a reputation for something specific, such as offering fast service.) Ask yourself how a customer would score a Rep. Better yet, ask some

Table 7-1. The Concept of Reputation
How would customers score this Rep on the scale below? Circle a number from
1 to 7 to indicate the Rep's subjective standing in the eyes of a typical customer.
Note this is the customer's *perception*, which may or may not coincide with reality.

Poorly regarded	1	2	3	4	5	6	7	Highly regarded
Unsuccessful	1	2	3	4	5	6	7	Successful
Unprofessional	1	2	3	4	5	6	7	Professional
Unstable	1	2	3	4	5	6	7	Stable
Poorly established	1	2	3	4	5	6	7	Well established

Add the scores and divide by 5 to take the mean.

A sample of over 250 relationships in the electronic components industry revealed
that manufacturers believe their customers score about half their Reps at 5 or better. In the same manner, manufacturers believe that customers score about half their
manufacturers at 5 or better. These estimates may be charitable: customers, when
asked, may give lower scores than manufacturers think they do. The electronic components industry is highly competitive, and customers are used to demanding and
getting high levels of service and performance. To be rated successful, stable, and
established in this industry is a feat.

From Weiss, Allen M., Erin Anderson, and Deborah J. MacInnis (1999), "Reputation Management as a Motive for Sales Structure Decisions," *Journal of Marketing*, 63 (October), 74–89.

customers! Today's customers are demanding and hypercritical:
they are loath to give any sales force (including a direct sales
force!) high ratings. Result: a good, solid sales force may score no
better than a 4. Customers are chary with their 5s, 6s, and 7s. The
closer the score to 7, the more this Rep is a pearl.

If you are fortunate enough to work with a highly reputable
OSP, you have an asset that is worth enhancing. Some manufacturers make it a point to bond with Reps that are on their way to
building a strong reputation. By allying with these Reps early, the
manufacturer makes it difficult for competitors to unseat them
once the Rep has gained prominence. By the same token, some
OSPs partner with up-and-coming manufacturers that they know
are well managed and are on the way to earning widespread customer recognition. Indeed, partnering is an excellent way to
speed up that recognition.

The second characteristic of the right Rep is its portfolio of
other principals. The OSP composes an assortment that is broad
(many categories) but not deep (only one brand per category).
The Rep will embed your brand in this portfolio: do your brands
fit? For example, if your brand needs premium positioning (high
quality, high image, but also high price), but the portfolio of products this Rep sells is targeted to customers with no-frills budgets,

your product won't fit. And if the portfolio doesn't fit, the Rep won't connect well with such customers.

The third characteristic of the right Rep is a compatible management philosophy. You should be in agreement on fundamentals. For example, if you are highly sensitive to even the appearance of a lapse of ethics, you want a Rep that feels similarly. This said, "compatible philosophy" should not be confused with "same management style." Managing salespeople *is* quite different from managing other types of roles. And outsourcing is an opportunity to break out of your own mold, to benefit from diversity of approach. You shouldn't want your OSP to be a clone of you.

BUILDING THE LONG-TERM STRATEGIC ALLIANCE: THE CIRCLE OF PERCEPTION

You've found the right OSP for you and built a relationship of confidence: your Rep expects your relationship to have some stability. Now you want to take it to the next level, quasi-vertical integration, in which your two firms collaborate so closely that they function almost as one. This is a long-term strategic alliance. How do you boost a stable relationship to practically a state of union?

Many people believe the secret is to put "the right people" in place and let them develop personal bonds, but that's not it. Organizations need bonds that go beyond ties between individuals. Personal ties do help, but the ability of individuals to keep a relationship performing at top grade is limited.[6] The relationship needs to be institutionalized. It needs to belong to both companies and to be resilient against the comings and goings of specific individuals.

When an organization is highly committed to a relationship with another organization, three elements are in place. The committed firm (1) desires the relationship to last, (2) is confident the relationship is stable, and (3) is willing to make short-term sacrifices to grow and maintain the relationship. Committed parties exhibit loyalty and view their counterparts as partners. They defend their partners from criticism and are patient with their partner's mistakes. They're willing to invest, to dedicate people and resources to do a better job for their partner. They expect to work with their partners for the long term and are so confident about this that they are willing to wait for payoffs to their investments. Often, they let their contacts wither, and therefore lose touch, with organizations that compete with their partners. They do this because they have dropped their guard: mentally, they are no longer

THE HIDDEN TRAP OF OLD RELATIONSHIPS
(A.K.A., THE SEVEN-YEAR ITCH)

If a Rep/principal relationship has survived the test of time, its history creates a long shadow of the past. Some relationships are startlingly old. For example, the origins of today's electronic components industry are in the radio industry of the 1920s. There are Rep/principal relationships today that date from radio. The OSPs are into at least their third "generation" of management, and the principals sell precious little that goes into a radio. Both sides have evolved to be unrecognizable to the originators of their relationship. Nonetheless, there is "something" there. Firms build social capital that is independent of (and in addition to) the people in them.[7]

Will that social capital keep the relationship going? On the whole, yes. Old relationships have inertia. Like long marriages, they have survived so much that it takes a great deal to envision undoing them. Further, old relationships have a considerable wellspring of trust behind them.

However, there is a hidden trap. The older the relationship, the less the parties make the effort to communicate. To some extent, they don't need to: they understand each other so well they can get their messages across faster and easier. Herein lies the trap. It's easy to take good communication for granted—and to let it erode. Old relationships are prone to letting the transfer of information slip, little by little, so gradually that neither side really notices. The players assume that they understand each other, that they are up to date. As they slowly slip out of contact, a knock-on effect occurs: the virtuous cycle of communication and trust turns in the wrong direction. As contact fades, so does trust, and that is the trap. Old relationships can let their asset of joint history wither away. Every Rep knows a story of an old relationship like this. By the time someone pulled the alarm bell, the arrangement was in trouble and its continuity was threatened.

The lesson is to continue to pay attention, not to take old relationships for granted. They need periodic renewal, which requires continuing efforts. When the two parties make the effort to keep transferring information, without assuming the other is up to date, old relationships do indeed have a much longer time horizon than young ones.

"in the market," even if it's just to keep up with the comings and goings of these competing firms. It sounds reckless, overconfident. Commitment to an independent company is indeed risky: the committed firm is vulnerable, at least on paper.

Signaling and Reciprocity

It takes reciprocity to get an OSP to develop these attitudes toward a principal. No Rep will commit to a principal unless it believes the principal feels the same way. And no principal will commit to a

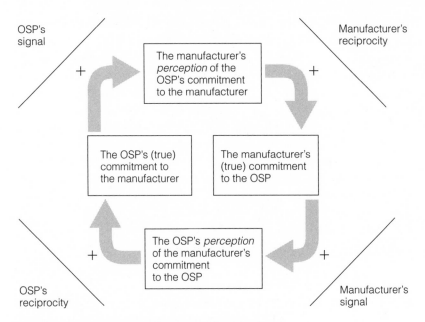

Figure 7-1. Pledges and the Circle of Perception

Rep unless it believes the Rep, too, is committed. It is essential that an organization *believe* its counterpart is committed.

That sounds logical—what firm would offer one-sided loyalty in business dealings? We have had managers ask us the logical next step: how can we persuade them that we are committed when we're not? How can we create the necessary perception without developing the corresponding attitudes? How can we keep our freedom but convince them to offer us their loyalty?

The answer is "you can't." In general, organizations are not "good actors." Unlike (some) people, organizations can't mask the truth very effectively. If a Rep is not committed, the principal will figure it out—and vice versa. This doesn't mean that principals and Reps figure each other out precisely—they don't. But organizations do sense accurately what zone of commitment their counterparts inhabit because each party gives off signals (usually inadvertently) that reveal its true intentions. A company (Rep or manufacturer, agent, or principal) that doesn't intend to stay in the relationship and invest in it will rarely be able to fool the other side for long.

Figure 7-1 shows the circle of perception. This is a process that builds—or decays—over time. Any change in any element of the circle ripples through the circle to influence the other elements. If any element increases, the circle accelerates. For example, if the manufacturer becomes more committed, it can't help but give signs of the change. The OSP picks up the signal (notices the change) and updates its perception. Then reciprocity kicks in. The OSP raises its own commitment. Over time, the manufacturer picks up signs of the change, updates its perception of the Rep's commitment, and reciprocates by increasing its own commitment another notch.

That's the good news. The bad news is that the circle is vulnerable to downward revisions as well. The alliance weakens if any element erodes. Thus, a drop in *commitment* works through to dampen the counterpart's commitment. A drop in either side's *perception* of commitment eventually becomes the truth—on both sides.

BUILDING THE LONG-TERM STRATEGIC ALLIANCE: PLEDGES

What creates actual commitment? There are two drivers: motivation and action. For commitment to happen requires both.

Motivation to Commit

The motivation side is calculative. You want to give commitment for one reason—to get commitment. If you are a manufacturer of goods or services, you want to get commitment when a normal commercial relationship with an OSP is not enough. If you are using an OSP under conditions that favor an employee sales force (see Chapter 3), you are asking a great deal of your Rep. To get what you need without the advantages of employing the sales force yourself, you must have the Rep's commitment. A long-term strategic alliance with an OSP is the next best thing to being vertically integrated. Bonding with a Rep approximates having an employee sales force while preserving many of the advantages of outsourcing.

What is the OSP's motive to commit to a manufacturer? The OSP is also calculative and is willing to give commitment only for the purpose of getting commitment. Like the manufacturer, the OSP wants to keep its options open: it would like to be free to switch to another manufacturer if this one turns out to be disappointing. Like the manufacturer, the OSP will commit only when a normal principal/agent relationship is not enough. These are circumstances in which the principal is likely to go direct someday, which would either take business from the Rep or ensure that the Rep is unable to find a good principal in a product category.

In short, OSPs and manufacturers are motivated to build a long-term strategic alliance in order to do business in circumstances that come close to favoring vertical integration of the selling function. The alliance is a way to continue enjoying the mutual benefits of outsourcing the sales force, even under conditions that make it difficult to outsource selling. These conditions (Chapter 3) include high levels of idiosyncratic investments or sales in which performance is difficult to benchmark. A long-term strategic alliance simulates being one company, not two. When circumstances put a strain on outsourcing, the alliance is a way to preserve the relationship and keep it working rather than vertically integrate the selling function.

Action That Builds Commitment

Motivation alone is insufficient. Creating an alliance also requires action. But what kind of action? A powerful way to forge a tight, stable bond between manufacturer and OSP is for each side to create "pledges" to their relationship.[8] Pledges are *actions* that *demonstrate* good faith and *bind* organizations to their relationship. There are three kinds of pledges: idiosyncratic investments, contracts, and selective use of business partners. We describe these categories and present the three mechanisms by which pledges build high levels of mutual commitment.

IDIOSYNCRATIC INVESTMENTS. In Chapter 3, we introduced the idea of company-specific capabilities, or what economists call "idiosyncratic investments." These are assets that are created over time on the job (that's the investment part) and that are tailored to a particular company (that's the specific part). Over time, manufacturers build assets that are particular to an OSP, while OSPs build assets that are particular to a manufacturer. For example, certain Briggs & Stratton motors have distinctive features. When salespeople get enough experience to acquire that product knowledge, they have picked up an idiosyncratic asset, one that is specific to Briggs & Stratton. The manufacturer must invest in training the salespeople, while the salespeople must invest their time in learning about the nuances of this very idiosyncratic product.

Idiosyncratic assets are significant not only because they are genuinely useful (they have productive value) but because they create a management challenge. For example, knowledgeable salespeople can't be hired in: they must learn by experience. Once they've learned, they are particularly valuable. Should they leave, the firm has a problem: there are no equivalent replacements available to be hired. *The firm has to start over.* Result: salespeople are in a powerful position because they generate benefits that are hard to find elsewhere. The firm depends on them.

Idiosyncratic knowledge comes in many forms. It may be about distinctive features of the product (how the product works with other products), the company (its routines and procedures), or even the customer (whether the customer does something out of the ordinary with it).

An extremely valuable asset is training. When Reps train their customers how to use a particular brand, and that training doesn't carry over readily to another brand, the Rep has created an idiosyncratic asset (specific to that principal) within its customer base. The Rep has made a pledge to the principal. Conversely, when manufacturers train Rep personnel about a particular brand, and that training is hard to transfer to another brand, the principal has created an idiosyncratic investment. The principal has made a pledge to its Rep.

Another idiosyncratic asset that arises by the investment of time and effort is relationships. These can be relationships with customers, within the firm itself (for example, with factory personnel, or with management), or with important constituents of the firm (for example, suppliers). The more these relationships help to get something done, they more they are valuable assets.

Table 7-2 presents nine statements that a Rep might make about a manufacturer. The better each statement fits the Rep/principal relationship, the more the Rep has invested in the principal in a way that is *difficult to transfer to another principal.* These investments are pledges the Rep makes to the principal.

Table 7-3 also presents eight statements that a manufacturer might make about a Rep. The better each statement fits the Rep/ principal relationship, the more the principal has invested in the Rep in a way that would be *difficult to transfer to another Rep.* These investments are pledges the principal makes to the OSP.

These statements have the same hallmarks. (1) Something durable has been created (knowledge, relationships, image, routines) by dint of investing while working together. (2) This creation

Table 7-2. The OSP's Pledges to the Principal

Ideally, your Rep is the best source, because these questions concern the Rep's actions vis-à-vis the manufacturer (i.e., the "principal").

From the Rep's viewpoint, circle a number to indicate how well each statement describes your relationship.

Strongly Disagree	1	2	3	4	5	6	7	Strongly Agree

1. If we switched to a competitive line, we would lose a lot of the investment we have made in this principal's line.
2. It would be difficult for us to recoup investments made in this principal's line if we switched to a competitive line.
3. If we decided to stop representing this principal, we would have a lot of trouble redeploying our people who presently serve this principal's line.
4. If we decided to stop representing this principal, we would be wasting a lot of product knowledge tailored to their brands.
5. We give extensive training to our customers on how to use this principal's product.
6. We have gone out of our way to align ourselves with this principal in the customer's mind.
7. We have invested a great deal in building up this principal's business.
8. We have made a substantial investment in facilities dedicated to this principal's product line.
9. We have made a substantial investment to create a reporting system that is similar to this supplier's.

Sum your answers and divide by 8 to get your score. The closer you are to 7, the more idiosyncratic investments your Rep has made in you. Among insurance firms in North America, the average is about 4.3. In general, scores should be considered high starting from about 5.5.

Adapted from Galunic, D. Charles, and Erin Anderson (2000), "From Security to Mobility: An Examination of Employee Commitment and an Emerging Psychological Contract," *Organization Science,* 11 (January/February), 1–20.

is not merely satisfying in itself: it has productive value. It serves to achieve a business goal. (3) The asset is difficult to put to another use if the relationship ends. These assets are the fruit of investments that are idiosyncratic: they don't travel well outside the relationship.

These idiosyncratic investments work to build commitment in three ways. First, making a pledge creates an asset, which has productive value. This asset raises the motivation of *both* sides. The company making the pledge (whether manufacturer or OSP) values the relationship because the firm is now more effective, hence

Table 7-3. The Principal's Pledges to the OSP

From the principal's viewpoint, circle a number to indicate how well each statement describes your relationship.

Strongly   I   2   3   4   5   6   7   Strongly
Disagree   Agree

1. If we switched to a competitive Rep, we would lose a lot of the investment we have made in this Rep.
2. It would be difficult for us to recoup investments made in this Rep if we switched to a competitive Rep.
3. If we decided to stop using this Rep, we would have a lot of trouble redeploying our people who presently serve this Rep.
4. If we decided to stop using this Rep, we would be wasting a lot of knowledge that's tailored to their method of operation.
5. We have gone out of our way to align ourselves with this Rep in the customer's mind.
6. We have invested a great deal in building up this Rep's business.
7. We have made a substantial investment in facilities dedicated to this Rep.
8. We have made a substantial investment to create a reporting system that is similar to this Rep's.

Sum your answers and divide by 9 to get your score. The closer you are to 7, the more idiosyncratic investments you have made in your Rep. Among insurance firms in North America, the average is about 4.5. In general, scores should be considered high starting from about 5.5.

Adapted from Galunic, D. Charles, and Erin Anderson (2000), "From Security to Mobility: An Examination of Employee Commitment and an Emerging Psychological Contract," *Organization Science,* 11 (January/February), 1–20.

able to make more money. *Both parties* stand to gain higher profits when either one increases its effectiveness by creating company-specific capabilities.

Second, a firm ties its own hands when it makes a pledge. The pledger is vulnerable. Should the relationship end, the pledger has much to lose. Therefore, the firm that posts a pledge is motivated to preserve the relationship, not only because the relationship pays off (the effect of productive assets) but because *there is much to lose if the relationship stops.* Termination is at best wasteful and at worst difficult. Result: the pledger works hard to preserve the relationship by being flexible, by treating its counterpart with consideration, and by continuing to perform to a high level. The threat of losing the pledge motivates the pledger to be committed, and not to be opportunistic.

If this sounds somewhat perverse (why would anyone tie their own hands anyway?), consider what we do in our personal lives. Psychologists have shown that the best way to change a habit is to put one's reputation on the line. Suppose you want to quit smoking. Being motivated to quit is not enough—you need action. A very effective action is to tell your entourage (colleagues, customers, friends, family) that you have quit. Now your image is at stake if you light up. Better yet, offer five dollars to anyone who catches you smoking. Now you don't just lose face, you lose money if your resolve weakens. You have created barriers to your own exit from your intended path of behavior. By tying your own hands, you have committed to quitting smoking.

In the same way, the company that invests in building assets that are tailored to its counterpart is making it difficult to get out of the relationship. This builds the company's resolve to make the relationship work.

So far, we have covered two ways that company-specific capabilities strengthen relationships: by creating productive value for both sides and by giving the pledger something to lose. There is a third mechanism. To the extent that the pledge is visible, the other side will see it—and will infer that the pledger is indeed committed. Unlike mere declarations of commitment, pledges are credible. A firm can proclaim commitment (good intentions) but fail to live up to it. Making an idiosyncratic investment is a credible signal that good intentions are real. The signal is credible because idiosyncratic investments go against the pledger's self interest—unless the pledger really is committed. To an economist, the only signal that is believable is one that is in your self-interest to honor. Hence, economists refer to pledges as "credible commitments."[9]

In short, idiosyncratic investments work three ways: (1) they create value for both sides, (2) they motivate the pledger to perform in order to preserve the assets by preserving the relationship, and (3) they signal the other side, thereby increasing the counterpart's perception of one's own commitment. Figure 7-2 summarizes this.

CONTRACTS. When Reps make pledges to manufacturers (or vice versa), they weaken their own position and therefore motivate themselves to perform to preserve the relationship. The principle of tying one's own hands can be applied another way. A party can sign a contract that ties its own hands by making it more difficult

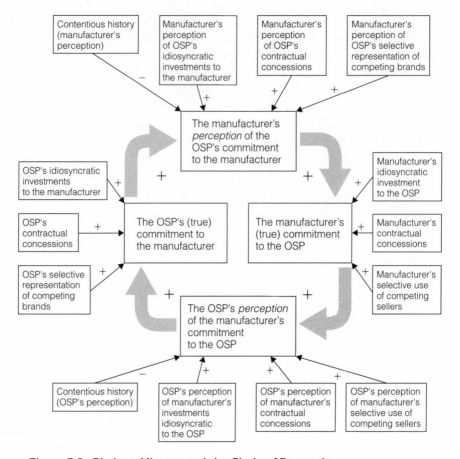

Figure 7-2. Pledges, History, and the Circle of Perception

to get out of a relationship. Let's look at the manufacturer's side first. A contract that restricts the manufacturer's freedom of action could, for example:

- Specify a long notice period before termination
- Guarantee renewal if certain goals are hit
- Set those goals to be attainable
- Set specific, observable goals that the manufacturer cannot manipulate (e.g., numeric sales goals, as opposed to verbal goals of "satisfactory sales")
- Guarantee a broad range of products or customers to the Rep
- Guarantee a level of support for the Rep
- Limit the principal's right to take house accounts

PERCEPTIONS—THE PRICE OF
A CONTENTIOUS HISTORY

Starting from a base of a normal-to-good business relationship, alliance building can work fast. Alliance building takes more time if you are starting from scratch, a new relationship. But the slowest and most gruelling alliance building happens when you are trying to repair a bad relationship. Here, history drags on your efforts by making the other party discount your commitment. A bad relationship leaves a legacy of conflict and doubt. It's possible to repair such relationships, but it takes a lot of time and a lot of pledging to offset the burden of acrimony.

It's very easy to wave this point away: "Business is business. That was yesterday. This is today. Besides, a lot of the people who were involved aren't in those jobs anymore." True. But organizations have memories that last beyond individuals: stories and conclusions get passed on for years. And a negative history makes management dubious of any new business proposition. Bad relationships can be mended, just be prepared to invest much more time and effort in building them back up.

In contrast, a manufacturer could preserve maximal flexibility by writing a contract that offers no protection to its Rep—or better yet, operate on a handshake (i.e., no contract at all).

Conversely, a Rep could tie its own hands by offering the principal a contract that limits the Rep's ability to change manufacturers or to take on new lines. Or, the contract could specify that the Rep assumes a high level of obligations to the principal. This makes it difficult for the Rep to contest a termination, for example.

In our estimation, these contract clauses are not as effective as idiosyncratic investments, for two reasons. First, contracts don't increase either party's ability to perform. Contracts are merely brute-force ways to create barriers to exit (which does motivate the pledger to preserve the relationship and does have signaling properties to the other side). Second, contracts tend to be out of sight and out of mind. Many managers don't know what their contract says, or even if they have one! What really governs a relationship is the series of understandings that grow up along the way.[10]

SELECTIVE USE OF BUSINESS PARTNERS. So far, we have discussed two types of pledges that can build commitment: idiosyncratic investments and contracts. Now we introduce the third: selective use of business partners. Take distributors as an example. A manufacturer that wants to create a tight, durable pact with a distributor can do so by limiting how many other distributors can carry the product line in the same territory ("market selectivity").

Conversely, a distributor intending to bond with a manufacturer can limit how many other brands it carries in the manufacturer's product class ("category selectivity"). The limit of selectivity is exclusivity (the manufacturer has only one distributor, or the distributor has only one brand). The more selective the use of business partners, the more potent the pledge.

This works for the same three reasons as idiosyncratic investments. If you have few business partners, they don't compete with each other as much, so they are motivated by the prospect of higher rewards. With fewer business partners, you can concentrate on working more effectively with each one, raising productive capability (again, the prospect of higher rewards). With fewer partners, it is harder for you to shift your business (terminate the relationship), so you value the relationship more and your selectivity sends a signal to your business partner.

When outsourcing the selling function, it is possible to have many agents, and for agents to sell competing brands, especially when selling to consumers (B2C markets). This is the norm in some industries, such as insurance. However, when selling to another business (B2B markets), it is customary for the OSP to accord category exclusivity to the manufacturer and for the manufacturer to accord market exclusivity to the OSP. This means that outsourcing selling begins with a pledge by both sides. This is appropriate: the selling function is intended to generate factory demand. Something this important demands a certain level of closeness, of coordination and collaboration between upstream and downstream.

But either party can weaken this pledge. The manufacturer weakens it by taking on house accounts, which effectively sets up another business partner (the manufacturer itself) in the Rep's market. The manufacturer also weakens the pledge of selective use of business partners by narrowly defining the product lines or markets entrusted to the OSP and then setting up other parties (other Reps, or the manufacturer's direct sales force) to cover the rest. The Rep is the principal's "exclusive route to market" only in a technical sense, by an artificial definition of product and market.

Two can play this game. The OSP can fudge giving the principal exclusive representation in the principal's product category by defining the product category narrowly, then taking on another principal that is uncomfortably close to the principal that occupies the "exclusive" position in the (nominal) product category.

In short, the more selective an organization is in its use of business partners to perform a given function, the stronger the pledge it gives to the other party. Conversely, the more a party "chisels down" its definitions, so that it is not really being selective, the weaker the pledge. Figure 7-2 shows the double effect: part one is that being selective boosts one's own commitment. Part two is that selectivity boosts the counterpart's perception of commitment, but only to the extent that the other side perceives genuine restraint in use of other business partners. A word of warning: perception is one thing and reality is another. We have seen many situations where one side considers itself selective and the other side disagrees. For example, some manufacturers state that they are highly selective because they don't use other Reps in a territory— but they do have extensive house accounts or encourage and enable distributors to compete directly for factory sales. Conversely, some Reps state that they don't carry competing brands: they give an exclusive to one brand for a red widget, to another brand for a blue widget, and still another brand for a green widget.

Calibrating the Balance

How much pledging should each side do? Logic says that both sides should pledge the same amount. But contrary to appearances, one side should usually be pledging more than the other. Why? Because the purpose of pledging is to make each side want to keep the relationship going. What will damage the relationship is when one side takes advantage of the other side. The one taking advantage is likely to be the stronger party, because the weaker party is less able to take countermeasures to defend itself. Therefore, *the stronger party should offer more pledges.*[11]

Who is the stronger party? It depends on the particularities of each relationship. Whether the Rep or the manufacturer is stronger rests on the specifics of their situation. But whichever one is stronger should pledge more in order to create a more even balance of power. Long-term strategic alliances work when both parties need each other. Dependence should be high and symmetric.

For example, who "owns the customer"? It could be the Rep, particularly if the Rep is well established and the manufacturer does not have a well-known brand with a favorable image (low "brand equity"). In this case, the manufacturer is vulnerable to exploitation by the OSP. To offset this threat, the Rep should post a pledge. Conversely, if the manufacturer owns the customer by virtue of brand pull, the Rep is vulnerable to manufacturer opportunism and the manufacturer should post some level of pledge.

In short, vulnerability should be calibrated, then offset. For example, the Rep may expand its operation to serve a principal. If the relationship ends and the Rep can find other ways to use its resources, there is little vulnerability. But if the Rep would be in a situation of excess capacity, faced with laying people off, it is vulnerable and the manufacturer should pledge.

Reps and manufacturer make these judgments, sometimes implicitly, and calibrate and recalibrate often. It pays to do so. For example, one study documents that when Reps make heavy investments specific to a principal, these OSPs are vulnerable. Some of them offset their exposure by cultivating the principal's prime customers more than is justified by current sales. By overinvesting in relationship building in the principal's best accounts, the Rep exerts more influence inside the account. This strengthens the OSP's position vis-à-vis the principal, thereby balancing the dependence of both sides. Reps that take precautions like this are more profitable than Reps that do not.[12] Offsetting your vulnerability is simply good management.

SUMMARY

There is much to be said for building a long-term strategic alliance. Reps that ally with principals improve their income statements and attract products that would otherwise be sold direct. Manufacturers that ally with Reps improve their P&L and sell effectively, even the sort of product or market that usually calls for an employee sales force. Both sides work together more effectively, creating strategic competitive advantage and growing the pie of rewards to share. Both sides are better positioned for the future, better able to change and to grow.

But there is a price. Long-term strategic alliances take time and resources to build and are encumbering. No firm can afford to develop and sustain large numbers of them. And these alliances pose a management challenge: because they are long-term and strategic, they are hard to exit. This opens the door to opportunism (failing to live up to the business understanding) by either or both sides.

Jumping into a high-level relationship, in which manufacturer and OSP are such a strong coalition that they operate as one company, can be done following the blueprint of Figure 7-2. In essence, each side needs to depend on the relationship and be motivated to make it perform and last. And each side must perceive that the other side is highly committed. Reality and perception create a self-reinforcing cycle of signaling and reciprocity, in which commitment becomes high and mutual. Unfortunately, this same cycle can unwind: any perceived or actual drop in commitment feeds through the system to weaken the alliance. Therefore, it is important to manage both perception (via persuasion) and reality (via action). It's possible, but more difficult, to do this in relationships that have had a contentious history. A legacy of acrimony makes it more difficult to restart the relationship on a better footing.

Potent commitment builders are pledges, which are actions that bind one party to another and that demonstrate good faith. Contract clauses are one type of pledge: they work by creating and signaling exit barriers. Idiosyncratic investments do the same, but have the added value of making the pledger more capable. This increases the size of the pie, which makes both parties value the relationship more. Being selective in how many business partners one uses to cover a market operates in the same way. Pledging balances up the power in a relationship. The stronger party needs to pledge more than the weaker one because the weaker party needs reassurance that its vulnerability will not be exploited. The very best, most effective partnerships are those in which manufacturer and OSP are highly empowered—and highly need each other.

ENDNOTES

1. The costs and benefits detailed here are documented in numerous articles. Some of the principal ones are noted below.

> Dyer, Jeffrey H., and Wujin Chu (2003), "The Role of Trustworthiness in Reducing Transaction Costs and Improving Performance: Empirical Evidence from the United States, Japan, and Korea," *Organization Science,* 14 (1), 57–68.
> Dyer, Jeffery H., and Harbir Singh (1998), "The Relational View: Cooperative Strategy and Sources of Interorganizational Competitive Advantage," *Academy of Management Review,* 23 (4), 660–679.
> Galunic, Charles D., and Erin Anderson (2000), "From Security to Mobility: An Examination of Employee Commitment and an Emerging Psychological Contract," *Organization Science,* 11 (January/February), 1–20.
> Heide, Jan B. (1994), "Interorganizational Governance in Marketing Channels," *Journal of Marketing,* 58 (April), 71–85.
> Heide, Jan B., and Anne S. Miner (1992), "The Shadow of the Future: Effects of Anticipated Interaction and Frequency of Contact on Buyer-Seller Cooperation," *Academy of Management Journal,* 35 (2), 265–291.
> Jap, Sandy D. (1999). "Pie-Expansion Efforts: Collaboration Processes in Buyer-Supplier Relationships," *Journal of Marketing Research,* 36 (November), 461–475.
> Mohr, Jakki, and Robert Spekman (1994), "Characteristics of Partnership Success: Partnership Attributes, Communication Behavior, and Conflict Resolution Techniques," *Strategic Management Journal,* 15 (1), 135–142.

2. Anderson, Erin, William T. Ross, and Barton Weitz (1998), "Commitment and Its Consequences in the American Agency System of Selling Insurance," *Journal of Risk and Insurance,* 65 (4), 637–669.
3. Adler, Paul S., and Seik-Woo Kwon (2002), "Social Capital: Prospects for a New Concept," *Academy of Management Review,* 27 (1), 17–40.
4. Williamson, Oliver E. (1996), *The Mechanisms of Governance.* New York: Oxford University Press.
5. Weiss, Allen M., Erin Anderson, and Deborah J. MacInnis (1999), "Reputation Management as a Motive for Sales Structure Decisions," *Journal of Marketing,* 63 (October), 74–89.
6. Jap, Sandy D., and Erin Anderson (2003), "Safeguarding Interorganizational Performance and Continuity Under *Ex Post* Opportunism," *Management Science,* 49 (December), 1684–1701.
7. Zaheer, Akbar, Bill McEvily, and Vincenzo Perrone (1998), "Does Trust Matter? Exploring the Effects of Interorganizational and Interpersonal Trust on Performance," *Organization Science,* 9 (March/April), 141–159.
8. The section on long-term strategic alliances is based on:

> Anderson, Erin, and Barton Weitz (1992), "The Use of Pledges to Build and Sustain Commitment in Distribution Channels," *Journal of Marketing Research,* 24 (February), 18–34.

Ross, William T., Erin Anderson, and Barton Weitz (1997), "Performance in Principal-Agent Dyads: The Causes and Consequences of Perceived Asymmetry of Commitment to the Relationship," *Management Science,* 43 (May), 680–704.

9. Williamson, Oliver E. (1983), "Credible Commitments. Using Hostages to Support Exchange," *American Economic Review,* 73 (September), 519–540.

10. Macneil, Ian R. (1985), "Relational Contract: What We Do and Do Not Know," *Wisconsin Law Review,* 483–525.

11. Fein, Adam J., and Erin Anderson (1997), "Patterns of Credible Commitments: Territory and Category Selectivity in Industrial Distribution Channels," *Journal of Marketing,* 61 (April), 19–34.

12. Heide, Jan B., and George John (1988), "The Role of Dependence Balancing in Safeguarding Transaction-Specific Assets in Conventional Channels," *Journal of Marketing,* 52 (1), 20–35.

8

The Cost Calculator©:
Determining the True Cost
of a Field Sales Force

The most frequently discussed topics among senior managers relative to field sales are performance and cost. Both are part of a crucial equation; sacrificing one for the other does not accomplish desirable results. Previous chapters have covered the performance issues; this chapter will focus on costs.

Today, it is more important than ever for senior managers, especially CEOs and CFOs, to have accurate cost information on all aspects of their business. Guesses, old school myths, and biased inputs can no longer be accepted. Competitive pressures and board-of-director scrutiny demand accuracy and completeness. The strategic decision whether or not to outsource field sales is no less important than the selection of other outsource partners—in fact, it is more important than most decisions.

In our research and experience, we have identified two major stumbling blocks that prevent managers from understanding the true costs of outsourcing the field sales role:

1. General lack of understanding of the real costs of a direct field sales staff
2. Misunderstandings caused by the "break-even" curve taught in many business schools.

We will address both in this chapter.

GENERAL LACK OF UNDERSTANDING OF THE REAL COSTS OF A DIRECT FIELD SALES STAFF

A direct field sales force costs a lot more than each salesperson's annual salary. These costs are vast and include medical and disability insurance, personnel or human resources support, technical support, automobile allowance, office space, marketing and PR support, and so on. In fact, there are more than 70 different expense items associated with any field (in-house or OSP) salesperson. In most companies, however, these costs are not pulled out and allocated to the field sales effort. Many costs are buried in the expenses of different departments and are impossible to retrieve or separate. Sometimes these costs will be buried in the catchall category of SG&A.

Figure 8-1 illustrates a few examples of where costs that should be attributed to field sales alone could be buried. By not having these costs properly allocated to field sales, many erroneous decisions and assumptions are made.

This problem led us on a quest to find a way to finally account for the real and complete costs of a field sales department. After several years of work, we figured it out and packaged it as the Cost Calculator, included in this book. Our methodology is not only unique but also more detailed than any study to date. It allows companies, for the first time, to look at their sales efforts and

Figure 8-1. Illustration of Departments Where Field Sales Expenses Can Be Incorrectly Allocated and Difficult to Retrieve

understand exactly what they cost, specifically pulling out the field sales costs.

The Cost Calculator

We were able to separate *field sales costs* from *total sales expense* by looking at OSP organizations. As it turns out, they are an ideal model since they are wholly contained and self-supporting examples of a field sales office. (See the sidebar on the development of the Cost Calculator.) The OSP firm does everything with the single purpose of producing sales. Every person within that firm contributes in some way to the selling effort. Every expense that is incurred is to support the selling effort. If a company has an employee who inputs data into their computer system, they are doing so to generate the sales reports, activity reports, financial data, tracking POS reports and split sales credits, and so on. OSPs have an inside sales staff to assist outside salespeople and offer customer support and service. They have clerical employees who do filing, typing, and other duties such as mailings, literature maintenance, and so on. All OSPs have an administrative staff that manages personnel records, accounts payable and receivables, insurance/ benefit records and policies, purchasing, dealing with outside vendors, and other administrative tasks. They require professional services and other outsourced services to maintain employee benefits, accurate accounting and payroll services, computer maintenance, and more (not unlike the principals whom they represent). Of course, they have an outside sales staff. The owner, in effect, serves as the equivalent of a district manager in addition to performing the many other managerial functions necessary to run a small, self-contained business enterprise.

A Rep firm is a selling machine! Its existence is exclusively dependent upon its ability to sell and get paid for its services. Its detailed financial statements account for all of the firm's expenses, and all expenses are in support of the field selling function. There are no other departments into which these expenses can be allocated.

A single Rep firm is comparable to, or an alternative to, one manufacturer's direct district office. The necessary functions that either an in-house or Rep offices perform are the same. Even if the in-house (district) office is a "trimmed down" facility with personnel working out of their homes, all of the supporting functions

DEVELOPMENT OF THE COST CALCULATOR

Well-managed Rep firms are known for their belief in the value of networking. Many of these firms form groups that meet regularly and share information regarding their businesses as well as trends within their industry. They are normally referred to as "no-name groups" because they have no official position within their particular industry trade association. Most of these firms consider these meetings (and the relationships that ensue) to be an extremely important part of their professional activities.

One such group in the electronics industry has been meeting for more than 40 years. Co-author Bob Trinkle was an original member of this group. The member firms are from different territories across the United States and do not compete directly with one another. Some member firms are now in their fourth generation of ownership/management. They share information openly, including detailed financial information that is supported with actual financial statements. Prepared in a uniform manner, these financial statements allow participants to benchmark themselves against one another, as well as create numerous statistical analysis and comparisons derived from this detailed data.

This group has allowed the authors to utilize their many years of verifiable data to create a database that is the basis for the formulas used in the creation of the Cost Calculator. The firms vary in size from 10 employees to over 40 employees.

The authors are grateful to this group for allowing us to utilize these data. Their contribution is the basis for establishing, for the first time ever, a method of explicitly calculating the actual cost of a *field sales organization*. Separating field sales from all other sales expenses allows management to make better strategic decisions that have a more meaningful impact on their company's financial statement.

---

of the sales office must still be performed. They are simply transferred back to the home office or some other regional facility. You cannot eliminate the necessary sales and administrative support functions; you can only relocate or transfer them.

In studying these firms, we were able to identify every possible cost associated with the field sales effort, create categories for these costs, and approximate their costs. With these costs finally accounted for, you can use the Cost Calculator to compare the costs of a Rep firm and a direct field sales force on an apples-to-apples basis.

Below is a detailed listing of all expenses identified in the Cost Calculator. (Please note that they do *not* include individuals such as a national sales manager or vice president of sales, their staffs, and all other associated expenses, which are part of overall sales costs. *We focus exclusively on field sales costs.* However, the Cost Calculator does provide a way to add regional and/or additional district managers and their expenses into your estimates.)

Expense Items for any Field Sales Organization

1. *Total payroll (US$):* The total W-2 expense for all employees in that office or serving that office, including all salaries, bonuses, and commissions.
2. *Travel and entertainment (US$):* Includes airfare, hotel/motels, entertainment, own meals, promotions, sales samples, sales meetings, conference attendance, etc.
3. *Automobile expense (US$):* Includes auto allowances, mileage allowances, auto rentals, gasoline, oil changes, car washes, parking, tolls, insurance, maintenance, etc.
4. *Advertising and sales promotion expense (US$):* Includes local advertising, trade advertising, customer promotion, customer outings, customer seminars, promotion and handout material, booth space, spiffs, etc.
5. *Communication expense (US$):* Includes telephones, fax, Internet, cell phones, beepers, PDAs, data networks, and their installation/maintenance, etc.
6. *Occupancy expense (US$):* Includes office rent/lease, utilities, landscaping and snow removal, janitorial service, general maintenance, etc.
7. *Group medical expense (US$):* Includes health care premiums, prescription reimbursement, deductibles reimbursed (less portions of premiums paid by employees).
8. *Other insurance expense (US$):* Includes liability, general business, salary continuance, accidental death and dismemberment, life insurance, etc.
9. *All company-paid taxes (US$):* Includes payroll taxes (FICA—Social Security—employer rate 6.2 percent up to $87,900 per employee), (FICA—Medicare—employer rate 1.45 percent up to no limit), (state unemployment and disability—varies by state), (federal unemployment—0.8 percent up to $7,000), (local business taxes—varies by locality).
10. *Office expense (US$):* Includes equipment rental/leasing, equipment maintenance, data processing services, dues, subscriptions, depreciation, supplies, software, software maintenance, payroll services, interest expense, postage, computer maintenance, etc.

RULES OF THUMB

- Total compensation of an average salesperson is 38.034 percent of total expense for that salesperson.
- Multiply total salesperson's compensation by 2.6292 to get average cost of a salesperson.
- These numbers do not consider start-up costs including equipment, recruiting, training, relocation, etc.
- These numbers do not reflect other soft costs referenced above.

---

11. *Professional services (US$):* Includes legal, accounting/bookkeeping, consulting, etc.
12. *Retirement plans (US$):* Includes pension plans, profit sharing plans, 401K plans contributions, cost of maintaining and updating all retirement/benefit plans in compliance with the laws and keeping employees informed.
13. *Employee relations (US$):* Includes any other employee benefits, employee testing and selection, interview costs, training, tuition reimbursement, child care, relocation expense, etc.
14. *Miscellaneous expenses (US$):* Includes all other expenses.

When you use the Cost Calculator, each of the above expense categories will be calculated automatically. The Cost Calculator will provide you with four different sets of calculations for each entry. The first set of calculations will be averages. Next will be median numbers and then two sets of smoothed numbers for both averages and medians (statisticians refer to these as "clipping outliers"), which eliminate both the highest and the lowest numbers in the database for each category of expense. When you use the Cost Calculator you can enter as many different scenarios as you choose, as well as change the circumstances. Let's look at an example using the Cost Calculator.

Suppose you plan to open a large sales office and hire ten outside salespeople. One of the outside salespeople will serve as a district manager with account responsibility. You estimate that the average salesperson, including the district manager, will earn $85,000 in total compensation, and you forecast that the average shipments per salesperson will be $3,800,000 in the first year. This example generates the following *average* results:

Total expense = $2,234,820
Shipment forecast = $38,000,000

Total office payroll = $1,417,868
Administrative expense = $1,384,820
Travel and entertainment = $100,665
Automobile expense = $89,021
Advertising expense = $5,712
Communication expense = $59,068
Occupancy expense = $85,761
Group medical expense = $65,515
Other insurance expense = $29,946
All company-paid taxes = $96,550
Office expense = $79,021
Professional services = $41,771
Retirement plans = $66,702
Employee relations = $7,549
Miscellaneous expense = $89,685
Cost of sales = 5.88%

If you utilize an OSP with the same sales forecast of $38,000,000 and paid a 5 percent commission on shipments, you would have the following cost results:

Commissions paid @5% = $1,900,000
Cost of sales = 5%

This *average* example illustrates a savings of utilizing an OSP of $334,820. The same illustration produces the three other analysis mentioned earlier (median, smoothed average, and smoothed median) on the Cost Calculator.

In addition, you would not pay the OSP until 30 days after shipments have been made. Also, the OSP buys its own equipment, which can represent a substantial up-front additional cost. These costs are listed below in the next list. These are costs and legal exposures that OSPs eliminate for their principals as part of their business responsibilities and expense. These can be quite burdensome, especially in this litigious society.

Other Cost Considerations . . . Not in the Cost Calculator

1. *Personnel selection.* Utilizing a personnel recruiter will add between 25 and 33.333 percent of first-year total compensation cost or future replacement cost.
2. *Personnel relocation.* Reps absorb all staff relocation expenses, such as moving costs (packing, traveling), insurance, etc.

3. *Equipment purchases.* Reps buy their own equipment (computers, printers, cell phones, PDAs, beepers, software, software updates, office equipment, furniture, supplies, etc.). This is a large initial expense as well as a recurring replacement expense.
4. *Recruiting.* Reps spend their own time and other resources to recruit employees; this includes testing, reference checking, interviewing, travel, and training.
5. *Trade shows.* Reps pay their own expenses to attend trade shows and sales meetings.

Soft Costs That Reps Eliminate or Minimize

1. *Legal issues.* Discrimination cases (age, sex, disability, racial).
2. *Legal issues.* Sexual harassment issues.
3. *Legal issues.* Reps select, train, compensate, discipline, and terminate their own employees.
4. *Legal issues.* Compliance with local and state laws, including filing of all required reports and fees.
5. *Legal issues.* Reps handle their own workman's compensation issues.
6. *Legal issues.* Reps handle all employee benefit issues including disputes and compliance.
7. *Legal issues.* Reps are responsible for the legality of their own policies and practices.
8. *Legal issues.* Reps are responsible for their own liability insurance issues.
9. *Legal and tax issues.* Reps approve and audit all employee travel and entertainment expenses.

OTHER COSTS THAT SHOULD BE CONSIDERED

In addition to those costs listed above that are not included in the Cost Calculator, two other important cost advantages to using an OSP need to be considered but are normally overlooked.

Financing the Cost of Sales

Reps are not paid at the beginning of the sales process, nor are they paid while the process is taking place, no matter how long it takes. They are not paid until the sales process is completed and the orders are shipped. And if products that are shipped are proven to be defective or not paid for, the previously paid commissions are deducted. The OSPs finance this entire sales process from beginning to end with their own resources and funds. They play the role of a banker for their principals at 0 percent interest. Try to find a banker who will match that arrangement!

The time between the first sales contact and the first shipment of an order can be substantial, especially when trying to break into a major customer with large potential who already has a few approved and satisfactory vendors. Similarly, some technical sales processes can take months and even years to become a qualified vendor. The in-house salesperson is paid from his or her first day on the project regardless of performance (success or failure to obtain a purchase order) and regardless of how long it takes. Of course, all of their associated expenses are also incurred for this period. In the case of the OSP, no sales cost is paid (usually) until 30 days after shipment. The substantial savings in expense can be invested in other projects, facilities, equipment, staff, R&D, or other products. That can accelerate the "bucks" to the bottom line, which is sure to please the stockholders.

If we use the example above, let's see how much money it costs to finance a sale. Suppose the following criteria:

Time between order and shipments = 1.5 months
Your cost of money = 4.25%
Customer pays in = 30 days
Cost for that period = $280,837
Rep cost for same period = $0 (paid 30 days after shipment)

Another example of Reps financing the cost of sales concerns a long, drawn-out time period to penetrate a customer, ship, or design a product. Other possibilities could be allocations issues, labor strikes, or relocation of manufacturing facilities.

Time between first customer contact = 6 months
    and shipment
Customer pays in = 30 days
Your cost of money = 4.25%
Cost for that period = $1,331,347
Rep cost for same period = $0 (paid 30 days after shipment)

The use of OSPs places considerable cash at your disposal for use in other areas within your company.

Face-to-Face Selling Time

There are different kinds of selling with varying amounts of non-selling functions. Industrial selling seems to require the salesperson to do more nonselling functions than other types of sales. It doesn't seem to matter whether the salesperson is a Rep salesperson or an in-house salesperson. The nonselling burden consumes a tremendous amount of time. In addition to these nonselling functions, today's salesperson is faced with the limited face-to-face (F2F) time available with customers. This was discussed in earlier chapters and presented some graphs and charts. Figure 8-2 was developed using data accumulated from electronic representative and in-house salespeople.

The calendar below is typical of salespeople who are engaged in industrial sales. It shows an average of 132 days per year in which a salesperson can visit customers. (The number of days may vary from one company to another, but 132 days is a good baseline to start with.) Many companies are becoming more alert to this issue. They are making changes in their method of operation to increase the number of available days by reducing many of the activities listed below.

The number of sales calls that a salesperson makes is not a good measurement criteria for industrial selling. A salesperson can spend an entire day with one customer if they've got a lot of business or potential business at that account. Some managers and academics still measure and teach the wrong thing. Quality and in-depth calls are the meaningful efforts that produce results.

In addition to the days available for selling, the next question is, how many hours in each of those days is a salesperson actually

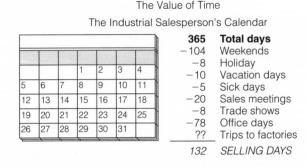

The Value of Time

The Industrial Salesperson's Calendar

365	Total days
−104	Weekends
−8	Holiday
−10	Vacation days
−5	Sick days
−20	Sales meetings
−8	Trade shows
−78	Office days
??	Trips to factories
132	*SELLING DAYS*

Figure 8-2. Typical Calendar of Salesperson Engaged in Industrial Sales

face to face with a buying influence? We mean *face to face!* Not waiting in the lobby or driving between calls, but actually face to face. The answer is, not many! (See Table 8-1 below.)

Many senior managers are surprised at the number of hours that a salesperson is actually doing what they are hired and paid to do. Often, the salespeople are a little reluctant to confess that during those 132 days of available selling, they spend only between 1 and 3 hours in front of a buying influence.

Consider the 3-hour day multiplied by 132 days per year, and then divide that number by 8 hours (normally you can call on customers only during the usual 8-hour workday); that equates to 50 full (8-hour) days for them to perform as we expect. They had better be good at their craft!

On the other hand, everybody can work together to increase the salesperson's efficiency. Eliminate redundant or unnecessary tasks, assign more tasks to support folks, and work to gain just 1 more hour of F2F time with customers. The results are dramatic in total sales effort; it's like adding additional salespeople without having to hire them, and they're already trained. It's worth everybody's effort.

If the calendar days could be increased by 6 days to 138 available days and the F2F time increased to 4 hours, the resulting difference is a 38 percent increase in F2F selling time (4 hours × 138 days divided by 8 hours = 69 days vs. 50 days = 38% increase).

To carry the F2F selling time for industrial salespeople to the ultimate level, consider that if we examine only those days that *could be* available for F2F selling versus working days available,

Table 8-1. Face-to-Face Selling Hours Rep or Direct (per day)

HOURS PER DAY	SELLING DAYS	ACTUAL SELLING
2	× 132	= 33 days per year
3	× 132	= 50 days per year
4	× 132	= 66 days per year
5	× 132	= 83 days per year

Example:
3	hours per day	
× 132	selling days	
/ 8	hour workday (when customers are available)	
= 49.5	actual selling days per year	

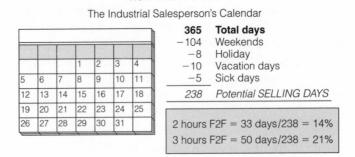

Work Time Available

The Industrial Salesperson's Calendar

		1	2	3	4	
5	6	7	8	9	10	11
12	13	14	15	16	17	18
19	20	21	22	23	24	25
26	27	28	29	30	31	

365	Total days
−104	Weekends
−8	Holiday
−10	Vacation days
−5	Sick days
_238_	_Potential SELLING DAYS_

2 hours F2F = 33 days/238 = 14%

3 hours F2F = 50 days/238 = 21%

Figure 8-3. Percentage of Maximum Selling Time Available Compared to Actual F2F Time with a Buying Influence

we come to a more dramatic set of facts as evidenced by the chart presented in Figure 8-3.

The obvious challenge for all managers of salespeople is to carefully inventory all tasks that salespeople are asked to do and then make sure that they are necessary or if other office staff could do them. Also, meetings should be well prepared and held only when necessary. Make every effort to maximize the F2F selling time of salespeople so that they can accomplish what they are hired to do and skilled at accomplishing. This can retrieve a considerable amount of hidden expense . . . the *taboo cost* of selling.

THE BREAK-EVEN CURVE

Business students who have become managers will likely recall the limited information that exists regarding the manufacturers' representative/agents function. The little that exists in textbooks is matched by the limited knowledge of professors concerning this widely used method of selling. A common thread in these textbooks, however, is the break-even curve. This curve is depicted in several ways, but they all portend the same message and illustrate the curve in the same manner: two straight lines intersect at a point defined as the "break-even point." At this point the authors say that a manufacturer should replace its Reps with a direct office. Short of this point, you need to stay with Reps. Figure 8-4 illustrates a typical example of this curve as it appears in popular textbooks.

A textbook example presents the following data:

1. A 5 percent commission rate to the Rep firm (regardless of sales volume).

2. Administrative (total) cost of $50,000 applicable for either a captive sales group or managing a Rep network (regardless of sales volume).
3. Company sales personnel receive a 3 percent commission on gross sales plus a salary.
4. Salary for 10 salespeople plus administrative expense is estimated at $550,000.

Using the above information and forming an equation:

Cost of company sales force = Cost of Rep firm
$0.03x + \$550,000 = 0.05x + \$50,000$
x = the break-even sales volume
$x = \$25,000,000$

Using this example and applying it to a break-even chart produces the results shown in Figure 8-4.

This kind of chart leads the reader to make unrealistic conclusions. To begin with, the chart implies that administrative costs, including the cost of an in-house sales force, remain constant regardless of sales volume. The total cost for their own in-house sales force is the same for zero-dollar sales to infinity. Absurd! Wouldn't that be every CEO's dream situation? The fact is that sales and administrative costs do increase with increased sales, but not in a linear fashion as the chart suggests.

The chart also implies that the commission rate being paid to the Reps remains constant regardless of sales volume. While that

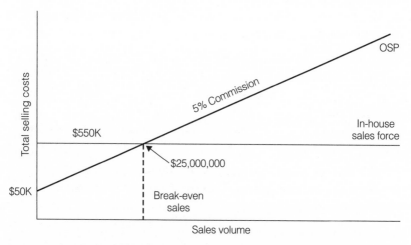

Figure 8-4. Typical Textbook Presentation of Trade-off: OSP versus In-House Selling

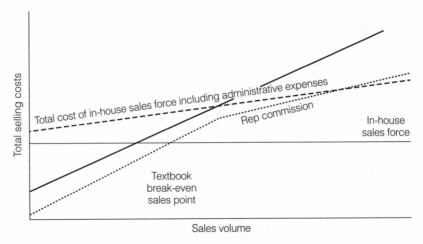

Figure 8-5. A Comparison: Break-Even Analysis

would be every Rep's most wonderful dream, it doesn't necessarily work that way in the real world. Again, the chart shows straight lines going out of sight without consideration of what the *average commission rate* is versus the contract rate. That is a critical consideration. Figure 8-5 depicts a more realistic curve.

These lines can be made to intersect at any point that you want. By adjusting commission rates or modifying administrative costs or both, you can literally keep the lines from ever intersecting. Manufacturers and Reps have worked together to keep the relationship a profitable one for both by intelligently adjusting commission rates or other means of compensation. A few examples that have been used are

1. *A sliding scale commission rate for very large customers.* Some have negotiated a reducing rate on a step-down basis on a *per customer basis,* not on total sales. Adjusting commissions downward on total sales can reduce the incentive to pursue new customers, which is the most expensive effort for any company, OSP or in-house. For example, on a per customer basis:

   a. Five percent commission on the first $1,000,000
   b. Four percent commission on $1,000,001 to $2,500,000, and so on.

2. *Same as above up to a fixed maximum dollar amount to be paid on very large customers.*

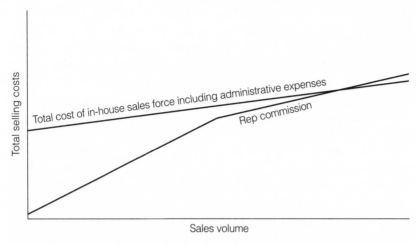

Figure 8-6. A More Realistic Break-Even Analysis

3. *Paying a fixed fee for certain customer locations where coverage is important but does not purchase anything.* Design centers, corporate headquarters, corporate purchasing locations, and manufacturing locations are just a few examples.

Many manufacturers have reduced some of their administrative costs by requiring their Reps to handle more customer service functions as well as more marketing functions, thereby reducing the principal's costs and passing them along to their OSPs. Depending on the amount of effort required by the Rep, manufacturers often pay fees to compensate the Rep firm for this additional requirement.

Figure 8-6 is a more realistic depiction of a "break-even" chart.

SOME FINAL POINTS TO PONDER

The Cost Calculator allows the user to play "what if" games. The user can bracket estimated sales performance and observe how the cost of sales can change under differing sales performance numbers. There are many "what if" scenarios: What if we don't make our forecast? What if the economy goes sour? How long will it take to penetrate these new markets or new customers?

Be sure to use an accurate average commission rate when inputting your numbers in the Cost Calculator. Split commissions, POS commissions on cost, special fees paid, and so on—all may differ from the contract commission rate. The contract may state a 5 percent commission, but when considering the actual monies paid against actual sales, the average rate may be less than 5 percent. Also, commissions are paid after the fact, after shipments are made, usually 30 days after shipment.

Determining the real cost of field sales is an important piece of information in the strategic decision-making process. The Cost Calculator gives the executive a tool by which to separate field sales cost from total sales cost. Until now, most companies have not had the tools by which they could determine these costs without exhaustive research and a lot of guessing. Some decisions can be made for the wrong reasons without examining all of the facets of field sales cost, including the soft costs and hidden costs of a field sales organization that are seldom considered as being significant until they are confronted.

CASE STUDY:
REP VERSUS DIRECT ECONOMICS

In 2003, we did an exhaustive pro-forma expense budget for each of the 16 territories in which we sell through Representatives. (Note: We are direct in our home territory, largely funded by one account that totals 13 percent of our sales in North America.) We looked at payroll and fringes including autos and expense reimbursement. We evaluated office locations and staffing, both selling and support.

In the end, we found our largest marketplace still favored the Representative model by 8 percent. As territory sales get smaller, the scale tipped more dramatically to the variable costs of Representatives, typically two to four times premium to staff a direct office. In aggregate, we estimated our costs to cover the United States and Canada would more than double, an estimated 122 percent premium over commissions expense, to staff a direct versus representative field sales organization.

[Figure 8-7 depicts the results that Bob Terwall references above.]

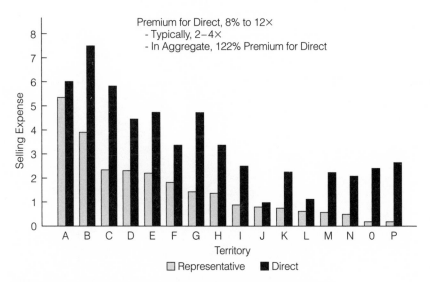

Figure 8-7. Cost Comparison: Representative versus Direct

Robert Terwall, President, Cherry Electrical Products, Waukegan, Illinois

9

Some Final Thoughts

Fierce global competition has given rise to reasons for *all* senior managers to consider new ways of thinking about the way companies manage and organize their business. The selling function should be a significant element of that evaluation process and should be considered without prejudice or preconceived opinion.

We have zeroed in on the two considerations that are the most important: performance and cost. Sacrificing one for the other has consequences; many of which may not be obvious. *Complete cost analysis of field sales has always been the most difficult to determine with reasonable accuracy.*

Today, most senior managers of companies are deeply concerned about the generation of revenue . . . *otherwise known as sales.* Without an adequate "top line," all other items of a financial statement are subject to significant revision. All senior executives recognize, without hesitation, that *"Nothing happens till somebody sells something!"* It's indisputable! Magnificent design, spectacular pricing, marvelous marketing, unheralded manufacturing capability, and so on, are meaningless if customers don't buy it!

Costs are everyone's concern, regardless of whether you are utilizing OSPs or direct employees. Managers who are paying attention know first hand that running a sales organization is difficult and is a constant experiment in cost containment. Good salespeople are hard to find, difficult to manage, a challenge to retain, and difficult and expensive to replace. There is no such thing as a good, unemployed salesperson these days. "They're as scarce as hen's teeth," as the saying goes.

There are several components of the sales cost that everyone needs to monitor. We have uncovered and explained the multi-faceted expense of the ever-rising cost of the selling business. In addition to the identifiable expenses shown in the Cost Calculator©, there are other costs (referenced in Chapter 8) that are rarely considered or discovered until they become part of a litigation experience. There is no escape from the reality of these expenses.

Some may be buried in different expense categories within a financial statement, but nonetheless, they can and do exist.

Once managers have a complete understanding of the real costs of the field sales role, we believe they are more likely to consider using an OSP, and the reasons for doing so are numerous. Outsourced sales professionals are entrepreneurs, private owners, and personally managed businesses. They are very cost sensitive and reactive. They insulate their principals from many "soft costs" and start-up expenses. Their compensation, based on performance, regardless of the economy, creates a fixed cost (or variable expense) that reduces the concern for cost getting out of control. The fact that OSPs finance the cost of the sale, no matter how long it takes, is a transparent cost that receives very little recognition or consideration. No banker on the planet would offer comparable rates or terms.

Because they are deeply committed to multiple manufacturers with differing management styles, OSPs must be nimble and quick to respond to changing times and circumstances as well as apply the "best practices" (learned from these multiple principal relationships) in their own operations. However, these attributes only apply to those Reps (OSPs) who are *"businesspeople in sales"* not the *"salespeople in business"* whose survival is dependent upon good economic conditions to survive. Outsourced sales professionals are no more insulated from failure than any other business. Their business acumen and instincts, coupled with their responsiveness to change, are vital characteristics to their survival and to their relevance.

After everyone has expressed an opinion as to whether or not to outsource field sales, utilize direct employees, and or a combination of the two, the bottom line is:

- Which options will produce the desired performance and at what cost?
- Which option has the best chance of serving your needs with minimum of turnover and supervision?
- Which option fits your management style and allows you to keep focus on your core competencies?
- What are *all* of the costs for these options?
- Will this cost be predictable, traceable, and consistent during good and bad economic times?

The manufacturers' representative function of selling (what we refer to as OSPs) has been proven to be dynamic, durable, and constantly evolving. For example, the vast majority of semiconductor manufacturers utilize OSPs, and that is a very demanding, technically challenging and dynamic industry segment.

They require very technically competent salespeople to sell their products. As semiconductor technology continues to advance with lightning speed, so does the skill level of the OSP, in sharp contrast to those who persist in promulgating an old myth that technical products require the total commitment of in-house employees. Additionally, semiconductor companies consider the representation of other compatible noncompeting semiconductor companies as an added synergy and offer a leveraging effect for their products.

When OSPs are utilized, most field sales costs, local management, and personnel responsibilities are transferred to them. Those principals can focus on assisting and promoting the performance of their outsource partner; they are freed up to do what they do best, whether it be manufacturing semiconductor parts or fabricating engines for helicopters.

NEXT STEPS

For Newcomers to Outsourcing

For those of you who have never worked with OSPs but are interested after having read this book, here are a few ways to get started. First, run the numbers. Use our Cost Calculator to find out the real cost of using an in-house field sales team versus outsourcing. Then consider some of the soft costs that aren't included in the Calculator (see Chapter 8). If the numbers look good, consider getting top management involved in the decision to outsource. Shifting to an outsourced field sales group is a critical, strategic decision and one that should involve managers in the highest ranks.

Once you've decided to go with an OSP, your next natural question should be, "How do I find an OSP?" And not only that, "How do I find a good OSP that's right for my business and knows my industry?" The best place to start is by asking other OSPs that you may know. Reps know other good Reps across the country and should only recommend other firms they feel will do a good job for you. A bad referral would reflect badly on them. Next, you can contact one of several professional trade associations, many of whom are listed on the Manufacturers Representative Education

Research Foundation's website, www.mrerf.org. They list many industry-specific trade associations, which in turn list their members and their websites. Also, ask major customers and other manufacturers for *several recommendations* of OSPs. Personal referrals are often worth their weight in gold, provided they are based on long-term performance-related criteria and not just likeability. Call those OSPs that seem to meet your needs.

Then, meet with the final group of OSP candidates *at their offices* for a first-hand observation of their staff and business operations. Listen carefully to their business philosophy, meet some of their salespeople, and see whether your ethics, attitudes, customer base, other principals, and goals match up. The right chemistry is so very important.

For Veterans of Outsourcing

You may have been using OSPs for some of your businesses, but now you would like to expand your use and enhance your experience. Review some of the case studies in Chapter 2 to see how companies like Intel, Honeywell, and Cherry Electric have used OSPs. We also reviewed ways to enhance your relationship with your OSP. Those principals who respect their OSPs and treat them as equal partners tend to get the most out of their outsourcing experience. As a goal setter, team coach, cheerleader, chief supporter, and scorekeeper you can become the emotional favorite of your OSP and achieve long-term relationships and higher performance.

INDEX

Page numbers in *italics* indicate figures or tables.

About TEXERE

Texere, a progressive and authoritative voice in business publishing, brings to the global business community the expertise and insights of leading thinkers. Our books educate, enlighten, and entertain, and provide an intersection where our authors and our readers share cutting edge ideas, practices, and innovative solutions. Texere seeks to cultivate, enhance, and disseminate information that illuminates the global business landscape.

www.thomson.com/learning/texere

About the typeface

This book was set in 11-point New Baskerville.

Library of Congress Cataloging-in-Publication Data

Anderson, Erin M.
 Outsourcing the sales function: the real cost of field sales/
Erin Anderson and Bob Trinkle.
  p. cm.
 Includes index.
 ISBN 0-324-31173-7 (text)—ISBN 0-324-311172-9 (data cd)—
ISBN 0-324-20748-4 (package)
 1. Manufacturers' agents. 2. Sales management. 3. Contracting out. I. Trinkle, Bob. II. Title.
 HF5422.A53 2005
 658.8'102—dc22